THE ARCHITECTURE
AND MEMORY OF THE
MINORITY QUARTER
IN THE MUSLIM
MEDITERRANEAN CITY

edited by

SUSAN GILSON MILLER
AND MAURO BERTAGNIN

THE AGA KHAN PROGRAM AT THE HARVARD UNIVERSITY GRADUATE SCHOOL OF DESIGN

CAMBRIDGE, MASSACHUSETTS

ISBN 978-1-934510-06-3

Book and cover design by Wilcox Design | www.wilcoxinc.com
Printed and bound by Kirkwood Printing, Wilmington, MA
Distributed by Harvard University Press

Cover image: A street in the Jewish quarter (Meschita) of Palermo

The Harvard Design School is a leading center for education, information, and
technical expertise on the built environment. Its departments of Architecture,
Landscape Architecture, and Urban Planning and Design offer masters and
doctoral degree programs and provide the foundation for its Advanced Studies
and Executive Education programs.

CONTENTS

HASHIM SARKIS

FOREWORD

FRAGILE: HANDLE WITH RIGOR

One of the ambitions of the Harvard GSD Aga Khan Program publications is to study the rapid erosion of vital aspects of the built and natural environments in the Muslim world. Widely acknowledged, this urgent matter is nevertheless understudied. The remaining few historic centers are fast receding in the face of large-scale development, the precarious restoration of the surviving few being further proof of their vulnerability. The agricultural landscape has given way to urbanization, and the desert and its oases are being stampeded by tourism. These urban and rural landscapes are equalized under increasing environmental, health, and security threats. Despite these serious encroachments, scholarship on the contemporary built environment in the Muslim world over the past ten years has focused primarily on monumental architecture, be it corporate or historic. The unprecedented economic and construction boom has no doubt veered research in this direction. In parallel, the few intellectual endeavors that have addressed the negative changes have been either fatalistic or nostalgic, seeking desperately to restore legitimacy to those endangered features. Cities are notorious for rediscovering their historic faces just as they are about to disappear.

The importance of this superb book, edited by Susan Gilson Miller and Mario Bertagnin, is that it does not fall into lamentation or sensationalism. With a very focused approach, both methodologically and regionally, it exposes several faults in the accepted wisdom on such central issues as the role of architecture in establishing identity and the morphology of the historic cores of Muslim cities. In the face of the fragility of the historic cities in the Muslim world, its authors propose rigor.

The rigor is applied to three key questions, all encapsulated in its carefully crafted title: *The Architecture and Memory of the Minority Quarter in the Muslim Mediterranean City.*

ARCHITECTURE AND MEMORY: Architecture as a locus of memory, as an *aide-memoire*, as an iconography that could be read like text, and as the mnemonic device that embodies historic evidence, has become as vulnerable as the memory that it encodes. Architecture is constitutive of memory, the authors seem to repeat after Maurice Hallbwachs in terms of collective memory and after Gaston Bachelard in terms of personal memory. Miller, Bertagnin, and the other authors in this volume slowly construe different kinds of complementarity between the historic document and the architectural document; in measuring distances, interpreting uses, mapping rituals, they reveal a unique disposition for architecture to embody history and propel it forward.

THE MINORITY QUARTER: Much existing scholarship on the minority quarter has tended to focus on isolation and differentiation as its most distinguishing features. Based on carefully gathered and compared historical evidence, the book refutes these generalizations. The different constructions of identity through architecture studied here expose a great dependency of the majority on the presence of the minority for self-definition. Such relative definition—or "narcissism of small differences," in the words of Sigmund Freud via Michael Ignatieff—finds in architecture and urban spaces a way of confronting the minority's vulnerability by highlighting the small differences in some instances (sequestering, clothing) or by hiding them in others (dispersal, camouflage).

THE MEDITERRANEAN MUSLIM CITY: From a stereotypical urban morphology point of view, the juxtaposition of the two terms, Mediterranean and Muslim, could be read as an oxymoron: the first urban model suggests openness and mixing and the latter suggests closure and segregation. However, the cities that are studied here through the lens of the minority quarters carefully complicate these generalizations. Each city, in its history, circumstances, and contingencies, responded differently to the issue of ethnic diversity. If there is a common message among the authors, it lies in their acknowledgment and celebration of ethnic and religious diversity in the geographic context of the Mediterranean and in the different ways in which Muslim cultures have historically embraced pluralism.

The loss of the urban quarters studied in this book may be irreversible, but their study is indispensible for understanding the role that these minorities played in the history of the region and the role that architecture played in shaping their identities. It is also indispensible in anticipating how new identities will inevitably be construed out of the homogenizing wave that continues to prevail.

SUSAN GILSON MILLER

MAURO BERTAGNIN

ACKNOWLEDGMENTS

The idea of studying minority quarters of Muslim Mediterranean cities began in the summer of 1998 with a joint Harvard-MIT studio on Islamic architecture held in Fez, Morocco. Coeditors Susan Gilson Miller, then Director of the Moroccan Studies Program at Harvard, and Mauro Bertagnin, Professor of Architecture at the University of Udine, along with Attilio Petruccioli, then Director of the Aga Khan Program in Islamic Architecture at MIT, directed a group of Harvard and MIT graduate students in a studio on the *mallāh,* or Jewish quarter of Fez. The intention was to conduct an architectural survey of the minority quarter that would shed light on its changes over time, while also establishing its role as a vital component of the larger city. In the sweltering heat of the Fez summer, a much grander project was conceived: a plan to study a series of minority quarters around the Mediterranean in order to develop a panoramic image of their evolution that focused on each one individually, but also considered them collectively and comparatively.

The broader context in which the project is situated relates to the rapid transformation of the Muslim Mediterranean urban fabric that has taken place in the last fifty years. The process of accelerated change that has so radically altered Middle Eastern cities such as in Cairo and Damascus has had its counterpart development in the Muslim Mediterranean world, in Fez, Marrakesh, Tangier, and Istanbul, as well as in and other places where Islamic culture once flourished, such as Sicily and southern Italy. Elements of a diversified urban life that for centuries included minority populations are fast disappearing into an anodyne urbanism lacking ethnic and religious variety. The idea behind our research was to document—through the use of written and visual sources—the multiethnic quality of these quarters at a particular moment in time, to provide a reliable resource to historians, historical preservationists, and anyone else interested in learning about forgotten aspects of their past. The project was founded on the belief that the preservation of a cultural heritage must begin with individuals working from the ground up, brick by brick and block by block, and not from the top down, by distant experts, donors, or planners. The result is the present volume, a first attempt to document the minority quarter of the Muslim Mediterranean as a historical and architectural phenomenon having distinctive and shared qualities across space and time.

It goes without saying that this book, like most complex efforts, is the product of many hands: students, colleagues, city officials, architects, librarians, technicians, authors, and friends. The book is above all a collaborative effort across disciplines, mediating among different methodologies and approaches. It is also a field-based work, founded on research carried out under frequently difficult conditions. Finding lodgings and feeding a large group of students, gaining permissions to enter places that were off-limits, working in the heat, dust, and dirt, using neighborhood photo and copy shops, arranging exhibitions in odd venues, and negotiating with sometimes reluctant officials were part of the daily routine. None of this would have been possible without considerable help from local supporters who deserve our gratitude for their patience and generosity.

Major financing was provided by the Lucius N. Littauer Foundation of New York City, led by Foundation President William Lee Frost, whose unstinting enthusiasm over the years turned our concept into a reality. The Littauer Foundation contributed to both the field research and publication phases of the project. Without its help, this book would never have seen the light of day. Other major patrons were the Maurice Amado Foundation of Los Angeles, the Council of American Overseas Research Centers, and the Graham Foundation for Advanced Studies in the Fine Arts, which provided funding for Susan Miller's research project, *Tangier and the Culture of Cosmopolitanism, 1860–1930, Architecture and Urban Form in the Age of Empire*. The Fondazione Cassa di Risparmio di Udine e Pordenone (CRUP) of Udine, Italy, contributed generously to the costs of publication. Our thanks also to Gerard Levy of Paris, who gave us access to his incomparable collection of rare Moroccan iconography, and Jamil Simon of Spectrum Media, who shared with us some of his own Moroccan Jewish photos.

Support for this project from various parts of Harvard University was outstanding, demonstrated by grants from the Center for Middle Eastern Studies and its most recent Directors, Cemal Kafadar and Steven Caton, and the Center for Jewish Studies, whose Director, Shaya J.D. Cohen, provided crucial support in the final stages with a grant from the William Landau Lecture and Publication Fund. No words are sufficient to acknowledge the contribution of the Aga Khan Program in Islamic Architecture at the Graduate School of Design and its Director, Hashim Sarkis, who recognized the relevance of our research to the broader field of Islamic architecture and urbanism and took the bold step of publishing our work. Melissa Vaughn, Publications Director at the Harvard Graduate School of Design, shepherded this volume into print, assuring both its beauty and exactitude. Jean Wilcox provided the graceful book design. Two colleagues at the Fogg Museum, Spriull Harder and Jeff Spurr, gave advice, material support, and technical help whenever needed.

In Morocco, our *mécène* was Saïd Mouline, formerly Chief Architect of the Ministry of Housing, who opened many doors for us. We are grateful for the generous hospitality that Saïd and his wife, Dr. Mia Balafrej, extended to us on many occasions. In Fez (summer 1998), our work was facilitated by the office of the Wali of Fez, Abdeslam Bekrate, and the Governor of Fez *madîna*, Mohammed Fassi-Fihri. Especially warm was the reception given to the Harvard-MIT group by the Jewish community of Fez, headed by Dr. Armand Guigui. We also wish to thank Prof. Mina El-Mghari-Baïda, architectural historian and now head of the Moroccan National Commission for UNESCO, who worked with us in the field, and Prof. Abdellatif Bencherifa, geographer, who contributed valuable cartographic materials. Dr. Mohammed Hajami and the personnel of the ADER-Fès redevelopment authority, Dr. Hassan Radouine, Prof. Driss Mansouri, and Engineer Sefrioui of the municipality of Fez, all made our task easier. Dr. Hajami's wise counsel was especially appreciated. Then graduate students and now colleagues Ilham Khuri-Makdisi, Jorge Ortero-Pailos, and Zack Hinchliffe made important contributions to the Fez chapter. Sahar Bazzaz's meticulous background research and knowledge of the sources helped immensely in writing up the Fez material. Our thanks to the editors of the *Journal of the Society of Architectural Historians* for permitting us to use our article, "Inscribing Minority Space in the Islamic City: The Jewish Quarter of Fez (1438–1912)," which appeared in vol. 60, 3 (September 2001), as the basis for the updated version that appears in this volume.

Trani in Apulia was the site of a summer workshop of 2000 that included Harvard students and students from the School of Architecture at the Polytechnic of Bari. Among those Tranesis who welcomed, fed, and advised us were Yuditta Bianchi, Marita Rodondi, Francesca Onesti, Steven T. Minnich, and Salvatore d'Assisti. Our thanks also to Fabio d'Andrea and Prof. Arch. Claudio d'Amato Guerrieri, Dean of the School of Architecture at Bari, and Prof. Attilio Petruccioli, who arranged the studio. Students from the Polytechnic of Bari who participated included Daniela Amoroso, Guiseppe Andriani, Michele Cacucciolo, Domenico Catania, Giacomo De Pinto, Rosalia Loiodice, Francesca Marino, Daniella Martinelli, Giovanni Masciave, Alessandra Paresce, Paola Traversa, Anna Vadacca, Marco Zezza, Roberto Di Tolla, Stefania Lanzidei, Guiseppe Panebianco, Michele Petruzzelli, Francesco Pirulli, and Massimiliano Roberto. Our special thanks to Prof. Nezar AlSayyad of the University of California at Berkeley, editor of *Traditional Design and Settlement Review*, who gave us permission to reprint "A Mediterranean Jewish Quarter and Its Architectural Legacy: The *Giudecca* of Trani, Italy (1000-1550)," which appeared in volume 14, 2 (2003). A revised version of that article appears in this book.

Our site visit to Palermo in the summer of 2002 was facilitated by Prof. Francesca Fatta, native of Palermo and our generous host, and member of the architectural faculty of the Mediterranean University of Reggio-Calabria. Thanks to her, we gained access to churches, rooftops, and the interior of the famous "*Meschita*." Vincenzo Arena contributed to the design work. We also wish to thank local historians Rosario De Luca and Giovanni Fatta, who led us to key documentation and provided some of their own materials to us.

The Istanbul field work in the summer of 2003 would not have been possible without Tony Hananel, who introduced us to the Jewish community of that glorious city and smoothed our way. Serra Emin-Levi was an efficient and able assistant whose interviews with former inhabitants of Balat enriched our research. Historians Naim Güleryüz and Rifat Bali, and Engineer Senem Kadioğlu of the Balat-Fener restoration project, gave us valuable insights gleaned from their intensive research on-site. Irem and Metin Bonfil hosted us and made our stay in Istanbul especially warm and fun. Invaluable informants were Balatlis Leon Brudo and Korin Suryano, who freely contributed their in-depth understanding of the place. We also wish to thank Cengiz Sisman, Nedret Kuran-Burçoğlu, Lina Filiba, and Leyla Navarro for their help in gathering documentation.

Our fieldwork in the *mallāh* of Marrakesh in 2004 was facilitated by Jacky Kadosh, President of the Jewish Community of Marrakesh-Essaouira. Thanks are due to the Haliwa family of Bâb al-Mallâh, who allowed us into their home for days on end to make drawings and take photos. The coeditors wish to pay special tribute to architect Enrico Pietrogrande of the University of Padua, who rendered the portfolio of exceptionally beautiful drawings of the *mallāh* of Marrakesh that appear in the chapter, as well as many of the maps used throughout the book.

Our research in Tangier had its home at the Tangier American Legation Museum and Institute for Moroccan Studies. This historic establishment, managed by curators Thor and Elizabeth Kuniholm, and TALIM librarian Yhtimad Bouziane, provided a congenial base for our operations. Our studies in the Beni Ider quarter of Tangier were aided by Sonia Cohen Azagury, Rachel Muyal, Lucette Marques-Toledano, the late Ramon Lourido-Diaz, Abraham Azancot, Dr. Nadia Erzini, Abdellah El-Gourd, Muhammad b. al-Hajj at-Tawfiq al-Mrabit, the late 'Abd Hamid Bouzid, Hanae Bekkari, Philip Abensour, Sidney Pimienta, Elena Coon Prentice, Georges Bousquet, Jacob Lasry, Farida Benalyazid, Bashir Skirj, 'Abd Hamid Skirj, and Khalid Amine. Thanks also to Prof. Ahmad Toufiq for his help in securing a copy of the Skîrij manuscript that was a primary source for our research on Tangier.

Warmest thanks to Pierangela Mazzon, who provided culinary comfort during our Palermo stay, and to David Miller, who never flagged in his enthusiasm for this project, though it added up to many miles and many days away from home. Architects Stefania Lanzidei and Roberto DiTolla did much of the on-site drawing in Trani, Tangier, and Balat, bearing up under less than ideal working conditions. And finally, a deep bow to our contributing authors who responded without complaint to our many demands: to Bill Granara, Emily Gottreich, Ilham Khuri-Makdisi, Attilio Petruccioli, and Karen Leal, a word of gratitude for your patience, cooperation and willingness to share our belief that this was a story that had to be told.

1-Marrakech
2-Fez
3-Tangier
4-Palermo
5-Trani
6-Istanbul/Balat

Location of research sites around the Mediterranean Basin.

SUSAN GILSON MILLER

AN INTRODUCTION TO THE MEDITERRANEAN MINORITY QUARTER

The city...does not tell its past, but contains it like the lines of a hand, written in the corners of the streets, the gratings of the windows, the banisters of the steps, the antennae of the lightening rods, the poles of the flags, every segment marked in turn with scratches, indentations, scrolls.

—ITALO CALVINO, *Invisible Cities*

In the same way that amnesia is not merely a local disturbance of the individual's memory but causes more or less serious perturbations in his personality, the absence, or voluntary or involuntary loss, of collective memory among peoples and nations can cause serious problems of collective identity.

—JACQUES LE GOFF, *History and Memory*

Cities of the southern Mediterranean region have their own particular trajectory. Located at the edge of the encounter between two great civilizations, they reflect the diversity of peoples who lived, traded in and traversed this vast region of vibrant cultural exchange over the centuries. This book is about the minority quarters of those cities, and how they functioned as living parts of a larger urbanity. Six chapters cover the medieval period to the early twentieth century, and cross the region from Morocco to Turkey. Five of them concern quarters found in Muslim cities (Fez, Marrakesh, Tangier, Palermo and Istanbul) where the population was either wholly Jewish or mixed, while one study is about a Jewish quarter in a Christian town, Trani in Apulia.

While Islamic urbanism has been the subject of intense scholarly interest for decades, the minority quarters that were a vital component of predominantly Muslim cities have been studied hardly at all.[1] Minority quarters were complex organisms that functioned not only according to a rhythm of their own, but also in concert with the tempo of the larger city. The few studies on this subject tend to deal with minority quarters as self-contained units, disregarding the many connections between the minority quarter and the rest of the city. Here we have deliberately set aside the notion of isolation, adopting instead a point of view that sees the minority quarter as a permeable space that had many extensions, pathways and openings reaching out into the surrounding environment. Exploring how the minority quarter sustained itself over time as a vital element both separate from and integrated with the greater Mediterranean city was the inspiration for this research.

PARAMETERS OF RESEARCH

In the broadest sense, this project is situated within the current effort to reexamine the composition of cities of the Islamic ecumene and to identify the influences that have contributed to what appears to be a hybridized form of urbanism. Among the sources of that hybridity was the minority quarter and the multiplicity of influences it brought to bear on the shape of the city. In North Africa, the principal religious minority in pre-modern times were Jews whose presence in North Africa pre-dated Islam. While the approximate moment of their arrival is unknown, their entrenched settlement in major cities as well as remote rural villages was an established fact. In Egypt and elsewhere in the lands of the Eastern Mediterranean, Greek Orthodox, Maronites, Assyrians, Copts, and Armenians as well as Jews proliferated alongside the Muslim majority. The *millet* system was the Ottoman state's answer to the problem of minority governance. In both form and substance, it differed markedly from the methods used to govern the Jewish minority in North Africa. Yet, as we shall see, certain continuities across time and space help bring the opposite ends of the Mediterranean spectrum into one unified field. Moreover, although our emphasis is primarily on the Jewish quarter, our discussion has ramifications for other ethnicities as well, and the theoretical conclusions reached here may be applicable beyond the circle of Muslim-Jewish relations.

Architecturally speaking, the methodology used was governed by the concept of the courtyard house, a dominant type throughout the region. Prior research on the

Muslim city suggested that cultural norms dictated the pervasiveness of this type, which could be expanded to encompass all the building styles in the pre-modern city. Minority architecture presents a new perspective on this problem, as well as an extension of it. Is there a distinctive Mediterranean Jewish architecture different from the dominant type, and if so, where does it differ and how did it evolve? Similarly, how did other minorities, such as Greek Orthodox, impress their identity on the building form? While the question of type is the starting point for our investigations, it does not represent the totality of our interest in the morphology of the quarter. We ask further questions, such as: What were the prevailing street patterns in the quarter, and what was their relationship with other important nodes in the city? How did economic activities dictate the shape of the quarter, and how were limits of the quarter evoked? Answers to some of these questions emerged in the course of this research, while others await a second round.

Another unique aspect of this study is the close collaboration between architects and historians with the aim of eliciting a vibrant portrait of life in the quarter at a given point in time. This approach is evident in the research methodology. Although our focus rested on the entire quarter, it was especially concerned with those parts of it that narrated domestic practices, patterns of economic life, forms of governance, evidence of solidarities and social differentiation, the boundaries between private and public, spaces of deviance, and factors contributing to growth and decline—that is, the human content. Research on site was principally an effort of surveying, drawing and recording aspects of the built environment. However, it was closely followed by the search for relevant historical documentation, including maps, archives, letters, memoirs, prints, photographs and postcards that helped to populate our vision of the cityscape.

Other research questions reflect the dual nature of the project by addressing the meeting points between material and social life. What physical aspects determined the building of the quarter? In the houses, how was internal space organized and used, and how did this compare with Muslim structures? Where was commercial space located, how did it relate to what we know about minority vocations? What is the hierarchy of streets and alleyways, and how are the transitions from public to semi-public to private space made? What form did landmark structures (synagogue, church, mosque, school, public bath) take, and what was their place in the urban fabric? Where did various social classes and categories reside within the quarter, and to what extent was the minority quarter a meaningful social unit? How did the physical fabric reflect social constraints placed on the minority?

Each of the chapters covers an expanse of time sufficiently long to witness the effects of historical contingency on the minority quarter. The reader will not find here conventional history of a sweeping nature; rather, this book is a collection of micro-histories tied together by a particular optic that concentrates on the intense interactions between minorities and majorities within a specific spatial and temporal context. We hope that this methodological constraint will not detract from the overall relevance of these episodes to more encompassing historical narratives. The earlier chapters are shaped by the dramas that accompanied the rise and fall of Hispano-Moorish civilization in the Iberian peninsula, while later chapters are concerned with the problems of modernity: how minority quarters were transformed by ideas arriving from outside, how their populations in turn became agents of that transformation. In all, the book spans almost 1,000 years of Mediterranean history.

Deciding on which sites to study was a further consideration. A comprehensive survey of all the remaining Mediterranean minority quarters would take several life-times. The southern Mediterranean region is rich in towns and cities that contain the vestiges of past minority quarters, in Iberia, North Africa, southern Italy, Greece, Turkey, Palestine and Egypt. They vary size from major agglomerations, such as Balat in Istanbul, to the miniature walled enclosures (*qusûr*) of southern Morocco. Sometimes the quarter is contained within the larger city and forms a microcosm of it; at other times, it is removed from the old city, as in Fez, where it was attached to the separate royal compound. There is no one pattern or template that determined our choice of site. We made a selection based on our own interests and biases: Morocco and Italy predominate. We worked where the existing fabric offered intriguing possibilities for reconstruction and interpretation. But numerous other sites fit our criteria and could be studied from the perspective of minority space. Our long-term goal is to achieve a balance between the Eastern and Western Mediterranean, between Muslim, Christian and Jewish communities. In this first volume, we have come down more heavily on the Western and Jewish side. We hope this bias will be corrected in future studies, with more attention paid to the Eastern Mediterranean and to non-Jewish minorities within Islam.

INTEGRATION VERSUS ISOLATION

A question that continually came to mind was that of integration versus isolation. Reading separation as ostracism, some observers have gone so far as to draw a parallel between the Jewish quarters of Muslim cities and the ghettoes of Europe. In our view, this is entirely inappropriate, because it ignores the profound distinctions between the Jewish experience in the lands of Islam and the European experience. Islamic culture differed from Christendom in many respects, but most noticeably in its treatment of minorities, who had a protected (if subordinate) status under Islamic law. The special legal status of Jews and Christians in Muslim society, as well as the practices of every-day life, allowed for a greater degree of interchange than was known in pre-modern Europe.[2] As a result, the minority quarter was often open to the surrounding city in ways not always immediately apparent to the Western eye. Each chapter in this book stresses the idea of porosity, underlining the many ways in which it was achieved. Moreover, because of the role minorities played in local, regional and supra-regional trade, their field of activity was not confined to the city and usually extended into the countryside or toward the sea. In our reading, the minority quarter can be imagined as the epicenter of a series of concentric circles that linked its inhabitants spatially and experientially to the city, the territory, and the greater region. This model allowed minorities to enter the wider city and the territory for economic reasons, while also permitting them to withdraw into their own enclaves that offered a sanctuary and the means to sustain a rich spiritual and associational life.

The concentric circle model works at a variety of levels, both spatially and socially. Personal identity was closely tied to minority space, with the quarter serving as epicenter of the individual's selfhood, as well as the point of reference through which the self was recognized by others. Leaving the quarter implied making nuanced shifts in the parameters of identity that are not easy to reconstruct historically. We can say, however, that in general, identity was flexibly adjusted as one moved outward from the quarter, from a situation in which minority status was self-evident, to one in which it was declared through various strategies of self-representation.[3] But it was inside the quarter that the individual felt most "at home." Here were the places of worship, the baths, the bread ovens, the grocers, the cobblers and butchers who provided the services needed to sustain a comfortable life. Here, too, were the human networks vital for performing the social and ceremonial practices, the transactions and negotiations, that inscribed a specific minority presence onto a Muslim context. An overriding concern was to not lose sight of the human dimension of our study; in terms of methodology, this meant a continual re-centering of our perspective to focus on the hypothetical subject, that is, the minority person.

THE HISTORIOGRAPHY OF MEDITERRANEAN MINORITY SPACE: ISSUES AND PROBLEMS

Older urban studies on the Muslim world paid little attention to places of minority settlement, viewing them as irregular exceptions to an otherwise rational and homogeneous urban fabric. An earlier generation of scholars, operating within the framework of colonialism, developed schemas of the "Islamic city" that were often reductive and lacking in finely grained detail.[4] They considered minority communities peripheral to what they thought was the real business of the city: to fulfill an essentialized version of Islam. In their view, minorities were a disturbing and inassimilable intrusion into the harmonious Eastern city of the European imagination, with its mosque, market, and *hammâm*: what place for a synagogue or church in this idealized Muslim space?

Behind this attitude of exceptionalism was the excessive attention given by scholars to Islamic law, which has much to say about urban social practices. The legal tradition had a two-fold influence: first, by way of emphasizing the strict rules governing the use of space in the city, and second, by underscoring specific regulations about minority access to it. Jurists of the Maliki school of legal interpretation (*madhhab*) that prevails in North Africa were especially influential in this regard, through their contributions to an extensive body of law that regulated conduct in the home, the neighborhood, and in public space. Conflicts over the use of space in the Maghrib, including disputes involving minorities, were usually resolved in conformity with a theoretical notion of urban "order."[5] Historian John Hunwick's study of medieval *fatwâ*s from North Africa shows that legal opinion emphasized the need for clear spatial distinctions between Muslims and non-Muslims, especially in regard to places of worship.[6] Height was an issue, in the belief that Islam should "stand tall," while other tolerated religions should not make a display of the symbols of their faith. The legal approach tended to polarize and oversimplify the tenor of the majority-minority relationship, reducing it to a contentious and unequal binary embrace.

It is indeed true that Islamic precepts were a major factor in determining the social environment of the city and the conduct of minority-majority relations, but they were not the only factor. Other, less prescriptive historical sources paint a more nuanced portrait of the interactions between social groups and bring out lesser-known aspects of the relationship. Diplomatic archives, court records, travel literature, chronicles and letters written by both Muslims and non-Muslims, the testimony of maps, archeology and architecture—along with other sources unknown or unavailable to an earlier generation of scholars— offer more detailed perspectives on the changing patterns of human relations. These sources show that depending on time and place, inter-group contacts varied widely from the peaceful to the agonistic, to the deeply conflict-ridden. Moreover, recent scholarship suggests that members of minority groups often acted with agency, negotiating with the political authorities, and even, at certain moments, exercising leverage over them.[7] A close reading of these new sources and a rereading of familiar ones bring unexpected elements to the surface and help us rethink long-standing views about the minority presence in the city.

Another particularly corrosive element affecting minority studies in the field of Islamic urban history was the post-colonial tendency to write histories that glorified the triumphant nation-state. In nationalist-inspired narratives, residual minorities were sometimes viewed as errant actors who preferred to follow their own path rather than the mainstream direction plotted by nationalist regimes.[8] Builders of the new Arab or Turkish nations, sometimes overtly, at other times subconsciously, regarded minority communities as a species on its way to extinction. When minorities entered the discourse of the city, their places of habitation were usually looked on as frozen in time and lacking any evolutionary trajectory of their own, not even one that moved in tandem with the wider society. The intention was to absorb them as quickly as possible into the social fabric and to literally make them disappear.

Because the study of minorities and minority space in particular was regarded as irrelevant to the task of nation-building, the field was abandoned to specialists of minority cultures, whether the topic was Jews, Berbers, Armenians, or Kurds. When ethnicity appeared in historical urban studies, as it did in the work of the so-called Syrian school, it was very often asso-ciated with notions of rivalry and discord.[9] This standardization of urban space avoided taking into account the historical variability that was far closer to reality. Cities of the past were reduced to flat, two-dimensional models devoid of the rough-and-tumble of living social content. Talking about the persistence of paradigms that smoothed out the irregularities in the Muslim city, André Raymond has remarked: "Old myths about the homogeneity of the social body die hard."[10]

The question of integration versus separation is another contested terrain, espe-cially within Jewish historical studies. It is not possible to discuss topics such as trade, migration, and the transmission of ideas in the pre-modern Mediterranean world with-out taking into account the Jewish factor. In fact, Jews were so omnipresent in pre-modern Mediterranean history that they merited the status of a "civilization" in the work of Fernand Braudel, the doyen of Mediterranean historical studies. Developing an inter-pretive framework for understanding Jewish Mediterranean history poses a major chal-lenge to scholars, evoking a range of opinions and interpretations. Medievalist S.D. Goitein painted a harmonious portrait of inter-faith cooperation in the Mediterranean region from the tenth to thirteenth centuries in his magisterial *A Mediterranean Society*. His main source was a trove of letters and other documents from the *geniza*, or storeroom, of a Cairo synagogue.[11] Focusing on this single source, Goitein narrated a story of close and mutually reinforcing cross-communal ties at a particular moment of Mediterranean time. On the other hand, Jacob Katz, a scholar at the Hebrew University of Jerusalem and the most influential Jewish social historian of his day, held a different view of inter-communal relations. Katz forwarded a theory of "exclusiveness" that was significantly different from Goitein's idea of symbiosis. Katz regarded the strict separa-tion of Jews from non-Jews as a positive factor and an instrument of cultural survival. On the basis of his studies of Ashkenazi Jewish communities in the sixteenth through eighteenth centuries, Katz argued that Christians and Jews were "two distinct soci-eties" situated in two separate worlds.[12] Without making reference to time and place, he maintained that the Jew was "ecologically" suited to the ghetto, which possessed, in his words, "all the characteristics of a distinct civilization....The Jew whose work took him out of the ghetto and among Gentiles for the day or the week felt as if he were leav-ing his natural environment."[13] For Katz, the ghetto was a nurturing space, the site of a "full-blooded Jewish life" and its "logical corollary" was an indifference to conditions and events in the outside world.[14]

Katz's reading removed the dark cloud from the historical image of the European ghetto by making a virtue out of necessity; but in so doing, he ignored evidence of the intense interactions between Jews and non-Jews in the Sephardic Jewish world that encompassed much of the southern Mediterranean region. He may have brought a new dimension to the study of Northern European Jewish communities, but he contributed little to understanding the situation of Jews in the lands of Islam. Moreover, he endorsed the notion of Jewish exceptionalism based mainly on the ghetto experience, thereby contributing to a historiography of difference that separated the histories of Jews from the histories of those who surrounded them.[15]

Fernand Braudel, co-founder of the French *Annales* school, had much to say about the Jewish role in the pre-modern Mediterranean economy, but little to say about the Jewish contribution to urban life. Culturally, he saw Jews as an exotic species ("an Asiatic people in Europe, foreign to our part of the world, inextricably the prisoners of an ancient law given to them under a distant sky") whose main utility came from their contributions to the growth of capitalism.[16] Although he agreed that Jews were important "agents of cultural change," he argued that their primary linkages were to each other rather than to the wider society. Echoing Jacob Katz, he asserted that the Jewish "destiny" was its need to be "irreducible" and its refusal "to become diluted, " even suggesting that calamitous events such as the Spanish Inquisition were self-induced. His comment, "Every civilization is its own heaven and hell," seems to best sum up his point of view.[17] Inspirational on other topics, Braudel has surprisingly little to say about Jews as an urban phenomenon.

Although each of these approaches brought something new to the discussion of minorities and their use of space, no single methodology provided the perfect model. We decided to circumvent these historiographical roadblocks and to take as our starting point the physical form of the quarter. The underlying assumption of our research was that the residual spatial and architectural components could provide a jumping-off point for reading the minority quarter as a fundamental constituent of the larger urban environment. By mentally stripping away the accretions built up over time, we hoped to return to a moment in the lifespan of the city that narrated the reality of the minority presence from a new perspective.

PRIVILEGING THE "SPATIAL TURN"

The initial objective was to document the physical form of the quarter; that is, the houses, streets, churches, synagogues, shrines and public buildings that were the settings for social interaction. Using the fabric as text and reading backward in time, we noted how each site offered new material evidence about the quarter as a living entity: the plan of the house, the rhythms of the street, the pathways that led to the outside. Concurrently, we considered other topics relating to the status of the minority community, such as demographics, economic situation, and relations with authority, mostly gleaned from archival and secondary material. Moving outward in ever-widening circles, we looked for crosscutting themes that contributed to building theories about the character and function of these quarters and their role in maintaining urban order.

Our book begins with a study of Palermo in the later Middle Ages, where Muslims, Jews, and Christians intermingled in an ever-changing mosaic that adjusted to rapid shifts in the configuration of power. Then we move to Trani in Apulia during the late medieval period and early Renaissance, when it was one of the last footholds of Jewish settlement in the southern Italian peninsula. Here the theme is the intersection of authority and communal stability, and the dismemberment that takes place when political structures no longer support the minority presence. The dissolution of southern Italian Jewish communities like Trani coincided with the waves of expulsions of

Jews and Muslims from Iberia and southern France. The *expulsados* found new homes in cities in the Maghrib and the Mashriq, in the Balkans and in Anatolia, where they rebuilt on the substratum of pre-existing communities. Fez was the recipient of many of these émigrés, as was Marrakesh, where a Jewish nucleus established a stable presence in the sixteenth century that continued for nearly half a millennium. Both of these cities and their Jewish quarters are discussed in chapters devoted to them. Then we move to Tangier and Istanbul, tracing the development of their mixed quarters from the sixteenth to the nineteenth centuries, in order to examine how Jews, Muslims, and Christians adapted as old categories imploded and reformed in novel ways. The contracts that minorities brokered with the new urban order that came with modernity form the background to these two final chapters.

A COMPLEX MORPHOLOGY

How were ethnic quarters created and what is their specific character? In what ways, if any, do they differ from the rest of the city? Separate ethnic quarters have always been part of the Mediterranean city, and the voluntary grouping of ethnicities is a fact of Mediterranean life. The great cities of the Muslim West contained minority quarters in medieval times. We have detailed information about the *juderías* of Cordoba, Seville and Toledo, while the sources tell us that Ceuta had a Christian quarter in the twelfth century, housing "its own ovens, baths, church, and even a cemetery."[18] These quarters bore different names, some of them specific to Jews, such as the *mallâh* in Morocco, while others referred to residential quarters in general, regardless of who lived there: *hawma* (in Morocco), *hâra* (in Algeria, Tunisia and Egypt) *mahalle* and *nahiye* in Turkey.[19] The variety of forms they took were a result of differing historical, topographical and political realities. Initially, they seemed to defy categorization, but as the cases accumulated, we began to see some regularities in their patterns of growth.

The *mallâh* of Fez, for example, is distinguished by a complex morphology that reveals its increase by increments over time. The main gate of the *mallâh* is oriented on a north-south axis that is not congruent with the main street, suggesting that the street was laid out at a later date. We presumed that the area closest to the gate was the oldest part of the *mallâh*, since the most ancient synagogues were located nearby. In Fez, and indeed in each quarter we studied, there was a principal or main street, with secondary streets leading from it, following either a grid or a spine-like pattern. The newer quarters tended to preserve the grid, while the more ancient quarters display the involuted street pattern associated with the old *madîna*. Balat of Istanbul shows a different trajectory: though the quarter dates to the fifteenth century, repeated conflagrations in the nineteenth century opened the way for a massive restructuring of all sections of the urban fabric, including a regularization of the street network.[20] In every case we studied, the main street of the quarter was more impressive than the rest by virtue of its width, the grandeur of the buildings, and the density of traffic.

Like other quarters of the city, minority space evolved around a central node, usually a religious site. In Palermo, the Aghlabid mosque (Arabic, *masjid*, Spanish, *mesquita*),

La Grande Rue du Mellah

later converted into a synagogue, served for hundreds of years as the nucleus of the quarter to which it gave its name. In the Beni Ider quarter of Tangier, the *zâwiya* (lodge) of the Wazzâniyya brotherhood, built on the foundations of a mosque, forms the central nodal point. All the streets of the quarter radiate out from it. Organic development outward from a religious center seems to have been a principle of growth in several of the quarters we studied.

In planned minority quarters such as the *mallâh* of Marrakesh, the religious sites are less consequential in terms of the morphology of the quarter than in other places, so that internal nodes or poles of attraction were rare. Here, the container of the walls and the hierarchy of the streets seemed to take on greater importance in the absence of specific nodal sites such as tombs or synagogues. We found both planned and spontaneous patterns of growth at work in these quarters, with the latter by far the more usual. We concluded that whether the quarter was laid out at one time or developed incrementally, whether it was part of the old urban core or situated on the periphery, it grew according to the same organic processes as the rest of the city, spreading outward from a central point over a period of time.[21]

Some quarters we studied were walled and gated, others were not; in some places, simply the gates remain. A narrowing of the streets and an intensification of religious sites, nothing more, marks the Jewish neighborhood of Tangier, while a high wall, impressive gates, and a *burj*, or watchtower, announce the entry to the Jewish quarter of Fez. Access to the *giudecca* of Trani is through a monumental gate. Most of the Jewish quarters of Morocco had well-defined boundaries, making the separation between the Jewish quarter and the rest of the city one of the most salient facts of *mallâh* architecture. It is seductive to read into the outer wall a semiosis of exclusion. If the wall were a feature unique to the minority quarter, this would perhaps be so. But it is not, for the walled compound is omnipresent in southern Mediterranean architecture, on an ascending scale, from the level of the house to that of the quarter, to the city.

On the other hand, the wall around the *mallâh* did have symbolic resonance. It not only marked a clear transition from an exterior Muslim to an interior non-Muslim space; it also defined the limits of privacy for those on the inside. The wall also served as the *eruv*, the physical boundary that set off Jewish space from the rest of the city. Within its territory, always defined by some actual physical element, such as a wire or a wall, Jews were allowed the convenience of "carrying" personal objects on the Sabbath.[22] Thus the wall was multi-purpose; from the outside, it established a perimeter and a point of transition; from the inside, it had a symbolic importance that was deeply imbricated into the ritual practices of the community.

SOCIAL FACTORS AND SPATIAL DEFINITION

Although our research privileged the spatial, a layered sense of the complexity of the quarter began only when we introduced the socio-historical dimension. For example, the sources helped us to understand the human factor behind the genesis of these quarters, and especially the importance of migratory movements in their formation. Urban growth is almost always associated with inward migration, and the development of minority quarters is no exception. In Fez, Marrakesh, and Istanbul, rulers responded to the influx of Jewish and Muslim migrants from Iberia in the late fifteenth century and the resulting competition for space by organizing the construction of new minority quarters. While Muslim arrivals melded easily into the existing social fabric, the Jewish newcomers were less easily absorbed, as Emily Gottreich explains in her chapter on Marrakesh, leading to the founding of the *mallâh* in that city. In Balat, waves of migration into Istanbul orchestrated by the state initiated new communities of worship. Balat is dotted with synagogues created in the fifteenth and sixteenth centuries by Jews coming from all parts of the Ottoman Empire, but especially from (present-day) Macedonia, Bulgaria, and Greece. The remains of these synagogues are still visible today.

Although migratory waves placed a strain on resources, there was a positive aspect to these movements. By controlling the settlement of new populations, the state could expand the bounds of the city. Moreover, the tactic of populating new or abandoned quarters with minorities enhanced state power while heightening minority self-awareness through their identification with a specific place. Moreover, it concentrated minority assets and permitted their efficient mobilization in the service of the state. Simply put, taxes and fees were easier to collect when the subject populations were gathered in one place. More than a brute tactic of exclusion, the making of the minority quarter was often a strategy that went hand in hand, in most cases, with a rise in state power and a burgeoning economy.

Was the minority quarter public or private space? A quarter has specific qualities, whether it houses a minority or not. While public space concentrated around the main urban institutions, quarters were more private. The street network usually reflects the transition, moving from wide to narrow, from open to closed, as it branches out into the neighborhood. The ideal residential street in the Muslim city, according to Stefano Bianca, is the *cul-de-sac,* where movement can be closely watched and intruders immediately noticed.[23] In Hanafi law, according to Baber Johansen, residential space has a different status than public space; social control in the neighborhood is more personal than legal, replicating the controls within the family.[24] Minority quarters also seemed to function according to these principles. The degree of privacy in a quarter was relative to its size; large minority quarters broke down further into small neighborhood units, while small ones constituted a neighborhood in and of themselves.

In Balat of Istanbul, for example, a very large area, identity with the local neighborhood superseded identity with the district as a whole. Solidarities emerged from association with a specific street or location. It was only when the individual traveled outside of Balat that he or she became a *Balatli*. Otherwise, it was the immediate streets, the local mosque, church, or synagogue that advertised one's affiliations. A feeling of being "at home" was probably the essential quality of the quarter. Women went from house to house "uncovered," food could pass from one house to another without arousing comment. The neighborhood was the place for a sociability that did not exist elsewhere in the city; it was both private and extremely public, in the sense that every activity was noticed by one's neighbors. The repeated face-to-face meetings, the daily contacts, made for a sense of well-being, as well as its opposite—an uncomfortable sense of being "watched." "Home" was not only one's dwelling, but the streets and places surrounding it.

This quality of intimacy did not necessarily depend on exclusivity. As Karen Leal points out in her chapter on Balat, non-Jews resided in the predominantly Jewish neighborhoods of Istanbul, and Jews lived in Muslim neighborhoods. Even in medieval Palermo, according to William Granara, neighborhoods were not composed of a single ethnicity. Among the great *yalis* (mansions) mentioned by Evliya Çelebi in mid-seventeenth-century Ortaköy, a suburb of Istanbul, was that of Sekerci Yahudi, a Jewish sugar dealer, Mimar Mustafa, a Muslim builder, and Safiye Sultan, an Ottoman princess, along with other high Ottoman officials.[25] In fact, pure exclusivity in pre-modern Istanbul's neighborhoods seems to have been a rarity, if it existed at all.

Nevertheless, one of the characteristic features of the southern Mediterranean city from the later Middle Ages onward was the presence of quarters claiming a certain religious, ethnic, or "national" specificity. As André Raymond points out, eighteenth-century Cairo was at least 20 percent occupied by what he calls "national" communities (Kurds, Syrians, Maghribis) or religious groups (Jews, Copts, Syrian Christians). These quarters were found "everywhere" in the city, according to Raymond. Their number and names fluctuated over time, but not their average size, which was about 2 hectares.[26] Naguib Mahfouz's portrait of the rowdy Cairene neighborhood in his famous *Cairo Trilogy* captures the tenor of daily life in these enclaves.

When the quarter was predominantly composed of people of the same religion or ethnicity, how was its character established? Did people choose to live there, or were they moved there by force? Sometimes the making of the separate ethnic quarter was ordered by the authorities, as in the case of Fez, while at other times it was an accumulation of micro-steps leading to the self-willed separation of a group within its own exclusive terrain, as in Tangier. At other times, both processes took place sequentially. Balat, for example, was initially populated by imperial fiat, but later, minorities gravitated there voluntarily. A general observation is that forced relocations were often associated with moments of upheaval and times when men in power would seize the opportunity to reshape the body social to suit their own purposes. But forced segregation was not the only instrument of minority quarter formation, for people often chose to live together and went to great lengths to seek out their co-religionists. Goitein cites a twelfth-century letter to Abraham the Nagid, the son of the eminent Jewish philosopher Maimonides, complaining that apartment houses inhabited exclusively by Jews in Fustat, a section of Old Cairo, were hard to come by and therefore prohibitively expensive. Goitein concludes that Egyptian Jews in that era preferred to live together, even though they were not compelled to do so.[27]

In the case of Morocco, the separation of Jews from Muslims was usually imposed from above and reported in the sources as being associated with some form of religious transgression. Wine poured on the steps of the mosque, a careless insult, a supposed assault on a Muslim woman, are some of the misdeeds mentioned to justify the banishment. On closer inspection, however, it appears that these misdeeds took place in the presence of other factors, such as fierce competition over urban space. Separating out minorities and forcing them to move was often a pretext for clearing out a neighborhood and launching a round of land redistribution. The creation of the Fez *mallâh* is instructive in this respect. Jews lived in Old Fez for generations before the fifteenth century in a quarter in the heart of the old *madîna,* where their segregation was voluntary. The creation of a compulsory and exclusive Jewish space was the outcome of a decision by the authorities to remove Jews from the city center, eliminate them as a commercial threat, and liberate valuable land for redistribution to Muslim clients of the ruling dynasty. These measures were adopted in a climate of political turmoil as the Marinid princes, in the twilight of their rule, sought various means to shore up their tenuous hold on power.[28]

Donatella Calabi noticed a parallel phenomenon in sixteenth-century Venice, where the enlargement of the ghetto was tied in with a planned urban expansion allowing wealthy merchants "to carry out a profitable financial operation."[29] Yet another example of minority quarter formation as part of a larger scheme of urban growth took place in seventeenth-century Constantine. Jews were scattered throughout the town, mixed in with the rest of the population, before Salah Bey (ruled 1771–1792) settled them together in a new quarter to the north of the city. He then built a Friday Market, a mosque, and a *madrasa* (school) near the same area, meeting the needs of both Jews and non-Jews while expanding the city to accommodate a population increase.[30] We found that the formation of minority quarters proceeded from an array of measures ranging from mild manipulation to harsh coercion, and their location and dimensions were most often—but not always—determined by the authorities.

THE WORLD INSIDE: ARCHITECTURE, DOMESTICITY, AND SOCIAL CLASS

On entering the quarter, our attention is drawn immediately to the domestic architecture. Our research confirmed the findings of others that challenge the theory of the pervasiveness of the courtyard house.[31] Minority architecture presents a new perspective on the problem, however, prompting further questions: Does the minority house differ from the dominant type, and if so, how? Is there such a thing as a "Jewish" or "Christian" house? The house type is deeply rooted in society and its ordinariness is a source of difficulty, because it has rarely been documented historically. Moreover, it is a living organism, and scarcely an old house exists that has not been modified in some way. All the houses we studied mediated between some older form and more recent modifications. In every case, they were built using the construction techniques similar to houses in other parts of the city. Equal-sized plots and a regular alignment with the street demonstrated an understanding of town planning adapted from the culture of the majority, confirming that minorities were aware of the prevailing building techniques, absorbed through living together, just as language, food habits, and other social practices were acquired. One could speak of a principle of *osmosis* in minority building, in which the dominant type was assimilated and adapted to meet the specific needs of the minority neighborhood.

On the other hand, according to our observations, we cannot say that the "minority house" is exactly identical with the houses of the rest of the population. Signs of an assertive self-identification emerge in all the quarters we studied. In the Fez *mallâh*, for example, the plan of a Jewish house varied from that of the Muslim house of a comparable size and age. The left-over spaces around the courtyard of the Jewish house were often transformed into a labyrinth of smaller rooms that opened onto half-levels reached via hidden stairways. Access to the stairway was often concealed in a cupboard, so that it was difficult to detect, creating a secret means of communication within the house. Another variation of the Fez *mallâh* house was the cellar, frequently divided into rooms and storage areas, and in some cases, with a door that led out into the street. Jewish sources indicate that these basement storage areas were used to stockpile foodstuffs to be used in times of trouble. Donatella Calabi noted this same characteristic in the houses of the Italian ghettoes; in both Ferrara and Venice, secret corridors joined one house to another in a manner that was atypical for the rest of the city.[32]

The Moroccan Jewish house does not have the usual *saqîfa*, or dogleg entryway that increases the privacy of the interior by preventing a direct line of sight from the street to the inner courtyard. One can only speculate why this feature that was fundamental to the Muslim house plan was not considered necessary. Perhaps the need for strict privacy among Jews was less important than the need to conserve precious interior space. In Istanbul, Minna Rozen identified a special type of dwelling inhabited by Jews that was not found elsewhere in the city. The *yehudihane* was a three-story structure densely packed with small apartments facing an inner courtyard. Individual units were connected to each other by a balcony on the courtyard side.[33] However, it is debatable whether this was an exclusively "Jewish" type; perhaps so in Istanbul, but not elsewhere in the region. Tenement houses were common in Cairo, where they were known as *rab'* and were primarily inhabited by the working class. They were often the preferred form of housing for new arrivals from the countryside and men without families.[34]

Breaking radically with Ottoman tradition, the nineteenth-century row houses of Balat are built on small parcels of land, using materials that were fire resistant, with entryways above street level. The houses reflect design principles imported from Europe that circulated within the Ottoman Empire at that time. A specific typology that stands out is the row house with an *oriel*, or bow window made of material different from the rest of the façade. In many cases, their construction was the product of state planning in cooperation with local communities—Greek, Armenian and Jewish—who held title to the land. Today, both the bow windows and the small size of the house plots distinguish the Balat district from other parts of this huge and sprawling metropolis.[35]

Elements not found in the contemporaneous dominant type appear also in the Beni Ider quarter, where the diplomatic buildings introduced innovations such as the use of iron girders for structural framing, serial windows facing the street, and the application of cement grouting instead of lime. The influence of European construction techniques in Tangier is also evident in residential architecture; European architects working in turn-of-the-century Tangier introduced new elements into the local building culture that were soon disseminated to other cities of Morocco.

Difference is also apparent in the decoration of houses, where markers of identity appear on both the exterior and interior. Some examples: in the *mallâh*s of Fez and Marrakesh, the niche that once housed the *mezuzah* (protective amulet) was still visible in a much-scarred doorframe; in Tangier, the date of construction according to the Jewish calendar was worked into grillwork above a door. Also in Tangier, doors were even more explicit: *menorah*s and six-pointed stars were molded into the decorative woodwork. In Istanbul, the Star of David figured prominently on the fronts of Jewish-owned houses, while an urn above the lintel was the sign of a Greek Orthodox dwelling. In every quarter we studied, the house façade announced who were its owners through subtle signs that projected private identity into public space.

From our contemporary perspective, one of the most important indicators distinguishing the minority quarter from the rest of the city was its greater density. Limitations on building space meant that transformations and extensions often reached abnormal levels. The question arises: Were minority quarters historically overcrowded, or is the density we read today a more recent phenomenon? It is important to note that in the pre-modern period, excessive overcrowding was not a serious problem in any of the quarters we studied. War, disease, and famine limited the population, both minority and majority, and relieved pressure on living space. As late as 1901, an epidemic of malaria reduced the population of the Fez *mallâh* by more than one-third.[36] Migration from the countryside usually replenished these losses. It was not until the end of the nineteenth century that the situation changed dramatically and density became a pressing problem throughout the Mediterranean region, as a massive movement from the rural areas to the city produced an urban explosion. It is from this point forward

that the discourse of excessive density enters the sources.

Density creates detritus, and visitors often commented on the insalubrious conditions in the minority quarter, giving rise to the conclusion that it was in far worse condition than the rest of the city. In 1889, Pierre Loti depicted the *mallâh* of Fez as a scene out of hell, with its dark and malodorous streets and its "ashen-faced" inhabitants; in his popular guidebook to late nineteenth-century Istanbul, Edmundo de Amicis used similar language when describing the "stench" of Balat. José Benech, writing in the 1930s, said that passing through the main gate of the Marrakesh *mallâh* was "like descending into the Paris metro."[37] Were these observations the product of inflamed literary imaginations, or was there a real substance to the suggestion that the minority quarter was dirtier than the rest of the city? French traveler Charles René-Leclerc remarked about the Fez *mallâh* in 1904 that it was "as dirty and as badly maintained as is the rest of Fez," suggesting that conditions in the quarter were not unusual.[38] Yet others went to the opposite extreme, commenting on the orderly state of the minority quarter. We may conclude that 1) conditions varied greatly according to time and place and 2) the testimony of the traveler is not always the most reliable historical source.

Another distinguishing quality of the minority quarter was the variety of services concentrated in a very small space. In every case we studied, the quarter was able to function to a large extent on its own, from its own commercial center. The local market attracted people from the wider city who came to buy products not available elsewhere. Even today, the prices of goods in the *mallâh* of Marrakesh are known to be cheaper than those found in the rest of the city. Houses frequently contained workshops, salesrooms, and storage space, so that the principal means of livelihood was accommodated within the architecture of the house. *Hammâms*, bread ovens, schools, places of worship, and in the modern era, dispensaries, were liberally scattered throughout the neighborhoods, enhancing their self-contained quality. No doubt the quarter was dependent on exterior sources of supply over the long term; however, in the short run, residents could easily meet their daily needs within their immediate vicinity.

To what extent do minority quarters show evidence of social stratification? Data from the built environment confirm the presence of all social levels, from the very poor to the very wealthy. Indicators of wealth in domestic dwellings, according to Nelly Hanna, include room size, the presence of large reception rooms and balconies opening to the exterior, built-in features such as closets and beds, the use of decorative elements such as colored tiles, wooden paneling, inscriptions, access to water via an interior well or cistern, multiple floors, and a *minzah* or summer pavilion on the roof.[39] In Fez, great houses containing many of these features occupy the choicest parts of the Jewish quarter, aligned to the outer wall and overlooking the Sultan's palace in New Fez. The uniformity of their dimensions indicates that they were probably planned and built at the same time, in the late nineteenth century, a period that corresponds with the rise of an elite class of Jewish merchants who reached unprecedented levels of wealth and prestige through their alliances with the royal court. In this block of old mansions in the Fez *mallâh*, windows open to a view of the palace gardens, giving residents of the house access to light and air while maintaining their privacy. The Trani Jewish quarter still contains several grand *palazzi,* dating from the thirteenth century. In Tangier's Beni Ider quarter, houses of the very wealthy stood out from the rest, their lavish exterior decoration extolling the status of the owner.

At the scale of the quarter, however, there was little social segregation, at least up until the end of the nineteenth century. Before that, rich and poor tended to live side by side. In Fez and Trani, the houses of the very wealthy clustered together on the "high street," but in Marrakesh the very rich lived scattered about the quarter, often next to humble dwellings. The indicator of wealth was more often plot size than location, with wealthier inhabitants buying up an adjoining plot in order to build a house larger than that of their neighbors. This was the case with the house of the rich merchant Yesh`ua Corcos in the Marrakesh *mallâh*; the size of this house relative to its neighbors is still impressive. The fundamental nature of the North African *madîna* did not invite segregation by class. In choosing a house, less attention was paid to the social surroundings, and more was paid to privacy, plot size, and access to services.

Seemingly insignificant details often yield the most provocative information about class and status. The gently faded name card on the back of a synagogue bench in the Beni Ider quarter, held in place by a rusty pin, announces who sat in front, who sat behind. Names and inscriptions on silver lamps and Torah covers, old photos of community leaders forgotten on the wall, tell a story about relative social position. In the old Tangier Christian cemetery, now erased, the size, inscription, decoration, and location of the headstone was a measure of rank. A careful study of seemingly minor visual facts reveals traces of former hierarchies of personal power.

The minority quarters we studied also contained places of vice, usually located at a distance from the homes of the rich. In a street along the edge of the Jewish quarter of Marrakesh, Jews and non-Jews mingled in noisy bars, where fiery doses of *mahiya,* Jewish-made fig brandy, fueled the conversation. Muslim men of a certain age in Morocco remember with nostalgia nights spent in the Jewish quarter, known as a place of transgression. Such places were in short supply in the rest of the city. Unlike the Ottoman Empire, where coffee-houses were a feature of public life, cafés were not as common in Morocco; instead, people gathered in private houses, in mosques, and for those seeking different pleasures, in the drinking dens of the *mallâh*.

Prostitution is a theme that runs like a wild card through the study of minority space, though very little has been written on it. In the Marrakesh *mallâh* in the late nineteenth century, according to Emily Gottreich, drinking, gambling, and extra-marital sex were rampant: "Sexual impropriety was a basic characteristic of life in the *mallâh*."[40] The Marrakesh *mallâh* was home to many women without men, according to an 1890 census. Officially recorded as *ayâm* ("widow" or "unattached"), these women were most certainly prostitutes.[41] In a suburb of the Fez *mallâh* known as *nawâla* (huts) from the rustic style of housing found there, poor Jews and non-Jews cohabited in the early twentieth century. It was also a place of prostitution that Protectorate authorities tried repeatedly to clean up, but without success.[42] Why vice raged so fiercely in certain minority quarters is an intriguing question. Surely poverty, restricted possibilities for employment, and the availability of alcohol all played their part. But other factors must also have come into play that promoted the use of minority space for transgressive activities. The study of this issue in a variety of historical contexts is needed before any sweeping generalizations can be made.[43]

THE WORLD OUTSIDE: INSTITUTIONAL STRUCTURES AND RELATIONS WITH AUTHORITY

Minority quarters were organized both internally and externally through relations with the central power. From the point of view of the state, the collection of taxes and the maintenance of public order were primary concerns when it came to minority affairs. Overlapping state institutions kept a close watch, belying myths that minorities enjoyed complete autonomy. Relations between minority structures and the authorities were mediated by local "strong men" who had ready access to power. Every quarter had its headmen, shaykhs, rabbis, or elders whose authority was rooted in space—in the church or synagogue, in the meetinghouse and community center. They were crucial in determining the outcome of the countless situations that required negotiation between minority and majority; without this layer of protection, the individual was reduced to near impotence. In every case we studied, access to the favor of the authorities was the *sine qua non* for creating a framework in which the minority as a group prospered. When that access was removed, their situation became precarious.

The well-kept Italian archives are especially instructive on this point, showing that Jews of Napoli and Bari in the thirteenth and fourteenth centuries frequently had exchanges with the local nobility, who were much involved in the day-to-day details of Jewish governance. Trani's Jews were granted personal and commercial protection by Frederick II *in perpetuo* in return for the payment of an annual tax. Although considered inferior to Christians, they nevertheless were given the right to appeal in the courts in their own defense. In sum, the *droit de cité* that minorities enjoyed was contingent on the attitude of the governing power, and without its approval, minority settlement was tenuous at best. The cosmopolitan Mediterranean city did not grow by chance; it achieved that status through official complicity, and it was unmade when that complicity was withdrawn.

This environment of acceptance should not be misconstrued as an argument for a generalized pattern of *convivencia* across time and space. In the Muslim Mediterranean world in pre-modern times, periods of violence often erupted, but they were infrequent, and widespread genocide on the European model was extremely rare. Only two major episodes qualify as systematic, state-sponsored genocide against minorities, according to Jacqueline Hadziiossef: the first was the Fatimid interlude of the eleventh century that lasted only a few years, and the second was the more intense Almohad persecution of the twelfth century. This latter event caused Jews and Christians to flee the Maghrib for the safety of Egypt and the Christian enclaves of Iberia.[44] The recollection of these persecutions shaped inter-communal relations for generations to come. More usual were the petty acts of aversion: the baleful look, the tossed stone, the snatched head covering. Inside the walls of the quarter, the boundaries were clear; on the outside, matters were less safe.

In an alternative reading, these less lethal forms of violence can be seen as a perverse form of social engagement, a dynamic recognition of the other and his importance as a reflection of the self. Inter-communal conflict, as David Nirenberg has shown, was usually situational, often springing from competition between individuals rather than differences over belief. And the target of aggression was more often property than people.[45] In the 1912 uprising that destroyed a large part of the *mallâh* of Fez, only forty-five Jews lost their lives out of a community of several thousand. Many of them were victims—not of rural marauders or fellow Fâsîs—but of the French bombardment of the quarter.[46] We may conclude that competition was a perennial feature of inter-communal relations in a mixed society, but not the only mode through which that society should be conceived. Any notion of permanent structural exclusion based on intermittent periods of violence would constitute a serious distortion of the past.

THE MINORITY QUARTER AND MEMORY

All across the southern Mediterranean region, the coming of the twentieth century witnessed a seismic shift in relations between minorities and the central power. Minorities were subjected to new rules and obligations as states attempted to modernize and make more efficient use of their resources. The rise of nationalism hastened this process of centralization, accelerating the breakdown of the protective social covenants that were the sinews of a multi-ethnic society. According to urban historian David Harvey, it was a moment of "creative destruction" that introduced a century of upheaval.[47] As the twentieth century matured, the cosmopolitan cities of the southern Mediterranean (and those of Western, Central, and Eastern Europe, for that matter) disappeared into the chaos of war, revolution, mass migration, and even genocide. Throughout the Muslim Mediterranean, members of minorities abandoned their habitual quarters and fled or were forced into exile. In the best of circumstances, they melted into the anonymity of the homogenizing megalopolis; in the worst circumstances, they escaped with their lives, or not at all. It was a period of rupture, not unlike the earlier crisis of the late fifteenth century, when the *convivencia* of Muslim Spain fell victim to the Catholic reconquest.

When places of minority settlement are assimilated into the urban landscape and the story of their specificity is forgotten, we must consider this a form of erasure and cultural loss. When sites that contain layers of human experience become an empty shell, they lose their capacity to evoke memory. Memory, as we know, is a means of cataloguing the past; as Lawrence Kritzman says, it is the medium "through which cultural communities imagine themselves."[48] Memory is not always constructed in terms of space, but when it is, the imagining of place becomes a complex process whereby sites achieve a symbolic value that reinforces collective identity. Recognizing these "*lieux de memoire*" not only vivifies our understanding of the past, but also strengthens our ties to each other, whomever that *other* may be—family, group, or nation. Thus, an understanding of how cities and their various parts evolved would appear to be fundamental to constructing and maintaining social cohesiveness. By the same token, when we forget or ignore significant places in the historical landscape, we not only impoverish ourselves, we also suffer a deficit at the level of the collectivity.

An important motivation for us in carrying out this work was our belief that historical documentation was essential to preserving some vestiges of the fast-disappearing minority presence in places such as Fez, Marrakesh, Tangier, and Balat. These spaces are not only the property of the specific groups that created them; they are also the part of the patrimony of society-at-large and should be treated as national treasures. Although not subject to the same racism and genocide that obliterated minority sites throughout Europe during World War II, the minority places of the Muslim world are subject to different kinds of threats, such as neglect, the ravages of time, and the indifference of custodians. One of our main goals was to draw attention to those hidden "places of memory," not only for their heuristic value, but also for the sake of the feelings and emotions that recovered memories awaken. Christine Boyer captures this sentiment when she says:

> Perhaps it is the elusive quality of these outmoded places or their precarious state of existence that offers the spectator pleasure. Or pleasure might be found because these fragments reawaken forgotten memories that have long been dormant, or because their original function and purpose have been erased.... Whatever it is, these fragments and remnants cause an unexpected shift of attention, allowing a reappraisal of their presence in the city.[49]

This owes much to Walter Benjamin, who deplored the debased and soulless mediocrity of the modern city. He collected the ruined arcades, the neglected street signs and broken cornices, the bricks and tiles of old Paris and pointed out their value as mnemonic devices awakening us to the pleasure of buried memories.[50] Similarly, our purpose here is not only to study ruins, but also to evoke some of the beauty and richness that minorities brought to the urban scene. The chapters that follow are aimed especially at a new generation of listeners, in the hope of contributing to a discourse of inclusiveness in which forgotten places in the city are given the chance to speak again.

Notes

1. Studies of minority quarters in the North African context with an emphasis on urbanism include: Paul Sebag, *La hara de Tunis; l'évolution d'un ghetto nord-africain* (Paris: Presses universitaires de France, 1959); Abraham L. Udovitch and Lucette Valensi, *The Last Arab Jews: The Communities of Jerba, Tunisia* (Chur, Switzerland: Harwood, 1984); Daniel Schroeter, "The Jewish Quarter and the Moroccan City," in *New Horizons in Sephardic Studies*, ed. Yedida Stillman and George Zucker (Binghamton, NY: SUNY Press, 1993), 67–81; Emily Gottreich, "On the Origins of the Mellah of Marrakesh," *International Journal of Middle Eastern Studies* 35 (2003):287–305; Kenneth Brown, "An Urban View of Moroccan History: Salé 1000–1800," *Hesperis Tamuda* XII (1971):5–106. The excellent article by Donatella Calabi sets parameters for research in this field: "Les quartiers juifs en Italie entre 15e et 17e siècle; quelques hypothèses de travail," *Annales ESS* (1997): 777–797. Further research relating to urbanism and minority quarters is cited in the individual chapters.

2. The "People of the Book" (*ahl al-kitâb*), specifically Jews and Christians, were believers in the holy books of the Torah and the Gospels who intentionally rejected the prophecy of Muhammad. Allowed to live within the Muslim polity without having to convert to Islam, they were nevertheless compelled to adhere to the laws and obligations that made manifest their subordinate status. While varying greatly depending on time and place, laws concerning matters such as special taxes, codes of dress, modes of habitation, and practices of daily life profoundly molded how minorities fitted into the urban scene.

3. The literature on ethnic boundary maintenance is vast. The author found the work of Fredrik Barth particularly helpful, especially the "Introduction" he wrote for a collection of essays entitled *Ethnic Groups and Boundaries* (Bergen, Universitetsforlaget, London, Allen & Unwin, 1969).

4. The "Islamic city" concept was developed by French researchers during the colonial period, first by William Marçais, in his article "L'islamisme et la vie urbaine," *Comptes Rendus de l'Académie des Inscriptions et Belles Lettres* (1928): 86–100, and further elaborated by Georges Marçais, "La conception des villes de l'Islam." *Revue d'Alger* 2, no. 10 (1945): 517–533. An oft-quoted critique by an urban sociologist is Janet Abu-Lughod, "The Islamic City-Historic Myth, Islamic Essence, and Contemporary Relevance," *International Journal of Middle Eastern Studies* 19 (1987): 155–176. A revisionist view based on more solid historical research is André Raymond, "Islamic City, Arab City: Orientalist Myths and Recent Views," *British Journal of Middle Eastern Studies* 21, 1 (1994): 3–18.

5. Akel Kahera and Omar Benmira, "Damages in Islamic Law: Maghribî Muftîs and the Built Environment (9th–15th Centuries C.E.)," *Islamic Law and Society* 5 (1998): 131–164.

6. J.O. Hunwick, "The Rights of Dhimmîs to Maintain a Place of Worship: A Fifteenth-Century Fatwâ from Tlemcen," *al-Qantara* 12 (1991):141, 149.

7. A particularly good example of Jewish agency on the political level is retold in Daniel J. Schroeter, *The Sultan's Jew: Morocco and the Sephardi World* (Stanford, CA: Stanford University Press, 2002).

8. French social historian Lucette Valensi critiques the "teleological" character of minority studies written to serve the purposes of the nation-state in her "Inter-Communal Relations and Changes in Religious Affiliation in the Middle East (Seventeenth to Nineteenth Centuries)," *Comparative Studies in Society and History* 39, 2 (April 1997): 252. Even influential thinkers who eschewed nationalist rhetoric had an aversion to an over-emphasis on minorities. Oxford Middle East historian Albert Hourani declared that minority history represented a "disproportionate concern" for historians and called for a redressing of the balance. Albert Habib Hourani, Philip S. Khoury, and Mary C. Wilson, *The Modern Middle East: A Reader* (London, New York: Tauris, 1993), 25.

9. André Raymond, "Islamic City," 5.

10. Ibid., 14.

11. S.D. Goitein, *A Mediterranean Society: The Jewish Communities of the Arab World as Portrayed in the Documents of the Cairo Geniza*, 5 vols. (Berkeley: University of California Press, 1967–1988).

12. Jacob Katz, *Exclusiveness and Tolerance* (New York: Oxford University Press, 1961), 22. On the Jerusalem school in general, see David Nirenberg, *Communities of Violence: Persecution of Minorities in the Middle Ages* (Princeton, NJ: Princeton University Press, 1996), 9 and "Introduction," notes 19 and 20.

13. Katz, *Exclusiveness*, 133.

14. Ibid.

15. Historian Mark Cohen has aptly labeled this tendency as "the neo-lachrymose conception of Jewish-Arab history," and we have many examples of this genre. See his *Under Crescent and Cross: The Jews in the Middle Ages* (Princeton, NJ: Princeton University Press, 1994) and the review by D. Lasker in *The Jewish Quarterly Review 88*, 1–2 (July–October, 1997) 76–78.

16. Fernand Braudel, *The Mediterranean and the Mediterranean World in the Age of Philip II*, transl. Siân Reynolds. 2 vols. (New York: Harper Torchbook, 1975): II, 805.

17. Ibid., II, 826.

18. Evariste Levi-Provençal, *Las ciudades y las instituciones urbanas del Occidente musulman en la Edad Media* (Tetuán: Editora Marroqui, 1950); Jean Brignon et al., *Histoire du Maroc* (Paris: Hatier, 1967), 121–124.

19. On the *hâra*, see Nadim al-Messiri, "The Concept of the Hara: A Historical and Sociological Study of al-Sukkariyya," *Annales Islamologiques* 15 (1979): 313–347. On the urban quarters of Istanbul, see Cem Behar, *A Neighborhood in Ottoman Istanbul: Fruit Vendors and Civil Servants in the Kasap Ilyas*

Mahalle (Albany: State University of New York Press, 2003), Introduction.

20 Zeynep Çelik, *The Remaking of Istanbul: Portrait of an Ottoman City in the Nineteenth Century* (Berkeley: University of California Press, 1993), ch. 3.

21. André Raymond, "La structure spatiale de la ville," in *Sciences sociales et phénomènes urbains dans le monde arabe : actes du colloque de l'Association de Liaison entre les Centres de recherches et documentations sur le monde arabe (ALMA), Casablanca, 30 novembre—2 décembre 1994*, ed. Mohamed Naciri and André Raymond (Casablanca: Fondation du Roi Abdul-Aziz Al-Saoud pour les études islamiques et les sciences humaines, 1997), 80.

22. *Encyclopaedia Judaica*, 2d edition, vol. VI, s.v. "Eruv."

23. Stefano Bianca, *Urban Form in the Arab world : Past and Present* (London, New York: Thames & Hudson, 2000), 38–39.

24. Babar Johansen, quoted in Raymond, "La Structure spatiale," 76.

25. Minna Rozen, "Public Space and Private Space among the Jews of Istanbul in the Sixteenth and Seventeenth Centuries," *Turcica* 30 (1998): 340.

26. Raymond, "Islamic City, Arab City," 15.

27. Goitein, *A Mediterranean Society*, 4: 21.

28. Mercedes García-Arenal, "Les Bildiyyîn de Fès, un groupe de néo-musulmans d'origine juive," *Studia Islamica* LXVI (1987):113–143. Many wealthy Jewish merchants refused to move to the *mallâh* and instead converted to Islam. Known as the *bildiyyîn* ("locals") or *muhajjirîn* ("those who departed"), they kept alive the memory of their Jewish roots and continued to play a role as a group in the complex politics of Fez up to the nineteenth century.

29. Donatella Calabi, "La cité des juifs en Italie entre XVe et XVIe siècle," in Jacques Bottin and Donatella Calabi, *Les étrangers dans la ville: minorités et espace urbain du bas Moyen âge à l'époque moderne* (Paris: Editions de la Maison des sciences de l'homme, 1999), 26.

30. André Raymond, "Les caractéristiques d'une ville arabe `moyenne` au XVIIIe siécle. Le cas de Constantine," *Revue de l'Occident Musulman et de la Méditerranée* 44 (1987): 138.

31. Raymond, "Islamic City," 16.

32. Calabi, "La cité des juifs," 35. How the Fez *mallâh* organized to combat food shortages is discussed in my article: "The Mellah of Fez: Reflections on the Spatial Turn in Moroccan Jewish History," in *Jewish Topographies*, ed. A. Nocke, J. Brauch, A. Lipphardt (Aldershot, Hampshire: Ashgate, 2008), 101–118.

33. Minna Rozen, "Public Space and Private Space," 342–343.

34. On the *rab'* in Cairo, see Hazem I. Sayed, *The Rab' in Cairo—A Window on Mamluk Architecture and Urbanism*. (Ph.D. diss., MIT, 1987), and J.-Ch. Depaule [et al.], *Actualité de l'habitat ancien au Caire: le Rab' Qizlar* (Cairo: Centre d'Études et de Documentation Économiques Juridiques et Sociales, 1985). I am grateful to Prof. Heghnar

Watenpaugh for providing me with these references.

35. Rémi Stoquart, *Réhabilitation des quartiers de Balat et de Fener (péninsule historique d'Istanbul: diagnostic et propositions d'aménagement, février 1998* ([Turkey?]: UNESCO, 1998), 24–32.

36. Moïse Nahon, "Les Israélites du Maroc," *Revue des études ethnographiques et sociologiques* (1909): 258–279. For more on epidemics, see Georges Vajda, "Un Recueil de textes historiques judéo-marocains." *Hespéris* 35, 36 (1948–49): 311–358, 139–388: in 35 (1948): 319, 326; in 36 (1949): 161–162, 188.

37. Pierre Loti, *Au Maroc* (Paris: Boîte à documents, 1988), 206; José Benech, *Essai d'explication d'un Mellah* (Paris: Maisonneuve, 1940), 2.

38. Charles René-Leclerc, *Le Maroc septentrional: souvenirs et impressions (été 1904)* (Algiers: Imp. Algérienne, 1905), 149.

39. Nelly Hanna, "Social Implications of Housing Types in 17th and 18th century Cairo," in Naciri and Raymond, *Sciences sociales et phénomènes urbains*, 85. In Morocco, houses that belonged to the *habûs*, or religious endowment, were often resold and their price recorded. E. Michaux-Bellaire, ed., *Les Habous de Tanger: Registre officiel d'actes et de documents, part 2, Analyses et extraits* (Paris: Ernest Leroux, 1914), *passim*.

40. Emily R. Gottreich, "Rethinking the Islamic City from the Perspective of Jewish Space," *Jewish Social Studies* 11,1 (2004): 131.

41. Emily R. Gottreich, *The Mellah of Marrakesh : Jewish and Muslim Space in Morocco's Red City* (Bloomington: Indiana University Press, 2007), 82.

42. Bibliothèque générale et archives (BGA) Rabat, Fonds du Protectorat, Carton 1046, Aménagement de Fès, Proces-verbaux reunion 21 Decembre 1925, "Eloignement des prostitutées du quartier des Nouail."

43. See comments by Omnia El Shakry in the *Encyclopedia of Women & Islamic Cultures*, III, "Family, Body, Sexuality and Health" (Leiden-Boston: Brill, 2006), 354.

44. Jacqueline Hadziiossif, "Les conversions des juifs à l'islam et au christianisme en Méditerranée XIe-XVe siècles," in *Mutations d'identités en Méditerranée: Moyen Age et époque contemporaine*, ed. C. Veauvy, E. Dupuy, and H. Bresc ([Saint-Denis]: Bouchène, 2000), 159–162. The Almohad storm is hardly mentioned in Arabic sources. The most explicit reference is a letter written by a Jewish merchant of Fustat (old Cairo) that records the testimony of eyewitnesses: H. Z. Hirschberg, *A History of the Jews in North Africa*, 2 vols. (Leiden: Brill, 1974–81), I, 127–129.

45. An important point made repeatedly by Nirenberg, *Communities*, 9, 30, 163–65, 177, 180, 201, 226–230.

46. Hischberg, *History*, II, 318. See the first-person account of this uprising by an unnamed woman who makes the allegation that the French artillery

was responsible for most of the deaths. Her account makes it clear that the Muslims who pillaged the quarter were tribesmen from outside. Louis Brunot and Elie Malka, *Textes judéo-arabes de Fès: Textes, transcription, traduction annotée* (Rabat: Ecole du Livre, 1939), 206–212.

47. David Harvey, *Paris, Capital of Modernity* (London and New York: Routledge, 2006), 1.

48. Pierre Nora and Lawrence D. Kritzman, *Realms of Memory : Rethinking the French Past,* 3 vols. (New York: Columbia University Press, 1996), I, ix.

49. M. Christine Boyer, *The City of Collective Memory: Its Historical Imagery and Architectural Entertainments* (Cambridge, MA: MIT Press, 1994), 19.

50. There are a few signs of the awakening of an interest in the cultural and touristic value of minority quar-

ters. In Palermo, the municipality recently erected signs with the street names written in Hebrew, Arabic, and Italian; in Trani, private citizens working with city officials have erected public plaques pointing out the Jewish quarter. Unfortunately, the jewel of the quarter, the Sant'ana synagogue (converted into a church, now abandoned) goes unmarked and unrestored. In Fez and Tangier, émigrés have financed the restoration of synagogues, and in Tangier, the Cathedral has been completely renovated. The thriving Istanbul Jewish community has renovated the Ahrida synagogue in Balat, but the more interesting Ichtipol synagogue, classified as a historical monument, is on the verge of falling into ruins.

WILLIAM GRANARA

1

FRAGMENTS OF THE PAST: RECONSTRUCTING THE HISTORY OF PALERMO'S *MESCHITA* QUARTER

Situated in the northwest corner of Sicily, the Mediterranean's largest island, Palermo was one of the most strategically important urban centers of the medieval Mediterranean world. Its stature as major metropolis began in 831 CE, when Muslim forces arriving from North Africa conquered the city and made it their Sicilian headquarters. Using Arabic chronicles and travelogues, Jewish personal narratives, and various historiographical, cultural, and visual information, here we reconstruct an account of the Meschita quarter of medieval Palermo, home to a mixed minority population of Jews and Muslims throughout the medieval period.

By scrutinizing one neighborhood to visualize the whole, we gain greater insight into how Arabo-Islamic, pan-Mediterranean, and European influences nourished Palermo's growth. The story of the Meschita quarter parallels the development of Palermo from its earliest stages as an Arab garrison town, based on a classical Roman *castrum*, to a bustling and diverse Mediterranean entrepôt. It also traces Palermo's transition from an exclusively military society, comprised mainly of Muslim victors and non-Muslim vanquished, to a complex, multi-religious, multi-ethnic, and multi-lingual society that commanded a leading place in commerce, industry, arts, literature, and governance. Finally, the reconstruction of the Meschita quarter in the medieval period will shed light on how different communities interacted and lived together. To what degree did the Muslims, Christians, and Jews of Palermo participate in collective institutions and public spaces? What were the contours and limitations of their private, separate, lives?

During the ninth through thirteenth centuries, Sicily was an arena of intense rivalry between Muslims and Christians, exacerbated by interference from the outside superpowers of Byzantium and the various ruling dynasties of North Africa. Meanwhile, the Jews, lacking any outside political patron, were treated by both Muslim and Christian overlords as a protected minority. Under Muslim rule, Jews had the legal status of "people of the Book" (*ahl al-dhimma*), while under the Christian authority, they were considered "possessions of the crown" (*servi regiae camerae*). However, laws governing inter-group relations fluctuated with circumstances, making legal status an imperfect lens for viewing the shape of minority existence. Rather, we turn to other sources to approximate an image of reality; a physical study, looking at the residences, religious and other public buildings, businesses, markets, streets, and squares, provides us with important evidence. The expansion and contraction of the Meschita quarter, its spatial, cultural, and demographic status relative to other parts of the city, tell us far more about the tenor of minority life than formal legal arrangements. In surprising ways, the story of the Meschita quarter of Palermo, read as *petit recit,* contests the *grand recit* of the medieval world as intolerant, violent, and resistant to cross-cultural contact. Palermo as *shared space* for Muslims, Christians, and Jews gives credence to S.D. Goitein's thesis of a "humane broadmindedness" that graced much of the medieval Mediterranean world.[1]

The location of the Meschita quarter within the urban fabric attests to its centrality. If we apply the "core and boundary zone hypothesis" and argue that political sovereignty began at the urban center and expanded outward to include "transitional zones" of agricultural lands and fortress towns, we see that this neighborhood housing a majority of the Jewish population was an integral part of the Palermitan core.[2] It also appears to have been a stable place of settlement; there is no mention of expulsions or forced movements of Jews in and out of the quarter throughout the Muslim period and early years of the Norman period (tenth to twelfth centuries). Because it enjoyed certain rights and privileges, and because its accumulated wealth was a rich source of revenue for the state, the Jewish community was closely guarded by the Muslim authorities. By contrast, the later Christian dynasties in the thirteenth and fourteenth centuries developed different strategies that led to erratic policies toward the non-Christian populations, based on political whim, economic necessity, and ideological cross-currents.

MAPPING PALERMO: IBN HAWQAL'S "SÛRAT AL-ʿARD"

The Muslim invasion of Sicily in the summer of 827, conducted with the fanfare of a full-fledged *jihâd*, changed the political and socioeconomic landscape of the island in radical ways. The autonomous Aghlabid ruling family from Ifriqiyya (modern Tunisia), faced with a host of domestic problems, turned outward and found an expedient solution by exaggerating the threat of a Byzantine-controlled Sicily. After four years of fierce Byzantine resistance, the Muslim forces succeeded in conquering Palermo. They called their new city *Balarm*, the Arabic pronunciation for *Panormo*, its name since ancient times. Like other foreign conquerors before them, Carthaginians, Romans and Greeks, the Muslims were seduced by Palermo's admirable situation, as well as its abundance of fertile land and fresh water. The decision of the Muslim commanders in 831 to make Palermo their military headquarters and new capital city had far-reaching repercussions. It shifted political and economic influence away from Syracuse, the political and economic capital of Byzantine Sicily for two centuries, and the island's major portal to the eastern Mediterranean since the time of the Phoenicians.

Moreover, the establishment of Palermo brought together the various segments of a new society that included both conquerors and conquered. Its urban-centered economy was largely dependent upon a semi-rural agriculture and a vibrant international trade, creating a confluence of town and a countryside whose natural and human resources now contributed to a prosperous and dynamic urban culture. The growth of Palermo, along with its satellite agricultural hinterland, was undoubtedly a major factor in the Arab conquerors' success in putting an end to the antiquated system of Latin-Byzantine *latifondi* (rural estates), with their baronial lords presiding over peasant farmers. Finally, the creation of Palermo as an urban center allowed different groups to settle in their own separate enclaves while affording them the opportunity to participate in a vibrant urban sphere. Jews left their Sicilian hometowns of Syracuse, Trapani, and Messina in search of greater opportunities in *al-Madina*, or "the City," as Palermo came to be called by the islanders. Like distant Baghdad during the same period, Palermo was being transformed into a city where "the varied ethnic and multiple religious population...was grouped by quarters and districts, with each remaining basic to the urban social structure."[3]

In 973, the traveler-geographer Abû al-Qâsim Ibn Hawqal visited the island of Sicily and recorded his observations in his masterful treatise, *Sûrat al-ʿArd* (The Configuration of the Earth).[4] Filled with astute scientific observations on the one hand, and acerbic comments on the peculiarities of Sicilian Muslims on the other, this account continues to draw the attention of modern scholars. His contempt for the arrogance, dim-wittedness, immorality, and cowardice of his co-religionists clashes wildly with an otherwise care-

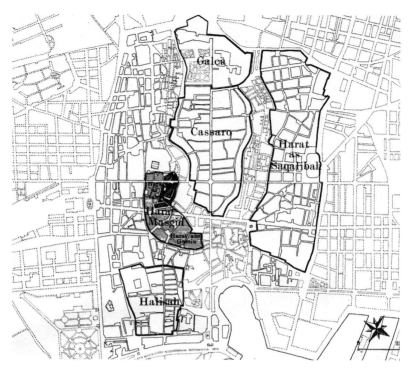

The medieval center of Palermo, after the *Sûrat al-ʿArd* of Ibn Hawqal. The Meschita quarter is at the center of the map.

ful and objective description of the island's physical features and social structures.

Ibn Hawqal provides us with the first comprehensive description of Palermo in the Muslim period. He verbally maps out five quarters: (1) Balarm, the old city center, called the "Cassaro" by modern Italian scholars, referring to the original walled city dating back to Phoenician and Roman times; (2) al- Khâlisa, today's Kalsa neighborhood; (3) Hârat al-Saqâliba , or the Slav Quarter; (4) Hârat Masjid Ibn Saqlâb, or the quarter of the Mosque of Ibn Saqlâb, that we now refer to as the Meschita quarter; and (5) al-Hâra al-Jadîda (the New Quarter). Ibn Hawqal describes them as contiguous but separate. Historian Rosario La Duca has reconstructed a map of Muslim Palermo that clearly shows these divisions.[5]

According to the Ibn Hawqal, Balarm or *al-Madîna* was protected by high, fortified walls. It was the seat of the Aghlabid governors of Ifriqiyya who ruled Sicily from 831 to 909. The economic and spiritual heart of the town, it was also the site of the Great Mosque (*al-masjid al-jâmiʿî*), a converted Byzantine church. Ibn Hawqal recounts that the coffin of Aristotle was once suspended inside, suggesting that the former church had even older roots, possibly dating back to pre-Roman times. Contemporary historians assume that the present Cathedral of Palermo, housing the burial places of both Roger II (d. 1054) and Frederick II (d. 1250) and located in the present-day Corso Vittorio Emanuele, is built on the site of the former Great Mosque.

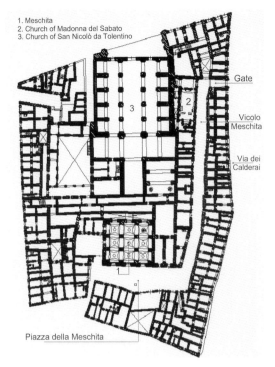

1. Meschita
2. Church of Madonna del Sabato
3. Church of San Nicolò da Tolentino

Gate

Vicolo
Meschita

Via dei
Calderai

Piazza della Meschita

Tissue of the Meschita quarter

The al-Khâlisa quarter survives today as the Kalsa. Situated on the Foro Italico, it extends south along via Lincoln and includes the Piazza Marina to the north. Al-Khâlisa was a fortified village built by Muslim naval commander Khalîl Ibn Ishâq in 940 to house the Fatimid sultan and his entourage. Khalîl was sent to Sicily from Ifriqiyya in 938 by the Fatimid caliph al-Qâ'im at the head of an armada to quell a local uprising that started in the Berber city of Agrigento and soon spread to Arab-dominated Palermo. The cause of the insurrection is not clear, and the usual explanation that the indigenous Sunni Palermitans were rising up against their Shi`î Fatimid masters is overly simplistic. After conquering the town, Khalîl appropriated material from the old city to build a new town closer to the sea, making it easier for the Fatimid rulers and their local clients to escape another attack.[6] The Khâlisa, according to Ibn Hawqal, had protective walls penetrated by three gates, except on the seaside, where there was no gate. Unlike the "typical" Islamic city, it had no marketplaces (*aswâq*) or hostelries (*fanâdiq*); however, it did have two public baths (*hammāmāt*), a small Friday mosque (*masjid jâmi` saghîr muqtasid*), a royal barracks (*jaysh*), an arsenal (*dâr sinâ`a*), and government offices (*diwân*).

The Slav Quarter was the most populous. It bordered on the sea toward the northeast, without any surrounding walls. It had many springs, and a waterway called the Pepiro separated it from old Palermo that lay to its south. As its name suggests, it may have been the most demographically fluid neighborhood, where new arrivals, traveling merchants, slaves [or Slavs] from the Dalmatian coast, and *dhimmîs* (Christians and Jews) may have lived.[7]

The fourth Quarter was called the *masjid,* the mosque quarter, or the Meschita as it is known today. It also bordered the old urban core to the south, it too was not walled, and it had a waterway running along its east-west border. Ibn Hawqal counted a large number of mills along its course. Finally, the New Quarter [al-Jadîda] lay at the south end of greater Palermo and sat adjacent to the Meschita with no discernible borders separating them. This quarter was also unwalled, and like the Meschita, it was a bustling commercial center. In fact, a major portion of Palermo's markets were located in these two quarters: olive vendors, grain merchants, wheat sellers, money changers, druggists, masons, sword makers, embroiderers and tailors, fishmongers, butchers, greengrocers and dry grocers, fruit vendors, sellers of herbs and spices, ceramicists, bakers, rope makers, tanners, carpenters, potters, and cobblers all plied their trades.

The city described by Ibn Hawqal in 973, almost a century and a half after its establishment as an Arab capital, had already undergone radical changes. In 909, the Aghlabids of Ifriqiyya were replaced by their Shi'î Fatimid enemies. These newcomers were quick to lavish their attention and resources on their new Sicilian province. On the popular level, the pervasive influence of Maliki Sunni Islam, introduced into Sicily by migrants from North Africa, continued to hold sway over large swaths of the Sicilian population. They remained devoted to their Sunni religious leaders as well as to the orthodox caliph in Baghdad. For Ibn Hawqal, an open rebellion of major segments of the population only thirty years before his writing was just one element disturbing his picture-perfect image of Muslim unity. Muslim Sicily had a glorious reputation for being a militant outpost (*thaghr*) of *jihâd;* what Ibn Hawqal found on his arrival ran counter to his expectations. Palermo was no longer simply a garrison town of warriors (*mujâhidîn*) answering the call to holy war; rather, it was a thriving urban center of merchants and artists, teachers and scholars, who lived far from events on the battlefield. Ibn Hawqal was deeply disappointed by their lack of religious zeal and accused the Sicilians of cowardice and debauchery. He complained that they "freeloaded" off the fortified monasteries (*ribâts*) built along the coast, and he hurled invectives against them for marrying infidels and shirking their religious duties. His bitter words read today like the diatribe of a self-righteous rustic against the evils of the godless metropolis.

Ibn Hawqal's visit coincided with a relatively peaceful period on the military front. Most of the island had by that time submitted to Muslim sovereignty, with only small pockets of Christian resistance in the northeast corner. Local governors, clients of the Fatimid rulers, had begun to establish some semblance of political order. A peaceful succession of local rulers held in check the latent tensions between the island's perennial oppositional forces: Arabs versus Berbers, urban versus rural habitants, and settled veterans versus newcomers. The Fatimid victory over Egypt and the transfer of the seat of government from Ifriqiyya to Cairo in 969 gave their Sicilian governors more autonomy. In these new circumstances, a powerful commercial triangle of Sicily-North Africa-Egypt began to dominate Mediterranean trade, continuing well into the eleventh century and beyond.[8] Palermo's location on this great trade route gave its local mer-

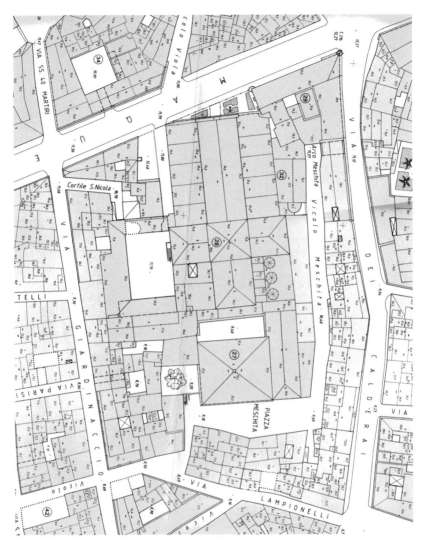

Plan of the Meschita quarter

chants and artisans, and especially those from the Jewish minority, a secure niche in the regional economy.

The area that Ibn Hawqal calls the Jewish neighborhood, or *Hârat al-yahûd,* was located within the Masjid Ibn Saqlâb Quarter. It was adjacent to the old city center, or Cassaro, and had access to it through the Iron Gate (*bâb al-hadîd*). On its south side lay the New Quarter, also a bustling commercial area. There is every reason to believe that the *hârat al-yahûd,* or Meschita quarter, was the principal place of Jewish residence and the focus of Jewish economic activity in the tenth century. However, the quarter was not exclusively Jewish, and there is also evidence that Jews resided in other parts of the

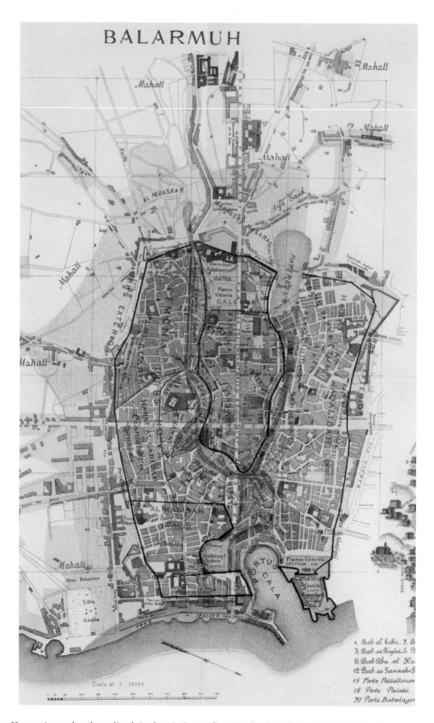

Palermo in 1889 superimposed on the medieval city, from *La Topografia Antica di Palermo* by Vincenzo Di Giovanni

city as well. Later, in the early fourteenth century, as Eliyahu Ashtor reminds us, Frederick III of Aragon expelled all the Jews from areas of the old city center surrounding the Cassaro, indicating that Jews lived dispersed throughout the old town. Nothing resembling a ghetto, either in physical form or social conditions, existed in Palermo at that time.[9]

The description of the *Hârat al-yahûd* by Ibn Hawqal resonates today. Vincenzo Di Giovanni's map of 1889, compared with a map of Palermo today, confirms the location of the borders of Palermo's medieval Jewish neighborhood.[10] The streets describing the limits of the quarter and the medieval gate, the Arco della Meschita (located on the site of the former Bab al-Hadîd), still serve as its entryway. Via dei Calderai, the major commercial artery of the Jewish quarter, snakes around the quarter in a semi-circle, defining its perimeter. Entering the quarter through the main gate from Via dei Calderai, the pedestrian immediately turns left into the quarter. Facing the opening of the gate is the diminutive Church of the Madonna del Sabato, built in a basilica style, most certainly a synagogue before its conversion into a church. Some historians speculate that this church was used by *marranos*, or Jewish converts to Christianity who continued to practice their former religion in secret. A residential street, Vicolo della Meschita, runs parallel to Via dei Calderai. It turns into the Piazza della Meschita, the open space in front of the main monument of the quarter, the Meschita, located at its center. This piazza then leads into Via Giardinaccio, the street that defines the southern limit of the quarter. The street pattern of the medieval quarter is easily discernable today thanks to the survival of nearly all the old toponyms. Indeed, it is remarkable how much of it has been preserved, given the transformations of later centuries that incorporated this neighborhood into the larger city.[11]

The Meschita neighborhood shares essential features with an eastern Arab city, with its open spaces, schools, baths, butcher shops, and cemeteries, and its streets ending in a *cul-de-sac*, according to Antonella Mazzamuto.[12] In the midst of the neighborhood was the great synagogue that gave the quarter its name, the main religious and social center of the medieval Jewish community. Recent studies based on its architectural features and its orientation suggest that the synagogue was originally a mosque (*meschita*),[13] and was most likely turned over to the Jews after the Norman conquest in 1072, when large segments of the Muslim population emigrated or were expelled from Palermo. Today the building standing on the site is the home of the Sicilian National Archives.

Via dei Calderai remains powerfully evocative of a medieval Arab *sûq*. The street and its surrounding alleyways are filled with shops grouped according to the goods and services on offer: potters, tanners, smiths, linen vendors. The shops are simple one-room storefronts, with residential apartments on the upper floors. A closer look reveals that the third—and is some cases, fourth floors—were later additions to the original two-story structures. The feeling of concentrated closeness in the street creates a level of intensity different from the rest of the urban fabric.

A metal goods shop on via dei Calderai

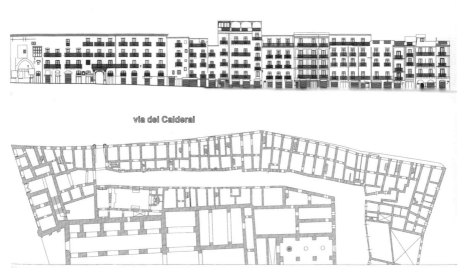

via dei Calderai

Survey of housefronts and tissue of via dei Calderai

In the first decades of the eleventh century, Muslim rule over Sicily began to unravel. Societal tensions that had plagued Sicily since the Muslim conquest, such as Berber resentment of the powerful Arab elite, urban interests as opposed to rural ones, hostility between the "first" settlers and the more recent ones, and perennial squabbles over political legitimacy, resurfaced with a vengeance. Moreover, the population remained divided between allegiance to the Fatimids in Cairo and to the upstart Zirid princes of Tunis (reigned 1016–1166), who were striving to regain control over Sicily and its highly lucrative economy.

In this period, our richest source for tracing Jewish life in Sicily, especially in the commercial sphere, are the documents found in the *geniza* of the Ben Ezra synagogue of Old Cairo (Fustât) in the late nineteenth century. S.D. Goitein, in his exhaustive study of this material, observes that most of the letters concerning Sicily dating from the eleventh century, when the collection is most expansive, refer to Palermo.[14] In addition to owning shops and contributing richly to the domestic economy, the Jews of Palermo were engaged in Sicily's flourishing overseas trade. Exports included luxury goods such as men's silken turbans, robes, carpets and brocaded covers, leather goods, and foodstuffs such as cheese, wheat, and shelled almonds. Imports included Egyptian flax, dyes such as indigo, brazilwood, pepper and other spices, drugs, medicinal plants, perfumes, Egyptian mats, pottery, jewelry, and clothing. The trade in luxury goods attests to a high standard of living. Moreover, the proliferation of marketplaces throughout the city, and the easy flow from one to another, speaks of a bustling economy generating revenues that were dispersed throughout the population. The importance of Jews to international trade and their settlement in the heart of the city tell us that this community played a pivotal role in commercial life.

The middle years of the eleventh century coincide with the Norman Christian conquest of the island. The *geniza* letters suggest that apart from some incidents of personal loss, the Sicilian merchant community of all faiths maintained a distance from the political upheavals and that business continued as usual, surviving and even expanding in this violent interregnum. Moshe Gil mentions Ibn al–Baʿbaʾ, a shipping magnate of Andalusian origin, who seized control of Palermo during the early years of the Norman conquest through his close ties to powerful Palermitan Jewish merchants. There is some suggestion that he, too, may have been of Jewish origin.[15]

Under the new Norman rulers, the hub of political, economic, and administrative power shifted from the Khâlisa district to the Galca quarter located at the western edge of the city. Site of the first Muslim royal palaces, the Galca is some distance from the port but sits on high ground with a good view of the city. The quarter has a circular shape, giving credence to the idea that "Galca" was a Latinization of the Arabic *al-halqa* (ring or circle). As for the Meschita quarter, there is no indication that either its physical boundaries or its human content were altered in any significant way during the transition from Muslim to Norman rule. The arrival of many Christians and a substantial decrease in the Muslim population through executions, expulsions, and self-imposed

Gate leading into the Meschita quarter

exile left room for the Jewish population to expand and fill the void. David Abulafia portrays the Meschita quarter in the Norman period, referring to it as *hârat al-yahûd*:

> Greeks, Muslims, Jews and northern Italian traders and other groups lived in the city in fairly well demarcated areas. The Jewish quarter, *hârat al-yahûd*, did not constitute a genuine ghetto, for the Jews gathered there by tradition and were not subjected to the sort of vexations, such as an armed guard on the ghetto gates, that were to be later typical of Italian ghettos. It seems that there was little change in the location of the Jewish settlement between the 10th century when Ibn Hawqal described the city and the late 12th century when the monastery of S. Maria of the Grotto received land adjoining the synagogue....This was not a city, unlike many in medieval Europe, where the Jews found it necessary to gather for safety in the shadow of the ruler's palace. The nearest Christian buildings of importance were the two surviving Norman churches of S. Maria dell'Ammiraglio and San Cataldo, which were both close to the principal synagogue. Thus we can see the Jewish quarter of Palermo as in many ways a survival from Islamic times, that is to say, it was an area of the city where Jews tended to live and work.... Ghettoization was a later phenomenon.[16]

The shift in the seat of power to the Galca neighborhood, the increase in royal palaces and Christian churches, and the judicious policies of the Norman princes of exploiting local talents and expertise contributed to shaping what has come to be referred to as the "Norman synthesis," an eclectic style that combines Arabo-Muslim, Byzantine Greek, and Latin Christian elements. However, we have little specific information about the Jewish quarter during the Norman period. Jews are infrequently mentioned in the sources and we have no indication of Jewish participation in the Norman Court.[17] The *geniza* documents shed light on business transactions between Jews, Christians, and Muslims, but they yield no information on the domestic lives of Jews and their neighborhoods. In 1172, Benjamin of Tudela, a traveling merchant from Spain who stopped in Sicily on his way to Jerusalem, estimated the size of the community at approximately 1,500 families.[18]

Other travelers are more informative, offering snippets that lead to broader conjectures about daily life in twelfth-century Palermo. The Muslim Andalusian geographer al-Idrîsî (1100–1166), patronized by Roger II, describes Old Palermo in the mid-twelfth century after the Norman invasion as having three major parts: the center, with its sumptuous, tall buildings and mosques, attesting to the survival of a Muslim community, and two smaller satellite zones with palaces, inns and springs.[19] This represents a great change from the city described by Ibn Hawqal nearly a century earlier. The immediate implication for the Jewish quarter in this new urban configuration is that it no longer existed as a discrete, homogeneous section of the Masjid Ibn Saqlâb Quarter that lay between the Old City (center) and the New Quarter, but rather was absorbed into a larger quarter called the Abergaria. It is difficult to say how these changes may have affected Palermitans of other ethnic groups. The existing documentation depicts no major ruptures. We may assume continuity in the city's multi-ethnic composition, with the Muslim minority, like the Jews, now living in various areas of the city.

Ibn Jubayr (1145–1217) was a Granadan traveler returning from the *hajj* whose ship took shelter in Messina on a stormy night in December of 1184. He spent several months in Sicily and his account, written a decade after that of Benjamin of Tudela, is far more detailed. He expresses the anxieties of a dwindling and besieged Muslim community and the precarious state of their affairs. His narrative gives voice to the growing antagonism and intolerance that marked Muslim-Christian relations in the later Middle Ages.[20] By this time, those Muslims who chose to remain in Sicily were restricted to several of the "suburbs" [*arbâd*] of Palermo. They were left alone to exercise their religion and professions, but in areas clearly separate from Christians. Still allowed access to government services and enjoying the favor of King William II, they were nevertheless increasingly subject to hostility from the Christian masses, especially those recently migrated from the Italian mainland.

For the moment, Jews were still exempt from restrictions and uncertainties. The arrival of the Provençal Jewish poet Anatoli Ben Yosef at about the same time as the Muslim traveler Ibn Jubayr, and Anatoli's warm reception by fellow Jewish poets in Palermo, offers a fleeting glimpse of a thriving community.[21] Culturally at home and politically quiescent, the Jews, unlike the Muslims, did not stage any popular uprisings or express other forms of discontent. Nor were they aligned with any foreign power that might intervene on their behalf.[22] In contrast with the widespread expulsion of rebellious Muslims, Jews continued to live in tranquility, providing the highly skilled services needed to maintain the Norman state apparatus. They still lived in the Old City, which included the Meschita, and elsewhere as well. Above all, they continued to be an important source of tax revenue.[23]

The rise to power of Frederick II (1198–1250) preserved the precarious balance between the extremes of tolerance and restriction. In his effort to strengthen the Norman empire, Frederick encouraged both Jews and Muslims to remain in Sicily and to practice their skills. But the minority "problem" was becoming increasingly difficult to contain; both the Sicilian Christian masses and the distant Papacy pressured Frederick to take a more militant "Crusader" position, and the Emperor responded by expelling as many Muslims as he could.[24] Sympathetic to Muslim and Jewish high culture, astute in utilizing non-Christian talent and skills, Frederick was nevertheless forced to respond to a growing Christian hostility toward Muslims, exacerbated by Islam's advances in the Crusader wars in the Levant. He was also forced to heed the ominous signs of the Fourth Lateran Council of 1215, presided over by Pope Innocent III, that coerced Jews to wear distinctive clothing and forbade them from cutting their beards.

The reign of Frederick II postponed for Jewish Sicilians a fate that had already been meted out to Muslims. Now the only *de facto* non-Christian segment of the population, Jews survived and even flourished, even though they were under the jurisdiction of the Church and had the legal status of "possessions of the crown." The Jewish elite contributed richly to Frederick's court culture. The King welcomed Jewish *literati* fleeing eastward from the ravages of the Spanish Reconquista, giving shelter to figures such as the eminent philosopher and mystic Abraham ben Samuel Abulafia (died around 1300), a poet, cabbalist, and translator born in Saragossa and raised in Tudela. He also encouraged Jewish migration from North Africa and the cities of southern Italy, offering to settle the newcomers and give them work on his various projects. Jewish migrants were sought after as physicians and accountants, and they even filled positions as farmers and vintners, not to mention their skills in the crafts and commerce.[25] This new wave of Jewish migration substantially changed the population of the old city. To accommodate the influx, Frederick granted the newcomers permission to build homes outside the Cassaro and to renovate their synagogue. But his persistent squabbles with the Papacy, and the failure of his policy to consolidate power over the Italian mainland, forced him to submit to a *realpolitik* that echoed in many ways his predecessors' vacillation between tolerance and repression.[26]

Frederick II died in 1250, and the great Norman cultural synthesis died with him. Although Jews and Muslims continued to live in Sicily and practice their professions, the political climate that supported a multicultural society was changing. The papal edict of 1265 granting the Angevins sovereignty over Sicily put an effective end to the era of the liberal-minded Norman princes. A shared hatred for the French Angevins bought the Jewish community into common cause with their Christian neighbors. Widespread discontent came to a head with the war of the Sicilian Vespers in 1282–1302, a popular uprising that succeeded in expelling the Angevins from Sicily altogether. Their departure, and the arrival of the Aragonese, ushered in a new period in which the island moved from a Mediterranean-oriented orbit into a European one. The reign of Frederick III of Aragon (1296–1337) saw the end to Sicily's long, close relationship with the Arabo-Islamic world.[27] The new ruler's assertive evangelism, tinged with apocalyptic symbolism, challenged all religious competitors. Hostile to Rome for other reasons, the government of Frederick III competed with the Papacy in its zeal to contain non-Christians. Since the Muslim community of Sicily had effectively disappeared, the Jews became the main target of his fervor.

Moreover, in the fourteenth century Sicily fell into economic decline. The wide variety of crops grown in Muslim times gave way to the monoculture of grain, making the island dependent on northern markets. The lucrative triangle of trade with North Africa and Egypt established during the Fatimid period and revitalized under the Normans could not be sustained in the new anti-Muslim "world order" of Frederick III. And finally, the power of northern Italian bankers grew as the Sicilian kings fell into their debt. Genoese and Venetian merchants came to dominate trade where local initiative had once ruled.[28] The northern influence was most forcefully felt in the coastal towns, while the countryside regressed to the pre-Muslim *latifondo* system. The once vibrant rural economy became "rigidly stratified, and rural people became more dependent on their lords."[29]

REQUIEM TO A FALLEN CITY

"Who would have believed that a wise man, a man who sought out God, would die so base a death?" With these words, Moses Remos begins his auto-elegy composed on the eve of his execution in Palermo in 1430.[30] Only twenty-four years old, this respected physician and Talmudic scholar was accused of poisoning his Christian patients. Given the chance to save himself by renouncing his faith, he refused. Moses asks in an anguished voice, why has fate turned against him so quickly? He laments the absence of justice, both divine and man-made, that extinguished the light that once guided his world. He begs his reader to transcribe his Hebrew poem and send it out in all directions so that it will reach the ears of his family in distant lands.

Moses Remos was in many ways typical of the sort of personality who had migrated to Palermo when it was a world capital of the high Middle Ages. He was born in Majorca, studied science and philosophy in Rome, and rose to prominence in the field of medicine.[31] The little we know about him comes mainly from his own words that illuminate the conditions under which Palermo's Jews lived at the time of his death. Jews like him from around the Mediterranean basin came to the city seeking the familiarity and comfort of a cosmopolitan culture, not to mention the opportunity to earn a lucrative livelihood. They continued to pour in from the Italian mainland and especially from Rome, but also from Malta and Marseilles. Sicilian Jews from Syracuse, Messina, Marsala, and Mazara also sought refuge in Palermo as social conditions of the smaller towns tilted irreversibly in the Christian favor. The survival of Latin vernaculars,

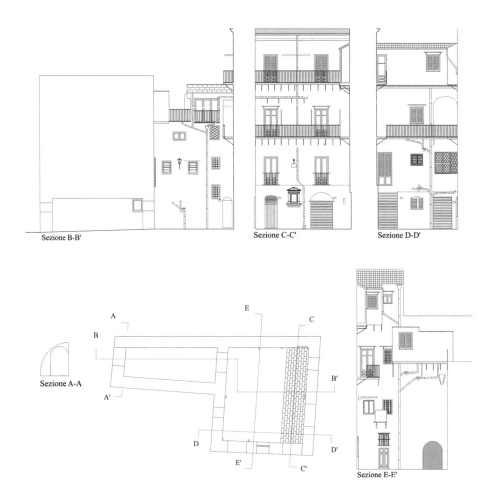

Sezione B-B'

Sezione C-C'

Sezione D-D'

Sezione A-A

Sezione E-E'

Survey of Vicolo Meschita

Maghribi Arabic, Hebrew, and to a lesser extent, Greek, allowed Palermo to evolve into a city of diverse customs and traditions.

This cosmopolitanism lived on as long as Palermo functioned as a major port for international trade in the Eastern Mediterranean. But the beginning of the fifteenth century ushered in a decline, overwhelming individuals like Moses Remos, an innocent victim caught in the web of events. In small but measured steps, the Jews of Sicily followed the Muslims into exile. In 1421, the position of chief judge of the Jewish community was abolished, and in 1425 the town council of Palermo asked authorities to prohibit the Jews from covering up their distinctive badges (*rotellae*). Sporadic anti-Semitic acts soon expanded into wide-scale violence encouraged by the Catholic Church; meanwhile, Church and the Palace fought over which of them would preside over the Jews and reap the profits of an overbearing tax system. By this time, Palermo and Sicily had

House fronts on Piazza della Meschita

Street signs in three languages

become increasingly dominated by Spanish barons whose ruthlessness and intolerance were consummated in the marriage of Isabella of Castile and Ferdinand of Aragon. These two vowed to complete the Christian Reconquista wherever "heresy" existed.

Moses Remos was among the many Spanish Jews who had fled to Palermo during the height of the Catholic onslaught. Abraham Abulafia found refuge in Palermo, as did Isaac Alhadib (died c. 1429), a native of Castile, who flourished there as a poet and astronomer.[32] Each arrived on one of the waves of migration that ebbed and flowed from the time the Arab armies first made Palermo their capital in 831 until the Edict of Expulsion in 1492. They came in search of a milieu where people of different provenances lived side by side, feeding off each other, competing, stimulating and antagonizing one another, finding refuge in one of the ethnic enclaves such as the *hârat al-yahûd* that offered a safe place to live both as a minority and as a citizen of the Mediterranean world.

Just as Moses Remos was lamenting his own cruel destiny, he was also giving voice to the loss of his city. "I am forced to walk backwards like a Crab, hands shackled, neck broken. At my right side stands the accuser, like Satan, a Lion eager for prey."[33] These bleak images may be read on the personal as well as public level. The murder of this prominent intellectual was tantamount to the unraveling of human progress, expressed graphically through the disturbing metaphor of a crab "walking backwards," an act of humiliation commonly used during the Inquisition. The violation of self and the feeling of betrayal Moses Remos conveys most assuredly resonated with his co-religionists and other humanistically minded Palermitans who saw their world crumbling in the face of religious and political tyranny. The fact that Remos was offered his life in exchange for his conversion to Christianity strongly suggests that his inquisitors were not convinced of his guilt, and that their true motives lay in religious hatred.

Fifty years later, on July 8, 1487, Rabbi Ovadia de Bartenura (Bertinoro) left Naples by sea and landed in Palermo. Ovadia describes the tenuous condition of Palermo's Jews on the eve of exile.[34] Impoverishment, discrimination, forced labor, high taxes, and inner divisiveness characterized a community on the precipice of annihilation. Paradoxically, the Meschita as an intact neighborhood continued to survive despite the upheavals that were already affecting the Jewish minority. Ovadia tells us that eight hundred Jewish families lived "all together on one street in the best part of town," clearly a reference to the *hârat al-yahûd*. His description of the square-shaped synagogue as having "no equal in the world," even if hyperbole, unequivocally refers to the Meschita. The synagogue possessed two courtyards, one within the other, replete with a sanctuary, a beautiful domed structure made of stone for the Torah scrolls, a ritual bath (*mikveh*) for the women, a hospice for the infirm and foreign travelers, a hall for deeds, and a cemetery. Twelve elders elected by the community presided over the administration of the synagogue complex. The tension in his vision between the splendor of the great synagogue, on the one hand, and an impoverished and defeated community on the other, informs our last glimpse of Palermo's Jewish minority. In 1492, the Jews of Sicily, now numbering 40,000, were compelled to leave by the Edict of Expulsion. Not long after, the old *hârat al-yahûd* was sold to a Christian noblewoman, Cristina DiSalvo.[35] The synagogue, courtyards, baths, inn, hospice, and adjacent residences and shops were transferred to Christian ownership at the same time Abu Abdallah (Boabdil) of Granada was handing over the keys of the Alhambra to Isabella and Ferdinand. The medieval world of Palermo came to an end just as Catholic sovereignty under the banner of Reconquista achieved its goal of removing the last non-Christians from the heart of Sicily.

Today, the cultural synthesis that characterized life in medieval Palermo is symbolically recaptured in the street signs hanging in the old Jewish quarter. Written in Hebrew, Arabic, and Italian, they evoke the memory of a long-absent multi-ethnicity. Contemporary historians have tried to trace the limits of the old *hârat al-yahûd*, and modern urban planners have recognized the value of the trilingual heritage that gave Palermo its particular history and identity. The result is a diligent signage of the streets and alleyways around the Meschita in all three languages that evokes, in the simplest of terms, a complex genealogy. The impulse to recognize Palermo's mosaic past, whatever its motivation, has produced the most modest of outcomes—a small yet significant *aide-mémoire* representing a multiplicity that is no more.

Notes

1. S.D. Goitein, *A Mediterranean Society: The Jewish Communities of the Arab World as Portrayed in the Documents of the Cairo Geniza*, 5 vols. (Berkeley: University of California Press, 1967–1988) 2, 299.

2. See Ralph W. Brauer, *Boundaries and Frontiers in Medieval Muslim Geography*, Transactions of the American Philosophical Society, 85, Part 6 (Philadelphia: The American Philosophical Society, 1995), 5–7.

3. Ira Lapidus, *Muslim Cities in the Later Middle Ages* (Cambridge: Cambridge University Press, 1984), xii.

4. Abû al-Qâsim Ibn Hawqal, *Sûrat al-`ard* (Beirut: Dâr Maktabat al-Hayât, 1979). This is a revised and enlarged version of Abû Ishâq al-Istakhrî's *Masâlik al-mamâlik*, both of which were compiled in the second half of the tenth century. See also Bernard Lewis, ed. and transl., *Islam from the Prophet Muhammad to the Capture of Constantinople*, 2 vols. (New York: Harper and Row, 1974), 2, 87–101.

5. Rosario La Duca, "Vicende topografiche del centro storico di Palermo" in *Bibliografia dell'Urbanistica e dell'Architettura Palermitana*. (Palermo: Facolta di Architettura, Quaderno no. 2–3, 1964), table 2, 32.

6. Adalgisa De Simone, "Palermo nei Geografi e Viaggiatori Arabi del Medioevo." *Studi Magrebini II* (Napoli: Instituto Universitario Orientale, 1968), 143. It is also well within the realm of possibility that Khalîl built al-Khâlisa in keeping with medieval Muslim political culture of establishing a new capital to announce a break with the past and to establish and legitimize a new government. On this practice, see Janina Safran, *The Second Umayyad Caliphate: The Articulation of Caliphal Legitimacy in al-Andalus*, Harvard Middle Eastern Monographs, 33 (Cambridge, MA: Harvard University Press, 2000), 53.

7. Other Italian cities such as Venice, Genoa, Pisa, Rome, and Naples also had quarters with this name. De Simone, "Palermo," 146, note 65.

8. Nadia Zeldes and Miriam Frenkel, "The Sicilian Trade; Jewish Merchants in the Mediterranean in the Twelfth and Thirteenth Centuries," in *Gli Ebrei in Sicilia dal tardoantico al Medioevo* (Palermo: Flaccovio, 1998), 248.

9. E. Ashtor, "Palermitan Jewry in the Fifteenth Century," in *The Jews and the Mediterranean Economy* (London: Variorium, 1983), 228.

10. Vincenzo Di Giovanni, *La Topografia Antica di Palermo*, 2 vols., (Palermo: Tipografia e Lagatoria del Boccone del Povero, 1889). Maps are attached at the end of the second volume.

11. Palermo began to take its current form toward the end of the sixteenth century, with the opening of Via Maqueda (1598) and the building of I Quattro Cantoni (1609). Giuseppe Bellafiore writes that these changes to the heart of the Old City (Cassaro) connected Palermo with architectural concepts of the Italian Renaissance: ("Riassunse a Palermo il concetto del Rinascimento italiano, quello dell'indissolubile relazione tra architettura singola e citta ") We should note also that the number of churches proliferated throughout the urban fabric in the fourteenth and fifteenth centuries. G. Bellafiore, "Architettura e forme urbane nella storia edilizia di Palermo," in *Quaderno dell'Instituto di elementi di architettura dell'universita di Palemo*, no. 2–3 (Palermo, 1964), 64.

12. In a panoramic view of modern Palermo, the Jewish quarter would be oval-shaped, with Via Roma to the east. The quarter would extend to

Via Maqueda toward the west. Its northern edge, above Via dei Calderai and Via L'Universita, is just south of the modern Piazza Bellini. See A. Mazzamuto, "L'insediamento ebraico in Sicilia dal periodo arabo all'espulsione del 1492," *Architettura judaica in Italia: ebraismo, sito, memoria dei luoghi* (Palermo: Flaccovio, 1994), 88.

13. David Cassuto, "La Meschita di Palermo," in *Architettura judaica in Italia,* 37. Ashtor also notes that C.B. Lagumina "surmised" that this was originally the Mosque of Ibn Saqlâb. See Ashtor, "Palermitan Jewry," 227, note 79.

14. S.D. Goitein, "Sicily and Southern Italy in the Cairo Geniza Documents." *Archivio Storico per la Sicilia Orientale,* Anno 67 (Catania: Societa di Storia Patria per la Sicilia Orientale, 1971): 9–33. For other studies on Jews in Sicily that draw extensively on these documents, see Moshe Gil, *Jews in the Islamic Countries in the Middle Ages,* transl. David Strassler (Leiden: Brill, 2004); and Shlomo Simonsohn, *The Jews in Sicily* (Leiden: Brill, 1997).

15. Gil, *Jews in the Islamic Countries in the Middle Ages,* 560–562. The fact that the name al-Ba'ba' is absent from the major Arab chronicles underlines the highly speculative nature of this assertion.

16. David Abulafia, "The Jews in Sicily Under the Norman and Hohenstaufen Rulers" in N. Bucaria, M. Luzzati, and A. Tarantino, eds., *Ebrei e Sicilia* (Palermo: Flaccovio, 2002), 76–77.

17. Jews are infrequently mentioned in Arabic and Latin sources of the twelfth century. With reference to the Norman court, see *The History of the Tyrants of Sicily by 'Hugo Falcandus' 1154–69* , ed. and transl. Graham A. Loud and Thomas Wiedemann (Manchester: Manchester University Press, 1998); S.M. Stern, "A Twelfth Century Circle of Hebrew Poets in Sicily," *Journal of Jewish Studies* 5 (1954): 60–79. Stern states: "We know very little about the Jews of Sicily at this period, but we may safely assume that their language and education were both in Arabic." [p. 61].

18. *The Itinerary of Benjamin of Tudela* (Malibu, CA: Joseph Simon, 1983), 137.

19. Abû ʿAbdallah al-Idrîsî, *Nuzhat al-mushtâq fî ikhtirâq al-afâq* (Cairo: Maktabat al-thaqâfa al-dînîya, 1990), 588–593.

20. Muhammad bin Ahmad Ibn Jubayr, *Rihla* (Beirut: Dâr Sâdir, 1964), 295–300.

21. Stern, "A Twelfth Century Circle," 65–66.

22. David Abulafia, *Frederick II: A Medieval Emperor* (London: Pimlico, 1988), 335. Abulafia also posits that the Jews had no political organization of their own nor were they loyal to any rival ruler.

23. Abulafia, *Frederick II,* 335–361. Abulafia points out that Jews, "like Saracens, were liable to the poll-tax of Muslim origin, and to taxes on wine and on knives," conjecturing that kosher and *halal* butchers were subjected to special taxes. Ibn Hawqal's mention of the numbers and various kinds of butchers in the *sûqs* in the Muslim period strongly suggests that this continued to be a lucrative profession, and thus one targeted by tax collectors.

24. In a brilliant attempt to make the best of a dire situation, Frederick devised a plan to build a massive agricultural business in the fertile plains of Apulia, drawing on both Muslim and Jewish skills. This would at once reduce the non-Christian population in Sicily and expand the Emperor's economic and political base in Southern Italy. For a recent comprehensive study, see Julie Taylor, *Muslims in Medieval Italy: The Colony at Lucera* (Lanham: Lexington Books, 2003).

25. Clifford R. Backman describes Frederick's policies as "enticing Maghribi Jews from Tunisia with royal protection, moderate taxation, religious tolerance, and opportunities for both administrative advancement and commercial prosperity. They returned where and when Arabo-Islamic influences were still strong; and they helped diversify the rural economy." *The Decline and Fall of Medieval Sicily: Politics, Religion, and Economy in the Reign of Frederick III, 1296–1337* (Cambridge: Cambridge University Press, 1995), 149.

26. Sicilian historian Giuseppe Quatriglio writes: "May of 1221, at Messina, Frederick convened a council during which he made it perfectly clear that he meant to reestablish full authority in Sicily and wrest power from the Sicilian Barons whom he deemed usurpers. The edicts issued by Frederick from Messina were drastic: gambling and blasphemy were outlawed, and prostitutes were forbidden to frequent public baths so as to have no contact with other women. Furthermore, Frederick forced Jews to wear emblems recognizable to all other citizens" *A Thousand Years in Sicily,* trans. Justin Vitiello (New York: Legas, 1991), 35.

27. The 20th-century Italian historian Benedetto Croce notes that the Vespers was a "permanent rupture between Sicily and its traditional political and cultural partner in Southern Italy, Naples." Cited in Backman, *Decline and Fall of Medieval Sicily,* xii.

28. Girolamo Arnaldi argues that this trend began with the Angevins and it continued under Aragonese rule. *Italy and Its Invaders* (Cambridge, MA: Harvard University Press, 2005), 114.

29. Tommaso Astarita, *Between Salt Water and Holy Water: A History of Southern Italy* (New York: Norton, 2005), 53.

30. Nahum Slousch, "Elegie de Moise Rimos: Martyr juif à Palerme au XVI siécle," in *Centenario della Nascita di Michele Amari,* 2 vols. (Palermo: Stablimento Tipografico Virzi, 1910) II, 186–204. Slousch records his death date as 1530, but T. Carmi records it as 1430 in *The Penguin Book of Hebrew Verse* (New York: Penguin Books, 1981), 122. Carmi's date is confirmed in the *Encyclopaedia Judaica* (Jerusalem, 1971), vol. 14, 70–71. *Encyclopaedia Judaica* [electronic resource.] Fred Skolnik, editor-in-chief; Michael Berenbaum, executive editor. 2nd ed. (Farmington Hills, MI: Thomson Gale; Detroit: Macmillan Reference USA, 2007.)

31. Carmi, *Penguin Book of Hebrew Verse,* 122.

32. Abraham Abulafia spent most of his time in the city of Messina, but his influence was great among

Palermitan Jews as well. See Moshel Idel, "The Ecstatic Kabbalah of Abraham Abulafia in Sicilia and Its Transmission during the Renaissance," in *Italia Judaica: Gli Ebrei in Sicilia sino all'espulsione del 1492*. Acts of the V International Conference: Palermo, 15–19 June 1992 (Rome: Fratelli Palombi, 1995), 330–340. See also Carmi, *Penguin Book of Hebrew Verse*, 118.

33.   Carmi, *Penguin Book of Hebrew Verse*, 438.

34.   *Pathway to Jerusalem: The Travel Letters of Rabbi Ovadia of Bertenura*, trans. Yaakov Shulman (New York: CIS Publishers, 1920), 16–21.

35.   Salvo Di Matteo, "La Giudecca di Palermo dal X al XV secolo," in R. Giuffrida, A. Sparti, and S. Di Matteo, eds., *Fonti per la Storia dell'espulsione degli ebrei dalla Sicilia* (Palermo: Accademia nazionale di Palermo, 1992), 78–79.

SUSAN GILSON MILLER,
ILHAM KHURI-MAKDISI,
AND MAURO BERTAGNIN

2

THE *GIUDECCA* OF TRANI: A SOUTHERN ITALIAN SYNTHESIS

 Jewish quarters (*giudecche*) were found in cities throughout the Italian mainland and Sicily in the early medieval period. The *giudecche* as a type had certain common traits, but each site evolved along its own path, refuting the notion of an all-encompassing "Mediterranean model." Every quarter had a distinct flavor, depending on the quality and extent of the architectural sediment left by its former inhabitants. This sediment still exists in many places, and can be evaluated through measurement, observation, and a careful reading of the written sources. The city of Trani on Italy's Adriatic coast has a beautifully preserved medieval core and a distinctive *giudecca* with streets, houses, and synagogues dating back to the period between the tenth and fifteenth centuries. Despite some modifications over time, the fabric of this section of the city has remained largely intact, making Trani's *giudecca* a living laboratory for exploring questions about the form and function of the medieval minority quarter.

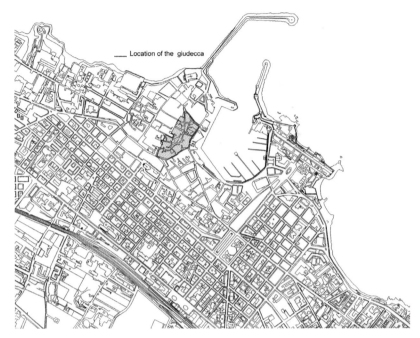

_____ Location of the giudecca

Map of modern Trani showing the location of the *giudecca*

THE SETTING

By virtue of its geographic position midway between the eastern and western halves of the Mediterranean, southern Italy was a meeting point for various traditions and ideas coming from Northern Europe, Spain, the Levant, and Northern Africa. It was a region of mediation, harmonization, and synthesis, not only for its Jewish population but also for other migratory peoples who arrived there. Jews have lived in Italy without interruption for almost 2,000 years, moving from place to place as conditions changed and new opportunities arose. Permanent Jewish settlement first appeared during the first century BCE, when Jewish slaves and merchants were counted among the heterogeneous population of ancient Rome.[1] After the failure of the Jewish revolt in Judea in 70 CE and the destruction of the Second Temple, captives seized during the Judean wars further increased Rome's Jewish population. These events are depicted on the Arch of Titus in the Roman Forum, where Jews are shown being led out of Jerusalem while carrying the ornaments of the destroyed temple. Jews lived in Rome after that, but left few traces of their presence. In the ninth century they appeared in southern Italy, where Jewish inscriptions in Greek and Latin suggest they took part in a wider cultural milieu that was Mediterranean and classical in origin.[2]

At this time a resurgence of Hebrew learning within the southern communities may have been stimulated by exchanges between local scholars and Jewish scholars from North Africa who arrived with the Muslim invasion of Sicily. The new arrivals maintained their contacts with the centers of Jewish learning in Palestine and other parts of the Islamic world. Acting as intermediaries, they reintroduced the Jews of the south to their cultural roots, and in particular, to the Hebraicizing tendencies of the Palestinian academy. Soon evidence of a revived interest in Hebrew culture became apparent in the south of Italy. In Venosa, for example, alongside the old Greek and Latin tombstone inscriptions, Hebrew writing appeared on gravestones starting from the first half of the ninth century.[3] Some time between the end of the seventh century and the middle of the eighth, Jewish names in southern Italy became Hebraicized. By the tenth century, the southern Italian Jewish communities were reintegrated into the orbit of Palestinian Jewish culture through their adoption of ritual, language, and intellectual tendencies originating further East.

Southern Italian Jewish scholars were also influenced by another important cultural trend of the time: the translation of Arabic texts into Hebrew and then into Latin. The transmission of classical learning to the West through the conduit of Jewish translations from Arabic into Hebrew was an important passage for Jewish scholarship in Italy and elsewhere in the Mediterranean basin. Ideas radiating outward from the small circle of translators permeated thinking at all levels and transformed Jewish production in philosophy, hermeneutics, mysticism, and *belles lettres*. Trani became the crossroads for an intense cultural interaction with Muslim and Christian influences from North Africa, Spain, and Byzantium.

TRANI AS A CENTER OF MEDIEVAL JEWISH LIFE

By the tenth century, Trani had become a seat of Jewish learning that reached out to Bari, Brindisi, Taranto, Venosa, and other towns along the Apulian coast. Jewish scholars in Trani did not constitute a school, but rather a concentration of erudition that reached a high point in the figure of Rabbi Isaiah of Trani (1200–1260), also known as the Rid, a Talmudic scholar of such importance that "no study of medieval rabbinic literature may claim any measure of comprehensiveness without integrating his contributions, attitudes and insights."[4] According to medievalist Isadore Twersky, his scholarly achievements were marked by a freedom of spirit that was unusual for his time.[5] Rabbi Isaiah's thinking was based on the works of the eminent French Jewish scholar Rashi, but he was also thoroughly inventive in his own right, writing volumes of legal opinions (*responsa*) that were marked by a "discriminating eclecticism."[6] He incorporated a broad spectrum of Jewish learning into his opinions, and was also influenced by non-Jewish sources. He was a "pivotal, powerful personality" who inspired a following that included his grandson, Rabbi Isaiah ben Elijah di Trani (d. 1280), also a scholar of great repute who was famous for his insights, or *novellae* (Hebrew: *chiddushim*) based on the Talmud.[7]

Thus we find in the *giudecca* of Trani precisely at the moment of its greatest physical expansion a rabbinical school that attracted Jewish students and scholars from all over the Mediterranean world. Traditionally, such scholarly centers, or *yeshivot,* are supported by wealthy men who seek to translate their worldly success into religious

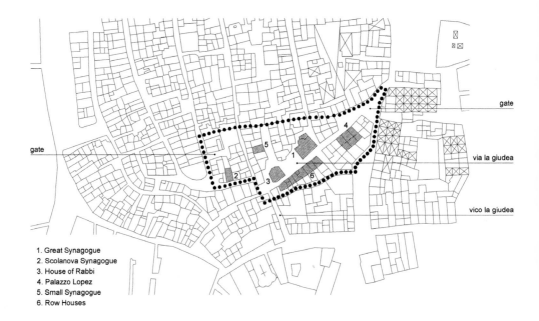

1. Great Synagogue
2. Scolanova Synagogue
3. House of Rabbi
4. Palazzo Lopez
5. Small Synagogue
6. Row Houses

gate

gate

via la giudea

vico la giudea

Plan of the *giudecca* of Trani

currency through acts of piety. In Trani, the presence of a rich Jewish merchant class engaged in overseas trade was a crucial factor in attracting Jewish scholars and providing them with the means to continue their studies. This intersection of intellectual vigor, economic success, and political stability is the setting for the expansion of the *giudecca* of Trani in the thirteenth century. An essential element in this conjuncture was the encouragement and acceptance offered to the Jewish minority by the ruler of Sicily and southern Italy, the renowned Frederick II.

FREDERICK II AND THE PROTECTION OF MINORITIES

Frederick II, King of Sicily and Apulia and eventually Holy Roman Emperor (1197–1250), cast an immense shadow across southern Italy in his day. Progeny of both Norman and German royal houses, Frederick's domination of southern Italy is the larger framework for understanding the situation of Trani's Jews. He was "a Mediterranean ruler, brought up in a world conquered from the Muslims, where Muslim traditions were still strong."[8] A cultivated intellectual with interests in natural science, literature, the arts and architecture, he knew some Arabic, encouraged the translation of scientific works from Arabic into Latin, and corresponded with Moses ben Solomon of Salerno about Jewish philosophy. He was also a promoter of the building arts. His rural retreat at Castel del Monte combined his curiosity about astrology with a passion for construction, producing an unusual eight-sided building that expressed both pragmatic and cosmological influences. He maintained a cosmopolitan court in Palermo, where the

Castel del Monte built by Frederick II in the thirteenth century

presence of lions and dancing girls, black musicians and a royal harem compromised his orthodoxy in the eyes of believing Catholics.[9] Strong-headed and independent, he engaged in a decades-long struggle with the Papacy for dominance over the Italian peninsula. When Pope Gregory goaded him to prove his Catholic credentials by partici-pating in the Holy Wars, he launched a crusade from the Apulian coast in 1228. This adventure ended with a ten-year truce negotiated with the Muslim rulers of Palestine, in which the cities of Jerusalem, Bethlehem, and Nazareth were ceded to the Christian side. As a result, commerce and exchanges with the Levant increased, stimulating Trani's role in the Eastern Mediterranean trade.

In contrast with the repressive and often unpredictable policies of the Papal States, Frederick's rule was equitable toward subaltern groups for sound political rea-sons. Directing a highly centralized state supported by a loyal nobility, Frederick was dependent on regular tax payments in return for legal protections.[10] In fact, Trani's Jews were granted personal and commercial protection by the King "in perpetuo" in return for the payment of an annual tax.[11] Documents in the archives indicate that the Jews of the south had frequent exchanges with the ruler and local nobility who were deeply involved in the everyday details of governance regarding fiscal obligations and other related matters.

Transferring the revenues from taxes paid by the Jews to the Church was a clever strategy used by Frederick to appease his clerical opponents and achieve a détente with his papal rivals to the north. But after 1239, the fragile truce between the Emperor and the Church dissolved, and Frederick launched an open war against his papal rivals.

The brunt of paying for this struggle eventually sapped the populace of their wealth and stifled their entrepreneurial spirit. Indeed, Frederick's protracted and costly conflict with the Church has been blamed for the retardation that afflicted the south for centuries. Yet this complex character was deeply admired by the southern Jews. He had a profound appreciation of Eastern cultures, and his peaceful opening to the Holy Land worked in favor of the Jewish minority by allowing it to maintain close ties with co-religionists in Egypt and Palestine.[12]

Perhaps the most significant aspect of Frederick's relationship with the minorities of Apulia was the fact that they were taken directly under the Emperor's protection and given a specific legal status.[13] The code of laws instituted in 1230 guaranteed sovereign protection for every subject, native or foreign, without discrimination with regard to birth, race, or religion. Although still considered inferior to Christians, Jews were given the means to appeal to the courts in their own defense. Furthermore, in 1236 Jews were protected against the false and deadly accusation of blood libel, and also against forced baptism.[14] Yet sartorial laws remained on the books, requiring Jews and Muslims to wear a beard and a blue shift covering their clothes. The extent to which these laws were enforced is not known, but their intention is clear—to maintain a strict separation between Jewish and Muslim minorities on the one hand, and the Christian majority on the other.

Was this a "golden age" for the Jews of Trani and southern Italy, as it has traditionally been depicted by Jewish scholarship? It is true that Frederick guaranteed a precise legal status to Jews, allowing them recourse to the civil law courts and thus moving them from the condition of a "marginalized" people to that of a "tolerated" one, a significant advance for that time. He also placed outside the law the most noxious local practices against the minority, such as the threats of blood libel or forced conversion. On these grounds alone, his reign must be viewed as an improvement over that of his predecessors. However, some historians have argued that by granting these concessions, Frederick was simply building on a tradition of protection of Jews and other minorities that was already present in southern Italy. To illustrate this point, historian Francesco de Robertis argues that the 1219 code of laws that preceded Frederick's legal code of 1230 was even more tolerant than the laws made later by Frederick. Before writing the code of 1230, Frederick sent a circular letter in which local magistrates were asked to transmit to the Emperor customs *en vigueur* in their districts, suggesting that the ruler was merely confirming in law certain practices that were already in use.[15] Although these observations may be accurate, they have not detracted from the historical image of Frederick II as a patron and protector of the Jews of southern Italy.

TRANI IN THE MEDITERRANEAN ECONOMY

Trani's role as a center of mercantile activity for the entire region was mentioned by the Jewish traveler Benjamin of Tudela, who passed through the city around 1166. He wrote: "Trani [is located] on the sea, [in a place] where all the pilgrims gather to go to Jerusalem, for the port is a convenient one. A community of about two hundred

Israelites is there, at their head being Rabbi Elijah, Rabbi Nathan the Expounder, and Rabbi Jacob. It is a great and beautiful city."[16] According to Benjamin of Tudela, Trani's position as an Adriatic port was the key to its economic prosperity.

How did the Jews of Trani make a living? Basing his conclusions on the granting of privileges by Frederick II, Italian historian Cesare Colafemmina deduces that during Svevian rule, the activity of Apulian Jews consisted mostly of long-distance trade and the dyeing of fabrics, especially silk. There were also moneylenders among the Jews, but this activity usually went hand in hand with commerce. "Some [were] also landholders, and [owners of] vineyards used to make wine for the Sabbath, and oil for [the lamps of] the synagogues."[17] Archival sources for the period also mention soapmaking.[18] On money-lending, Colafemmina remarks that although some Jews were moneylenders, they usually lent only modest sums. The larger banks and money-lending institutions that appeared later in the south were controlled not by Jews but by Tuscans, Lombards, and Genovese, "all foreigners and all Christians."[19] The presence of Venetian Jews in Trani is a reminder of the close ties between Trani and Venice, the most important center of Adriatic trade. Relations were closest in the period of Frederick II, but even later, Trani continued to serve as an outpost for Venice and was firmly fixed within its economic orbit. There was a Venetian consulate in Trani in the thirteenth century,[20] and the names of Venetian Christian families begin to appear in the local archives in the fifteenth century.[21]

THE ARCHITECTURE OF THE GIUDECCA

The thirteenth century was the period in which the most concentrated building took place in the Jewish quarter, including the two largest synagogues, the Sant'Anna and the Scolanova, the most important buildings visible in the *giudecca* today. The solidity, grandeur and variety of buildings in the *giudecca* dating from that period speak of a wealthy community that enjoyed economic prosperity, access to power, a stable legal status, and an optimistic view of the future. Few documents have survived, so that an imaginative reading of the built environment is essential for filling out the fragmentary evidence provided by the written record.

On entering the *giudecca,* the visitor is greeted by the grand palaces that were the homes of the wealthy families whose business activities set the rhythm of daily life. The facades of these impressive buildings show *bugnato*-type stonework, the same used in the great *palazzi* of Florence and Venice. Passing through the wide doors of the Palazzo Lopez, one finds oneself in a spacious courtyard where goods were stored and other domestic and commercial activities took place. A staircase leads from the courtyard at street level to the main living quarters located on the floor above. The floor plan of this grand house shows that it was most likely inhabited by a single extended family. The rooms flow into one another without interruption, allowing freedom of movement throughout the entire complex; they are of a substantial size and do not appear to ever have been sub-divided for multi-family use. The main salon faces the port, its large windows framing a view of the harbor.

Finding such a large palace within an Italian Jewish quarter is unusual, for generally speaking, Italian Jewish housing was small in scale, densely packed, and crowded. There are only two or three such palaces in the *giudecca* of Trani, indicating that the number of very wealthy families was very small. The contrast in scale between these grand houses and the modest residences lining the main street suggests a multi-layered society accommodating various social and economic strata. The ground-floor plan of the *palazzo* shows a series of vaulted spaces used as storage rooms, reminding us of the floor plan of the great commercial houses of Venice and Florence (the *casa bottega*). It speaks clearly of an active world of work incorporated into the domestic environment. The number of these rooms in the *giudecca* is impressive; in many cases they are not accessible from the interior of the house and the only entry is on the street level. They could be rented out, providing a source of income. These storage areas are found in almost every house, including even the more modest ones, suggesting that the quarter was alive with commercial and artisanal activities.

Interspersed throughout the quarter, but especially in the area of the great synagogue and in a *cul-de-sac* behind it, are row houses consisting of two levels of living space built above a commercial area at the ground level. These structures are remarkably modular, varying only slightly in elevation and in width. They march along the street front, filling the lot and giving the distinct impression of having been built at one time. The ground floor was used as a storage area or workshop, with wide entry doors to facilitate the movement of goods. Additional vaulted rooms at the underground level were also used for storage. Access to the upper levels of the house is by means of an external staircase. The second and third floors are two rooms deep, making for four-room living units. The kitchen is on the second floor of the house, and the roof area is an important addendum to the domestic space.

The quarter is anchored at its center by a complex of religious and communal buildings built around a large open space. The two largest synagogues of the quarter were built in the thirteenth century and close to one another. The Sant'Anna synagogue is unusual because of its size; it was originally planned as a synagogue and is not con-

Row houses facing the Great Synagogue of Trani

verted domestic space. It was built with the intention of accommodating the entire community. The structure was converted into a church in the late fourteenth century, and then abandoned as a house of worship in recent years. Today this magnificent edifice is boarded up and a near ruin.

The inspiration for the design of the Sant'Anna synagogue is the Byzantine church, with a main hall almost perfectly square (38 x 40 feet) enclosed by four immense arches that support a 26-foot-high dome, reminiscent of the Hagia Sophia, although on a far smaller scale.[22] The dome gives a feeling of spaciousness, although the building itself is no taller than the surrounding buildings. This was no doubt intentional, to avoid making a Jewish house of worship too conspicuous. In the western arch is a semi-circular niche that held the *tevah*, the platform supporting the reader's desk. The main doorway today is on the eastern wall, where the ark containing the Torah scrolls (*aron ha-kodesh*) would have been placed. The building underwent numerous transformations over the years, and the eastern doorway is most likely a later addition, according to Ernst Munkácsi, for two reasons: first, its unusual placement on the wall marking the direction of prayer, and second, because it leads out directly to the street. The more usual practice in synagogue design was to have a mediating space between the street and the interior. Munkácsi speculates that the original entrance was on the northern side, where the doorway led into small hallway that was a sacristy at the time of his writing.[23]

Another curious feature of this synagogue is the complexity of the space beneath its main floor. The subterranean zone was excavated to allow for two additional levels in which rooms were constructed. What activities might have taken place in these rooms? A ritual bath (*mikveh*) perhaps, or a room for preparing the dead for burial—activities not carried out at home. The use of underground space is part of a pattern of use that also appears in Jewish quarters elsewhere in the Mediterranean region.[24]

The adoption of the Byzantine style of construction is a statement about Tranesi Jews' self-perception as a cosmopolitan community having strong ties with the historical centers of Jewish culture located further to the East. During his visit to the synagogue in the 1930s, Munkácsi noticed a marble tablet embedded in the southern wall, probably placed there when the synagogue was built.[25] Its words shed light on the builders' motives in realizing what must have been a very ambitious project for a community of that size. In addition to mentioning the impressive dome, the inscription also makes note of the mosaic floor, two features that set the building apart from others of its type:

> In the year 5007[26] after the creation
> This sanctuary was built by a *minyan*[27]
> Of friends, with a lofty and splendid dome and a window
> Open to the sky, and new portals for enclosing it,
> And a pavement on the upper floor, and benches
> For seating the leaders of the prayer, so that their piety
> Would be watched over by the One who dwells in the glorious heavens[28]

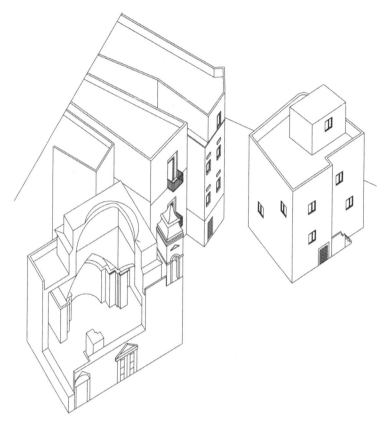

Axonometric drawing of the Great Synagogue of Trani

Doorway to the Great Synagogue of Trani

Thirteenth-century Hebrew inscription marking the construction of the Great Synagogue

The apparent ease with which the Byzantine church aesthetic was translated into a Jewish idiom speaks of a community comfortable with its cultural diversity and open to non-Jewish influences in the material sphere.

The rabbi's house located across a large open area from the Sant'Anna synagogue shows a first-floor plan having a semi-public space, with separate entryways leading to each of the rooms. It may have been a *yeshiva* (study house) or a school. It may also have filled other functions, such as a guesthouse for itinerant rabbis, a hostel for alms seekers, or a rest house for visiting scholars. Building a guesthouse attached to the main synagogue was a known practice in southern Italy. Simonsohn reports that the remains of a hospice were also found as part of the building complex of a medieval synagogue in Palermo, Sicily.[29]

Another synagogue is the Scolanova, a simple, unadorned building whose thick limestone walls are pierced by several small windows. Access to the interior is through a door on the south side reached by mounting a tall staircase.[30] Inside, the synagogue is a single, long nave-like hall with a niche on the eastern wall where the Torah scrolls were stored. An upper story may have been a women's gallery. The elongated nave of the Scolanova is a form of synagogue construction found in Islamic Spain and northern Italy; it was the style used in the building of the ancient synagogue of Ostia near Rome. It also bears a remarkable similarity to the El Tránsito synagogue of Toledo, a private synagogue built in the mid-fourteenth century by court official Samuel Halevi Abulafia as an addition to his family house.[31] Thus the prototype could have come to Trani from either northern Italy or Iberia. The Scolanova was probably built after the Sant'Anna, as its name, the "new" synagogue, suggests. Its smaller size indicates that it was not intended as the gathering place for the entire community but served a different purpose. The adjoining house is also noteworthy; its plan suggests that it was dedicated to synagogue-related activities, such as the baking of *matzot*, prayer rooms, and so on. There is also the possibility that the rabbi or patron of the synagogue lived in the

Bird's-eye view of the Scolanova synagogue

house. Perhaps it was part of a larger study complex presided over by a famous rabbi, such as Rabbi Isaiah.

A third synagogue found nearby in a block of residences represents yet another type—domestic space converted into religious space. The congregation that met here was smaller and again represented a faction of the community. The sources speak of *tedeschi* (German) Jews in Trani in the late fifteenth and early sixteenth centuries, perhaps arriving from Venice, when the Jewish community was already in decline. They followed a different ritual than the local population and therefore had just cause for forming a separate prayer meeting. This smaller synagogue is distant from the others yet enjoys a connection to them by its proximity to the open piazza.

The open space between the synagogues was dedicated to public use. A number of Jewish rituals take place in the open air, such as the celebration of the holiday of *simchat torah* and the procession that often accompanies a *bar mitzvah* or a wedding.[32] The space could also be used for public prayer, such as a service offered in the time of drought or calamity. We have no written evidence of how the *piazza* was used,

Main gate entering into the *giudecca* of Trani

or even a memory of it. However, we do know from other contexts that the area around the synagogue could on occasion be appropriated for public events. The surrounding buildings also relate architecturally to this open space, forming a complex whole that was conducive to the staging of ritual performances.

EXPLORING THE FABRIC OF THE QUARTER

The entry to the quarter was protected at both ends by a gate that is still visible at the southern end, while the closure at the northern end is marked simply by a narrowing of the street. The turning into the gate and the gate itself indicate the entry into a new and distinctive place within the fabric—not necessarily isolated, but different. The quarter was on the periphery of the larger town, close to the port that was the center of Jewish business activity. It is worth noting that other major southern Italian coastal towns, such as Naples and Bari, also contain Jewish quarters located adjacent to the port. [33]

Inside the main gate

The fact that the *giudecca* is not walled is significant. Jewish and Christian populations lived side-by-side, and there was constant exchange between them in the shops, the streets, and the port. The streets of the *giudecca* flow naturally into the rest of the urban fabric without interruption. Christians came to the Jewish quarter for certain essential services found only there, and the memory of these activities is still preserved in the toponyms. Via del Cambio, a small street leading to the port, was the center of operations for Jewish moneychangers and bankers. The shops and storehouses of the quarter specialized in weaving, dyeing, and selling luxury cloth, and drew their clientele from the entire town. We also know that the Jews of Trani spoke Italian, used it among themselves and with their Christian neighbors and business associates, and engaged in a wide variety of contacts with non-Jews. The *giudecca* was not a zone apart but was thoroughly integrated into the rest of the city.

CONVERSIONS AND OTHER CALAMITIES AFTER 1400

The century following Frederick's death in 1250 was one of ever-increasing turmoil and disintegration, as large state structures gave way to small-scale, local ones. In 1266, the French Angevins took over in the south of Italy, imposing their influence and creating new axes of exchange between Apulia and Provence. With the departure of the Papacy to Avignon and the demise of the Hohenstaufens, a power vacuum was created in southern Italy that had a catastrophic effect on the local population, and especially on the vulnerable minorities. In the countryside, the absence of authority led to a complete breakdown in order; in the cities, where the nobility took charge and continued to raise the necessary taxes, the situation was only slightly better. The huge tax burden placed on the people was the dominant feature of state-societal relations in this period. Much of this wealth flowed out of the region to the absentee Papacy that continued to confer legitimacy on the temporal rule.

In economic life, the center of gravity began to shift toward the north, where city states having a strong tradition of self-governance successfully weathered the transition from a centralized rule to greater fragmentation. A major population shift was driven by a combination of push-pull factors, including the attraction to the new centers of commercial activity and the desire to flee the political instability of the south. Jews active in banking and money-lending were invited to towns such as Ancona, Livorno, and Venice to provide the capital badly needed for commercial expansion, and Jewish artisans were drawn there to provide manpower for a burgeoning crafts industry.[34]

After 1290, Apulia experienced violent anti-Jewish revolts that led to a massive conversion of Jews in many locales. In fact, the Jews of Trani disappear from the historical record for more than a century.[35] They reappear again in the state archives of Bari and Naples after 1400. Some documents relate to individuals, while others concern the *giudecca* as a whole and treat the Jews as a collectivity. Many documents relate to Trani's Jewish converts, the *cristiani novelli*, who were considered by the authorities as part of the Jewish community.[36] Jewish complaints about oppressive taxation produced documents that deal with fiscal issues. Transactions of a commercial nature, such as disagreements over unpaid loans, broken contracts, and failed partnerships are also found in the archives. Notarial documents relate to matters of personal status such as marriage, inheritance, and divorce, and depict a Jewish population that would occasionally refer to non-Jewish civil authorities to resolve disputes instead of to their own rabbis. Often the sources concern Christians as well as Jews, revealing the intricate ties between the two groups, especially in the commercial sphere, giving us insight into the tenor of inter-communal relations. Jews are easily identified by their names and also by the use of the word *iudeo* following the name. It is clear from the language of these documents that the central authorities made little distinction between the recent converts to Christianity and those who had remained Jewish, perhaps because they doubted the sincerity of the conversions.[37]

What changes took place in Jewish life within the urban environment? How did Jews inhabit the city in this later period, and how did the city shape the life of the Jews? Weaving together information that is both spatial and textual, we are able to build a picture of the Jewish presence in Trani after 1400, keeping in mind that it is only a partial image, constructed from evidence that is fragmentary at best.

The initial question that comes to mind is that of the legal status of the Jewish community, and the extent to which it was integrated into the larger framework of urban life. Here the archives indicate that the Jews of Trani continued to enjoy a precise legal status within the formal structures of governance. In the fifteenth century, Jewish notables *(proti)* elected by the community served as the main conduit between individuals and the state. These notables were charged with the all-important task of supervising the collection of Jewish taxes.[38] The election of the *proti* took place in the public square of the *giudecca*, next to the main synagogue.[39] The *proti* of each town then met in Bari, where they formed a regional committee, or *Sommaria*, that represented Jewish interests at the state level. [40] Thus each *giudecca* had direct access to the king and the central administration; conversely, through the *Sommaria*, the authorities had the means to bring state power to bear on local matters, such as forcing delinquents to pay their share of the communal tax.[41]

The payment of taxes was the chief nexus between the state and the individual Jew. The archives contain many documents regarding taxation, indicating that the state played a role in assuring justice toward the community as a whole and toward individuals who felt aggrieved. While the *giudecca* as a collectivity was required to pay a set sum, an individual could still protest to the state about the amount of his or her share. The *Sommaria* reached down to the level of the individual in its interpretation of the law. The procedure went as follows: the *Sommaria* would order the Captain of Trani or other official to investigate the financial situation of the plaintiff. Sometimes the *Sommaria* would order the notables of the Jewish community to meet with the person under review in order to look into his financial abilities. The case of the banker Mose Todisco provides useful information on how this process worked:

> Mose Todisco, a Jew coming from outside...has a good sum of money...and we command you [to] congregate together in the said town of Trani according to your

custom…and require that the said Mose give under oath…a public declaration of the fortune that he possesses in Trani, and for which he should pay taxes.[42]

Not only were individuals investigated, but from time to time, the fiscal burden on the entire *giudecca* was reexamined. In 1482, the Jews of Trani went through a period of economic hardship and part of their communal tax was reassigned to the *giudecche* of several neighboring towns.[43] Again, in 1495, the economic situation of the Jews of Trani and of Apulia in general was so bad that the *Sommaria* ordered its preceptor "to insure that an examination of fiscal contributions take place, especially those of Trani… because of their poverty."[44] In 1490, the *Sommaria* ordered the Università (town council) of Trani to make sure that the Jews were exempted from contributing to a new salt tax:

> We command that [the Jews'] privileges [of exemption] be strictly maintained…
> you should in no way coerce or punish them to pay the salt tax…you should main-
> tain their exemptions and privileges…for as you know, the Jews, in addition to the
> other payments they make to the Università, already contribute to an annual pay-
> ment made by the *giudecche* of this kingdom to the Royal Court.[45]

The payment of taxes was a constant preoccupation, especially for rich Jews. This becomes clear in the story of Stella Astruc, who lived in the latter half of the fifteenth century. Stella had married into the distinguished Astruc family of Iberian origin, who belonged to the Jewish aristocracy of Apulia. She was the wife of Marsilio Astruc, who first appears in the archives in 1463, when he served as spokesman for the town of Gravina at the court in Naples. To achieve this status, he must have been a man of considerable wealth and influence.[46] The family reappears twenty-five years later when Stella, now a widow, was denounced for not having paid sufficient taxes.[47] Under threat of having her wealth confiscated, Stella asked to leave Gravina for Trani, but the Duke of Gravina was reluctant to see her depart and refused. Not one to submit mildly to her fate, Stella took her case to court and won. The *Sommaria*, ruling in her favor, stated that "the Jews of this kingdom are not vassals except to the King…and they can come and go as they see fit."[48]

Stella's troubles did not end here, however, for when she reached Trani, the Jewish community demanded that she contribute to the communal tax in her new place of residence, without being afforded the normal grace period offered to other newcomers. Again she resisted, claiming that her wealth had been depleted by war and the need to pay large dowries for her two daughters. We do not know the outcome of her case in Trani, but it is clear that her wealth, its advantages notwithstanding, was a great source of personal anxiety and the cause of a public debate. The last trace of the family is a tombstone found in the wind-swept countryside outside Trani, embedded in the wall of a stone farmhouse, the Masseria San Elena, which may have been used to mark the grave of one of Stella's daughters. The inscription in Hebrew reads: "Here lies Dvora Estrina, daughter of Maestro Astruc, who died on the 24th day of Kislev in the year 5252 (1492 CE). May her soul be released from the chains of life."[49]

A street sign in the *giudecca* of Trani, "Lane II of Judaea."

The gravestone of Dvora Estrina Astruc, died 1492

We may draw broad conclusions from this discussion about the status of the Jews of Trani between 1400 and 1550. Jews as individuals had rights before the law and could appeal to the civil authorities for redress when they felt mistreated. The authorities in turn placed a value on fairness and tried to constrain local officials who had tended to exploit Jewish vulnerability. Jews as a group had the power to elect officials, who could speak for them at the level of the city and the state, although their choice of representation was limited to a small group of wealthy men. This hierarchical structure allowed Trani's Jewish notables to join with the Jewish *proti* from other *giudecche* of Apulia to form a Jewish representation at the state level. Thus it seems that the Jews of Trani were organized in such a way that they enjoyed a protected legal status, access to power, and the assurance of fair governance.

Yet there was a dark side that included lapses in public order and violence against Jews. Although we have no indications of a major persecution, the Jews of Trani were on occasion so tormented that the state had to intervene. The people of the *giudecca* wrote to the King in 1494, complaining that the clergy of Trani were harassing them. The King responded by sending an order to the Captain of Trani "to forbid during Holy Week, or any other days of the year, that Jews be seized and stoned (*presi e sassate*) or in any other way injured."[50] A few days later, again at the request of the *giudecca*, the *Sommaria* sent a second letter, this time to the Bishop, "invit[ing him] to abstain from inciting (*aizzare*) priests and others against the Jews of the city."[51] Although the Bishop is addressed respectfully as *venerabilis* and is politely "invited" to cease making trouble, the language of the letter is unequivocal:

> It is a fact...that you are still making many false statements, vile slurs, and other injurious acts that are causing personal harm to the Jews of this *giudecca*, against the customary privileges and legal rights of the Jews of this kingdom...hence we ...command you that when you receive it [this letter], you should stop causing injury, and likewise your priests and laymen...let [the Jews] stay at home and go about their business.[52]

Four months later, the *Sommaria* again sent an order to the Captain of Trani, asking him to prevent the clergy from acting against the Jews, along with the reminder that "it is the intention of his Majesty the King that the Jews not be treated badly."[53]

Speaking about the condition of the Jews in northern and central Italy at that time, Renata Segre has noted that "Jewish existence was governed by contractual forms that were generally respected, and only rarely were they shaken by serious episodes of violence."[54] If this is so, then what triggered the attack in 1494, and how frequently did such incidents occur? The fact is, in the eighty years spanned by the Napoli archives (1463–1540), such attacks were mentioned only three times. To understand the 1494 incident, we must look at the general situation of Apulia at that time. After the fall of Granada in 1492 and their final expulsion from Spain, many Iberian Jews migrated to Italy. Two years later, in 1494, Aragonese rule ended and was briefly replaced by French, then Venetian rule, before the Spanish finally imposed their authority on the kingdom of Naples in 1510. It was a period of great political upheaval in the region. According to Colafemmina, "the problems of 1495 brought to Molfetta (another Apulian town) many *cristiani novelli* from Trani, where they had been massacred and their houses sacked."[55] Among the refugees were the de Buctunis family [56] that had provided members of the communal council of Trani, and the de Gello. Both were families of Tranesi converts. The political instability of the times offered the opportunity to attack the more vulnerable elements of society whose wealth was evident but whose status was unclear.

Conversion seems to have been a widespread phenomenon among Italian Jews during this period, so that our idea of Tranesi Jewish life must include the situation of these *cristiani novelli,* or "new Christians."[57] Changing one's religion was a viable choice for a Jew vexed by heavy taxes and continuous pressure from a militant church. Rich Jews more than poor ones were attracted by conversion because of the possibility for greater personal freedom it implied.[58] *Cristiani novelli* represented 120 households in Trani at the end of the fifteenth century; that is, roughly 15 to 20 percent of the total population of 600 to 700 households, which included both Jews and non-Jews.[59] According to a contemporary view, the reason that the *cristiani novelli*, some of them men of high status holding honorific chairs in the Università, continued to live within the Jewish quarter was that "once a Jew, always a Jew" (*semper judarizarunt et adhuc judaizant*).[60]

In any case, it was not unusual for Jews and Christians to live side-by-side. In the archives we find a case from neighboring Bitonto, where a Jew and a Christian who were neighbors entered into litigation over property rights.[61] However, the Jew in question was a member of the elite, which may explain his desire to reside among Christians. Less common was a Christian choosing to live among Jews, lending weight to the idea that the "Christians" living in the *giudecca* of Trani may have once been Jews. We may conclude, then, that the borderline between Jew and "new Christian" was a blurred one, at least in the late fifteenth century. Conversion could mean entering an intermediary stage in which one no longer prayed, broke bread, or married with one's former co-religionists, although it was possible to remain as neighbors. The resonance of "once a Jew, always a Jew" is that decades, and perhaps even centuries, had to pass before the mark of a former Jewish identity had completely disappeared.

Apart from the isolated periods of tension already mentioned, Jews and Christians generally lived in peace. They entered into business transactions and contracts, owned property in common, and lived in adjoining houses. The small and compact size of the Jewish quarter, its openness to the larger city, its proximity to the port, and the existence of important commercial services such as banking and money-lending within its precincts meant that Christians had to come regularly to the Jewish quarter for their affairs. We have to assume that Jews also entered the Christian part of town with equal facility: they were represented on the important governing bodies of the city, they engaged in crucial trades, and even held lands outside the town. Renata Segre, writing about the interactions between Jews and Christians in Italy in the late Middle Ages and during the Renaissance, concludes that the relationship established between Jews and Christians shows how their religious and (in some respect) ethnic differences, though certainly noticed, did not stand in the way of habits of civil coexistence. The sheer existence of such an enormous gap between the letter of the law and the reality of daily life is rich with implications. In fact, the law defined in extremely rigorous terms the gulf that ought to separate the Christian faithful from the people that the church so often called "the killers of Christ." And yet the very measures that could not help but have had repercussions on Jewish life—the decrees of the Fourth Lateran Council, the first burnings of the Talmud, the establishment of the Roman inquisition—seem to have had little effect on ordinary relations.[62]

INTELLECTUAL CURRENTS AND A SHARED CULTURAL PERSPECTIVE

Perhaps the most important common denominator between Jews and Christians was their shared appreciation for the richness of Italian culture as it developed in the southern part of the peninsula. From the period of Frederick II onward, the Jews of Trani participated in the intellectual ferment caused by the interaction of Muslim, Christian, and Jewish philosophical currents that converged on southern Italy at that time. The thinking of Maimonides and Rashi had dominated Jewish intellectual life at the beginning of the thirteenth century, but by mid-century, new ideas based on translations of Greek rationalist philosophy emanating from Spain and Provence had reached Trani. Emerging from this ferment was a common Arab-Jewish-Christian philosophical discourse that gave rise to "a genuine intellectual harmony between the new trends in Jewish philosophy and the Aristotelian conclusions of Dominican theologians."[63]

The fifteenth century was another period of intellectual excitement, with the arrival of many new immigrants from Spain, France, Germany, and central and southern Italy. Among the newcomers to Trani was the scholar and translator Tanhum ben Moshe from Beaucaire in Provence, who died in Trani in 1450 and whose tombstone has been preserved in the courtyard of the church of the diocese.[64] Tanhum is said to have translated Hippocratis's *Prognostica,* completed in 1406. The presence of such an illustrious figure in Trani suggests that even in the fifteenth century, there were enough Jews left to attract scholars of standing who acted as carriers of ideas and material culture. The archives speak of three *tedeschi iudi* (German Jews) who came to Trani "some years and months ago...to reside in this city with their goods and family." [65] As late as the sixteenth century, when the community was reportedly in its decline, Trani continued to attract Jewish intellectual personalities such as Rabbi Moses of Trani, the author of *Kisath Sepher*, and the famous Rabbi Yitzhak Abarbanel.[66]

THE FINAL YEARS

The process that eventually led to the disappearance of Jews from Trani gathered momentum at the beginning of the sixteenth century, when southern Italy came under the rule of Ferdinand the Catholic, who had expelled the Jews from Spain in 1492.[67] In 1510 the Inquisition was installed in the region of Naples, and Ferdinand ordered all Jews and new Christians to leave. But the edict was unequally applied, and some remained behind, especially those who had the wealth and the influence to acquire protection.[68] However, it was a short reprieve, and in 1541, Charles V made a clean sweep, wiping the community out of existence by forcing those few who remained to convert.

How does the Jewish remnant in Trani's urban fabric reshape our understanding of Italian urban history and the Jewish role in it? A concept of Jewish separation and even isolation has been central to our notion of the Italian city, particularly after the sixteenth century, when the prototype of the ghetto appeared in Venice. Was the *giudecca* of Trani like a ghetto, a place of exclusivity? Our research in Trani makes it clear that the ghetto model was limited in time and space. In the south, in cities such as Trani, we found examples of more integrated forms of co-existence that pre-existed the ghetto and offered possibilities for exchange far more extensive than the ghetto situation would allow.

Which leads directly to another question: Were the Jews of Trani considered "real Tranesi"? Not only does the archival evidence show that the Jews enjoyed a certain legal status; there are also signs that the Jews held significant social capital within the town. In addition to their pivotal economic role, their participation in public life, their ownership of shops and property, and their tax contributions, we have the evidence of the material goods they bestowed on the built environment. The remarkable aspect of this story is that although the last Jews left Trani nearly five centuries ago, an awareness of them is still a vivid part of local memory, coloring the popular perception of urban space. Street signs, tourist maps, and a renewed interest in local history are places where the former Jewish presence is explicitly evoked. The *giudecca* is still inhabited by Jewish ghosts after the passage of nearly five hundred years. The boldly cosmopolitan style of the great synagogue speaks of a Jewish community not cut from one cloth, but rather one that was diversified in its personalities, opinions, and aesthetic tendencies, enriching the local mix. One of the functions minority groups have performed throughout history is to provide a mirror in which the majority can reflect upon itself to achieve greater self-understanding. The image of difference that the minority held up to the rest of the population—preserved in the built environment—may be the most important gift Trani's Jews gave to their non-Jewish neighbors.

Notes

1. David B. Ruderman, "At the Intersection of Cultures: The Historical Legacy of Italian Jewry," in *Gardens and Ghettos: The Art of Jewish Life in Italy,* ed. Vivian Mann (Berkeley: University of California Press, 1989), 2.

2. Cesare Colafemmina, "Gli ebrei nel Mezzagiorno d'Italia," in Rosalia La Franca, ed., *Architettura Judaica in Italia: Ebraismo, Sito, Memoria Dei Luoghi* (Palermo: Flaccovio, 1994), 247–249.

3. Shlomo Simonsohn, "The Hebrew Revival among Early Medieval European Jews," in *Salo Wittmayer Baron Jubilee Volume,* 3 vols. (Jerusalem: American Academy for Jewish Research, 1975), 2: 843–848.

4. Isadore Twersky, "The Contribution of Italian Sages to Rabbinic Literature," in *Italia judaica: atti del I Convegno internazionale*: Bari 18–22, maggio 1981 (Roma: Ministero per i beni culturali e ambientali, 1983), 99.

5. Ibid., 392–393.

6. Ibid., 390. Rashi is the acronym of Rabbi Shlomo Yitzhaqi, medieval commentator on the Bible and Talmud, born in Troyes in northeastern France in 1040 and died there in 1105.

7. Ruderman, "At the Intersection of Cultures," 10.

8. John Larner, *Italy in the Age of Dante and Petrarch: 1216–1380* (London and New York: Longman, 1980), 24.

9. Ibid., 22.

10. Ibid., 27.

11. Cesare Colafemmina, "Gli Ebrei in Puglia al tempo di Federico II di Svevia" in C. Colafemmina and Luigi Palmiotti, *Aspetti della storia degli Ebrei in Trani e in Biscelie e vicende tranesi dal secolo IX* (Trani: Centro regionale di servizi educativi e culturali, 1999), 12.

12. Larner, *Italy,* 28–30.

13. Colafemmina, *Aspetti,* 12.

14. The blood libel accusation was based on the notion that Jews were responsible for the abduction of Christian children to obtain their blood for ritual purposes. In the case of baptism, the new laws required a three-day waiting period between the time a Jew declared his intention to be baptized and the actual ceremony, to assure that the conversion was not a coerced one. Colafemmina, *Aspetti,* 12, 14.

15. Francesco De Robertis, *Federico I Di Svevia nel mito e nella realta: notazioni critiche e ricostruttive sulla figura e l'opera, spesso tutt'altro che esaltanti, del maggior dinasta dell'occidente* (Bari: Societa di storia patria per la Puglia, 1998), 138.

16. Benjamin of Tudela, T*he Itinerary of Benjamin of Tudela,* edited and translated by Marcus Nathan Adler (London: Henry Frowde, 1907), 9. These figures are probably based on heads of families rather than on individuals. If we assume an average of six persons per family, we arrive at a community of about 1,200 people in the year 1160.

17. Colafemmina, *Aspetti,* 17; See also Cecil Roth, *The History of the Jews of Italy* (Philadelphia: Jewish Publication Society, 1946), 87–90.

18. *Documenti per la storia degli Ebrei in Puglia nell' archivio di stato di Napoli* (Bari: regione Puglia - assessorato alla cultura Istituto Ecumenico S. Nicola, 1990), Napoli, 16 March 1475, 34, #9 .

19. Colafemmina, *Aspetti,* 19.

20. Guido Malcangi, "La Giudecca di Trani," in G. Malcangi, *Trani: pagine di storia, ricordi di vita e altre divagazioni pugliesi* (Fasano: Schena, 1983), 16.

21. Benedetto Ronchi, *Indagine sullo sviluppo urbanistico di Trani dall' XI al XVIII secolo* (Fasano: Schena, 1984), 61.

22. Noemi Cassuto, "The Italian Synagogue through the Ages," in *Synagogues Without Jews and the Communities That Built and Used Them*, eds. Rivka and Ben-Zion Dorfman (Philadelphia: Jewish Publication Society, 2000), 301.

23. Ernst Munkácsi, *Der Jude von Neapel* (Zurich: Verlag Die Lica, 1939), 65. The interior was twice renovated in the nineteenth century, in 1841 and 1888, according to Munkácsi (p. 67). Munkácsi's description of the synagogue is very detailed and fills in the blanks posed by the semi-ruined edifice one sees today.

24. Jewish builders in Fez also made maximum use of underground space in their homes.

25. Munkácsi, *Der Jude von Neapel,* 67–69: the plaque has been removed to a nearby church.

26. This Hebrew date corresponds to 1247 CE.

27. *Minyan* is a Hebrew word meaning the quorum of ten males over thirteen years of age required for formal Jewish worship.

28. We have compared Colafemmina's Italian translation with the Hebrew text in making this English translation, which is our own. See his *Aspetti,* 23–24. For an alternative translation of the inscription, see Umberto Cassuto, "Iscrizioni ebraiche a Trani," *Rivista degli studi orientali,* vol. 13, 2 (1932), 178–179.

29. Simonsohn, *Hebrew Revival,* 851, note 54.

30. This synagogue was converted into a church and is currently being used for worship as Santa Maria di Scolanova.

31. Carol H. Krinsky, *Synagogues of Europe: Architecture, History, Meaning* (New York: Architectural History Foundation, 1985), 335.

32. A Jewish holiday marking the end and beginning of a new annual cycle of reading from the Torah.

33. Munkácsi, *Der Jude von Neapel,* 64 note 91.

34. Benjamin Ravid, "A Tale of Three Cities and Their Raison d'Etat: Ancona, Venice and Livorno and the Competition for Jewish Merchants in the Sixteenth Century," *Mediterranean Historical Review* 6,2 (1991): 139–162.

35. Umberto Cassuto argues for the date 1292–93 as the moment of massive conversion, based on fragmentary evidence from the archives of Naples and a manuscript found in the British Museum. In 1306, the Jewish representative body "Universitas

Judaeorum" was replaced by that of the "Universitas Neophytorum," or "new Christians." For this reason, Roth claims that after 1306, the Jews of Trani existed only as converts (*History*, 269). This interpretation seems a bit extreme. While the community as an entity may have disappeared for a time, individual Jews and families survived, perhaps by secretly practicing their faith as Cassuto suggests. See his "Iscrizioni," 175–176.

36. The Bari archives consist mainly of notarial documents, while the Naples archives are executive orders from the *Sommaria* of Naples to local officials. The language of these documents is generally Italian, with formulaic introductions and conclusions in Latin. The documents for Napoli appear in *Documenti per la storia degli Ebrei in Puglia nell' archivio di stato di Napoli* (Bari: regione Puglia - assessorato alla cultura Istituto Ecumenico S. Nicola, 1990), hereafter cited as ASN, and for Bari, *Archivio di Stato di Bari, La Presenza ebraica in Puglia: Fonti Documentarie e bibliografiche* (Bari: De Pascale, n.d.), hereafter cited as ASB.

37. ASN, 13.

38. In 1488, the *Sommaria*, or state governing council located in Bari, upon the request of certain Tranesi Jews, sent instructions to the Captain (chief officer) of Trani, advising him that only "wealthy Jews" (*giudi facoltosi*) should be selected to represent the *giudecca* as *proti*: "In previous times it has been the habit of the *giudecca* to elect two or three *proti*, the wealthiest and most competent, to govern....But some have been acting against custom, and the *giudecca* has been electing poor and insufficient men with the result that its interests have been harmed...[We] order the Jews of this *giudecca* to choose as *proti* the richest, best and most competent...as was the habit in previous times, so that the *giudecca* will be governed well and taxes will be paid, either weekly or monthly, according to habits and norms of the *giudecche* of this kingdom...under the authority of these notables. And if some Jews of the *giudecca* disagree and refuse to follow the orders of the governing *proti*...they should be punished as an example to others." ASN, 1 October 1488.

39. This was the practice in the neighboring town of Bitonto, and we may assume it was the same in Trani. ASB Bitonto, 2 March 1469, 54, #29.

40. Ibid.

41. ASN, 16 August 1491, 89, #76.

42. Ibid.

43. ASN, 20 July 1482, 42, #17.

44. ASN, 20 November 1495, 180, #193.

45. ASN, 10 December 1490, 81, #65.

46. ASN, 3 November 1463, 26, #2.

47. ASN, 4 March 1488, 62, #41.

48. Colafemmina, *Ebrei*, 20-21.

49. The site where the gravestone was found is described in Francesa Onesti, *La Campana di Trani* (Trani: CRSEC Trani, 1999), 105. Parts of Jewish tombstones, the Hebrew letters still visible, are found scattered throughout the old town of Trani, in lintels, embedded in walls, and used as doorsteps.

50. ASN, 11 March 1494, 127, #127.

51. ASN, 20 March 1494, 128, #129.

52. Ibid.

53. ASN, 3 July 1494, 154, #160.

54. Corrado Vivanti, "The History of the Jews in Italy and the History of Italy," *Journal of Modern History* 67, 2 (June 1995): 340.

55. Colafemmina, *Aspetti*, 39.

56. In *his Guida di Trani*, Salvatore Carlo Capozzi writes that the Palazzo Covelli on via Statuti Marittimi, popularly known as Lo Sciale, was the residency of the Jewish family of Troiano de Boctunis, president of the Regia Sommaria of Napoli in 1466 (Trani: ditta tipografica editrice vecchi, 1915), 216.

57. Renata Segre says the difference between "new Christians" and "neophytes" in the fifteenth century was one of origin: "new Christians" came from the Iberian peninsula, and "neophytes" were Italian. Both were Jews by birth who were later baptized. For a more extended discussion of this issue in its historical setting, see her "Sephardic Settlements in Sixteenth Century Italy: A Historical and Geographical Survey," *Mediterranean Historical Review* 6,2 (1991): 112-137.

58. Roberto Bonfil, *Jewish Life in Renaissance Italy* (Berkeley: University of California Press, 1994), 116-119.

59. Quoted in Malcangi, "La Giudecca di Trani," 18.

60. Capozzi, *Guida*, 39.

61. ASB, 13 February 1459, 34-35, #16.

62. Quoted in C. Vivanti, "The History of the Jews in Italy," 330.

63. Ibid., 327.

64. Colafemmina, *Aspetti*, 39.

65. ASN, 15 October 1478, 35, #10.

66. Malcangi, "La Giudecca di Trani," 16.

67. For a discussion of this problem, see Danièle Iancu, *Les Juifs en Provence (1475-1501); De l'insertion à l'expulsion* (Marseille: Institut historique de Provence, 1981), 55-59.

68. An exception was made for 200 Jewish families to remain in Naples in return for an annual payment of 3000 ducats to the Royal Treasury. The reluctance to seal the fate of the Jews was based not only on their ability to pay bribes but also on their skills in money-lending, which were essential to the local economy. Iancu, *Provence*, 58-59.

SUSAN GILSON MILLER,
ATTILIO PETRUCCIOLI,
AND MAURO BERTAGNIN

3

THE *MALLÂH,*
THE THIRD CITY OF FEZ

The view of Fez from afar, with its emerald roofs shimmering in the mist, can induce a state of poetic exuberance even in the most jaded traveler. But how many visitors to Fez are aware that it is actually a series of cities, strung together from east to west? Old Fez (*fâs al-bâlî*), the original place of settlement built in the ninth century, is the site of the countless mosques, oratories and colleges that make the city renowned for its building arts. The richness of this architectural heritage earned Old Fez the designation as a UNESCO World Monument in 1980, together with its neighbor, Fâs al-Jadîd or "New" Fez, the second city of Fez. But New Fez itself is hardly new. It was built in the thirteenth century to house the sultan and his court in serene and sumptuous surroundings far from the hurly-burly of Old Fez. The powerful complementarity of these two cities, one of the palace and the other of the bazaar, created the image of Fez as Morocco's preeminent city—the source of its government, commerce, religiosity, and intellectual life.

mallâh

Map of Fez showing location of the *mallâh*

.

Yet a third city of Fez is the *mallâh*, or Jewish quarter, home to the Jews of Fez for more than five hundred years. Thickly settled in the fifteenth century, the *mallâh* was built in the shadow of the royal compound of New Fez. Here the Jews lived within their own separate walled quarter, surrounded by the services needed to sustain ritual and communal life, such as synagogues, schools, ovens, and bathhouses. Covering about 5 hectares or 12.5 acres, the *mallâh* of Fez survives today as a distinct walled quarter, although it is no longer the home of Moroccan Jews. It was abandoned in stages in the early twentieth century: initially for apartments and villas in the French-built *ville nouvelle*, later for permanent exile in Israel, France, and North America following Moroccan independence in 1956. Today, the quarter that housed 7,000 Arabic-speaking Jews in 1900 is inhabited by migrants newly arrived from the countryside. Many of the great houses where the art of living in the Fâsî Jewish manner was practiced for generations have been subdivided into apartments or fallen into disrepair.

Despite its delapidated state, the *mallâh* of Fez retains its place in local memory as the first separate Jewish quarter of Morocco, the origin, at least in name, for all the many other Jewish quarters that followed. Even though its presence looms large in the Moroccan *imaginaire*, basic facts about the *mallâh* of Fez are still unclear. Scattered monographs treat certain aspects of *mallâh* history, but an overall portrait explaining the circumstances of its foundation, the events that shaped its early history, and the evolution of its material form are still lacking. Moreover, the sources for reconstructing a reliable history are contradictory and episodic. On the Jewish side, the chronicle *Dibre Ha-yamim*, a history of Jewish Fez compiled by members of the Ibn Danan family, is the preeminent source. Covering the fifteenth through the nineteenth centuries, this manuscript provides an inside view of life in the *mallâh*, written by members of a distinguished rabbinical family seeking to assure its place in history.[1] Arabic sources also speak of the *mallâh*, but in a tangential manner, since the inner life of the quarter was not of primary concern to the Muslim chroniclers. Nevertheless, the *Anîs al-Mutrib*, a fourteenth-century narrative by `Àli Ibn 'Abî Zar' al-Fâsî[2] and Muhammad al-Qâdirî's *Nashr al-Mathânî*,[3] a seventeenth-century chronicle of the ruling `Alawi dynasty, offer fleeting glimpses of Jewish life in Fez. Closer in sentiment to Jewish concerns but even more problematic in intent are the polemical tracts written by Fâsî Jewish converts to Islam.[4] On the whole, the written record has large gaps, placing heavy demands on the historical imagination.

Information as rudimentary as the date of the founding of the *mallâh* is contested. Some sources claim the thirteenth century, 1276 to be precise, as the founding date, while others place it nearly two centuries later, in the 1430s. The Arabic source *Anîs al-Mutrib* puts forward the thirteenth-century date, saying that "On the second of Shawwâl of this year [674 AH, corresponding to 20 May 1276] the Jews were killed in Fez when the common people rose up against them and 14,000 perished. If it had not been for the actions of the *amîr al-mu'minîm*, (the sultan, commander of the faithful), they would have finished them off."[5] Following this massive attack, the source goes on to say, the *mallâh* was established as a safe haven for the Jews. Here we have some of the perennial themes associated with *mallâh* creation in the Moroccan canon: a violent attack on the Jews, the sultan as savior and protector, and the removal of the Jews to a separate quarter, presumably for their own safety.

But this account is problematic for more reasons than one; for example, there is a longstanding claim that the great Jewish philosopher Maimonides lived in Old Fez at the end of the thirteenth century, casting doubt on the assertion that *all* the Jews had been removed to the *mallâh* in 1276.[6] Moreover, the traveler Leo Africanus, writing in the early sixteenth century and close to the events that he reports, says that "King Abusabid [Abu Sa`id Uthman III, ruled 800-23 AH/1398-1421] caused [the Jews] to remove into new Fez, and by that means doubled their yearly tribute." His account raises further doubt that all the Jews were removed to the *mallâh* in 1276, and introduces yet another date for the founding, at the end of the fourteenth century.[7]

This confusion is compounded when we look at the Jewish sources that uniformly place the founding of the *mallâh* two hundred years later, although the circumstances are remarkably similar to those citied in the Arabic accounts. The nineteenth-century chronicler Abner Hassarfaty lists 1438 as the year in which the Jews were expelled from Old Fez, citing as the purported cause of their banishment the sin of spilling wine on the steps of a mosque.[8] David Corcos, a modern Moroccan Jewish scholar, places the founding a year earlier, corresponding with the discovery of the tomb of Mawlây Idrîs at Fez, and mentions the instability associated with the last days of the Marinid dynasty as a principal cause of their removal.[9] Thus we have several conflicting dates for the founding, and different reasons for the expulsion from the *madîna*, each associated in some way with the themes of transgression, punishment, and eventual redemption.

One reason for the confusion may be that the founding of the *mallâh* was not a singular event based on the politics of the moment, but rather the culmination of a series of steps that had fundamentally altered Jewish-Muslim relations in Fez over the course of time. Jews were deeply implanted in Old Fez, where they had lived for hundreds of years. At its founding in 808, the city had attracted a diverse population from the Islamic East and Muslim Spain, and among them were Jews who were welcomed for their skills, artisanship, and facility at trade due to their far-flung family networks.[10] The Jews settled in the *madîna* of Fez, in a place known as *funduq al-yahûd*.[11] From the outside, the community may have appeared monolithic, but internally, Jews created their own social pyramid layered by occupation, family affiliation, and place of origin. After meeting their fiscal obligations, Jews were generally allowed to govern their own affairs, following their rabbis in matters of law and comportment, even as they built extensive economic ties with the Muslim community. Over time, Muslims and Jews had become intertwined in a dense set of mutual relations inflected by an array of dependencies, obligations, and avoidances that were in turn subject to events in the wider world.

This was especially true in the economic sphere, where Jews filled a vital niche vacated for them by the majority. Jewish peddlers traveled the countryside serving as a link in the chain of production and distribution of goods that made Fez an important regional trading center. A small elite with the capital and skills to conduct long-distance trade rose from the mass by dint of their wealth and connections, facilitating trade between the hinterland and the markets of Fez, and between Fez and the coastal ports. Jews were also central to the closely controlled process of producing wealth for the royal treasury. Leo Africanus describes the mint and the workshops of Jewish goldsmiths located close to the palace where coins were stamped and sealed. "The greatest part of goldsmiths dwelling in New Fez are Jews...for in old Fez neither gold nor silver is coined, nor are any [Muslims] suffered to be goldsmiths, because they have usurers among them."[12] Jews also paid heavy taxes, more than 400 ducats a month, according to Leo Africanus, and were a chief source of revenue for the palace.

Philologists, jurists, alchemists, and commentators on the Torah flourished among the Jews of Fez, contributing to the intellectual vitality that gave the city its reputation as a center of learning. As early as the ninth century, Jewish scholars of Fez were corresponding with rabbis in Babylon, seeking their advice on finer points of the law. The distinguished Algerian-born Talmudist Isaac Alfasi (d. 1103) taught in Fez for many years, although he eventually left Morocco for Spain. His legal opinions written in Arabic were famous throughout the medieval Jewish world.[13] The most famous Jewish scholar of Fez was Moses Ibn Maimon, known as Maimonides, whose writings on Jewish philosophy, law, and ethics had an influence on both Jewish and non-Jewish circles. Maimonides fled to North Africa from Córdoba in 1159 and lived in the *madîna* of Fez for five years.[14]

The preferential status of the Jews of Fez evaporated in the twelfth century under the rule of the Almohad dynasty, who were militants bent on eliminating all "heresies" from the broad swath of territory that fell under their rule. After annulling the validity of the *dhimma* contract, they left standing "neither church nor synagogue" in the whole of the Maghrib, forcing non-Muslims to convert and driving into exile those who refused.[15]

Jews who stayed behind practiced their faith in secret and nurtured a double identity to survive. These resisters eventually became the nucleus of a revived community in the thirteenth century, when the first of several rebirths that Fâsî Jews underwent over the centuries took place.

At the end of thirteenth century, the more tolerant dynasty of the Banû Marîn became the masters of Fez, and the Sultan Abû Yûsuf began an ambitious project to build the new royal city of Fâs al-Jadîd. Designed as an elaborate fortified camp, it contained a palace, several mosques, extensive gardens, a market, and a garrison for the royal guard. Just south of the palace was a marshy ground known as the *mallâh*, or "salty place," where a contingent of Syrian archers had their barracks.[16] At some point, Jews began to inhabit this quarter as well; employed in the palace service and engaged in the minting of gold coins, it was reasonable that they would live in proximity to their workplace. Meanwhile, Jews also continued to reside in Old Fez in the *funduq al-yahûd*, with its easy access to the main commercial center (*qaysarîya*). We may surmise that between the thirteenth and the mid-fifteenth centuries, these two places of Jewish settlement existed concurrently. However, the toponym *mallâh* was associated only with the dwelling place of the Jews adjacent to the palace in New Fez, and thereafter, each new Jewish quarter built in Morocco was called the *mallâh*.[17]

The course of events leading up to the transfer of all the Jews from the Fez *madîna* to the *mallâh* in the mid-fifteenth century can be traced through the Jewish sources. At the time, the power of the Banû Marîn was being eclipsed by that of a collateral dynasty called the Banu Wattâs, who controlled much of the country. Even in Fez itself, the ruling dynasty had become one among several rival factions competing for control. Caught in the middle of these violent crosscurrents were the Jews of Fez, whose numbers had grown considerably over the years, augmented after 1391 by consecutive waves of refugees fleeing Spain. Perhaps because of the Jews' increasing numbers and their growing importance to the economy, other contenders for power, namely the *shurafâ'* (nobility) and the wealthy merchants of the *qaysarîya*, saw them as rivals and sought to use them as pawns in a bitter struggle for dominance.[18] Caught in the crossfire of competing social groups and momentarily exposed because of the failing sultanate, the Jewish population of Old Fez was left open to manipulation. The "rediscovery" in 1437 of the tomb in Old Fez of its sainted founder, Mawlây Idrîs, sealed their fate. The *madîna* was declared holy ground and off-limits to unbelievers, forcing all the Jews to leave the Old City and to abandon their houses, shops, and places of work to Muslims.[19]

How did Fâsî Jews regard the move to the *mallâh*? An early-twentieth-century Hebrew text, *Ner Hama'arav*, gives some of the flavor of the event:

> In the year 5198 [1437-38] Jews who had been living in the Fez *madîna* since the foundation of the city were expelled from it with a fierce brutality. Some Jews were killed, while others embraced Islam. A few families left the *madîna* and built the *mallâh*. This event was provoked by the fact that Muslims found a bottle of wine in their mosque and wrongly accused the Jews of having placed it there.[20]

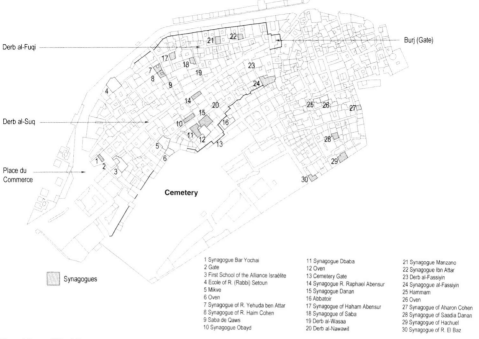

Derb al-Fuqi ——————

Derb al-Suq ——————

Place du
Commerce ——————

Burj (Gate) ——————

Cemetery

Synagogues

1 Synagogue Bar Yochai	11 Synagogue Dbaba	21 Synagogue Manzano
2 Gate	12 Oven	22 Synagogue Ibn Attar
3 First School of the Alliance Israélite	13 Cemetery Gate	23 Derb al-Fassiyin
4 Ecole of R. (Rabbi) Setoun	14 Synagogue R. Raphael Abensur	24 Synagogue al-Fassiyin
5 Mikve	15 Synagogue Danan	25 Hammam
6 Oven	16 Abbatoir	26 Oven
7 Synagogue of R. Yehuda ben Attar	17 Synagogue of Haham Abensur	27 Synagogue of Aharon Cohen
8 Synagogue of R. Haim Cohen	18 Synagogue of Saba	28 Synagogue of Saadia Danan
9 Saba de Qaws	19 Derb al-Wasaa	29 Synagogue of Hachuel
10 Synagogue Obayd	20 Derb al-Nawawil	30 Synagogue of R. El Baz

Plan of the *mallâh* of Fez

The story of the wine in the mosque is a recurrent motif that often appears in Muslim texts as the preamble to an anti-Jewish attack, justifying violence on the grounds of preserving the *sunna*. Its appearance in a Jewish text underscores the irrationality of events as they unfolded from the Jewish point of view. Clearly, the expulsion was a catastrophe for the Jews of Fez. The fact that only "a few" families left the *madîna* for the *mallâh* suggests how widespread was their determination to avert displacement, even if it meant converting to Islam. From the Jewish perspective, the order to leave was the culmination of a series of events calculated to cripple them economically and to marginalize them from the centers of power by placing them outside the urban core.

In the eyes of their Muslim antagonists, on the other hand, the banishment of Jews to the *mallâh* was a démarche that accomplished several goals at once: it elimi-nated Jewish competition from the crowded central markets; it cleansed the sacred precincts around the tomb of the revered saint; it caused Jews—a prime source of taxes and other supernumerary fines—to be gathered in one, closely supervised envi-ronment; it advanced political and social ambitions of rivals for power under the guise of upholding the religious law; and finally, it inscribed in space a clear distinction between Jews and Muslims, and perhaps even more important, between normative Jews and those Jews who had "dubiously" converted to Islam.[21]

In the aftermath of these complex maneuverings, the new quarter gradually became home to the Jews, as it filled out with houses, workshops, and the other elements of urban life—a town within itself, separate from the rest of Fez, yet attached to it through filaments of economic, social, and political dependency. In 1540, a Belgian Catholic priest, Nicholas Clenardus, took up residence in the *mallâh* for a year, and his correspondence offers a glimpse into life there in that period. He studied Arabic with Jewish scholars and estimated the population at 4,000, as compared with the 50,000 people in Old Fez.[22] The small group of original settlers had grown considerably in the hundred intervening years, augmented by Jews exiled from Spain in 1492, who carried with them the rich legacy of Sephardic culture in the form of special customs, language, and jurisprudence.[23] Another well-informed visitor was the Spaniard Luis de Mármol, who wrote in the 1540s that the quarter had a "grand plaza with many shops, syna-gogues, and well-built houses." Many Jews had reached powerful positions in the palace; no noble household, he wrote, was complete without a Jewish "majordomo" in charge of day-to-day affairs.[24]

As a consequence of the influx of Spanish Jews, the Fâsî Jewish community became divided along "ethnic" lines. On the one hand were the worldly exiles, the *megorashim*, immensely proud of their Spanish heritage; on the other were the Arabic-speaking *toshavim*, or local Jews, deeply immersed in the Moroccan Arabo-Berber tradi-tion. Members of each group worshipped in its own synagogue, revered their own rabbis, followed their own distinctive traditions in prayer, married within the group, and were buried in their own separate cemetery. It was not until the 1700s that the two communities finally melded together, with Arabic becoming the common language, while the Spanish *minhag*, or ritual, prevailed in religious practice.[25]

Over the next two centuries, the size of the community fluctuated wildly, as years of relative peace and prosperity were followed by calamities in the form of epidemics, famine, or war.[26] In 1723, an extended drought turned the *mallâh* into a ghost town, as Jews fled Fez for safer places: "The houses of the rich are empty, their inhabitants have disappeared, the gates of the courtyards are closed, weeds grow up and robbers enter, stealing the doors and the beds. Many houses have been demolished, their stones and rafters taken away...Most of the streets of the *mallâh* are deserted."[27] During this period, hunger killed more then 2000 people, according to the register of the communal burial society, and 1000 more apostatized.

Another calamity deeply incised in popular memory was the two-year exile of the Jews from the *mallâh* in 1790-1792, during the brief and infamous reign of the cruel sul-tan Mawlây al-Yazîd. The community as a whole was forced to move to the *qasba* Shrarda on the other side of Fez, abandoning the *mallâh* to tribal contingents allied with the sultan. The dismantling of the Jewish presence in the *mallâh* during this time was more or less complete. A mosque was built on the site of the main synagogue, using tombstones from the Jewish cemetery, and the cemetery itself was moved to Bab Gissa at the entrance to the Muslim quarter. The sources recount how the bones of sainted rabbis were transported to the new cemetery in clay vessels. The exile lasted almost two years, until the death of Yazîd, when the *qâdî* (chief judge) of Fez ordered the mosque to be torn down and the Jews returned to their quarter.[28]

Maroc
28. - Le Mellah, vue prise du sommet du ravin Oued Zitoun

un coin de la ville de Fez. le Mellah ville juif.

View of the *mallâh* from the south, c. 1920

Conversion was an ever-present option in extreme cases of suffering, and according to Jewish sources, many adopted that course. Yet as a group, Jews continued to
form a strong solidarity under the leadership of their rabbis, who served not only as
spiritual guides but also as their representatives vis-à-vis the central power. The rabbis
managed community affairs, counseling restraint, moderation, and public humility as
the most effective means of collective self-preservation. In moments of distress, they
organized prayers and fasting, and in times of famine, they supervised the stockpiling
of food for community-wide distribution. When the sultan was angered with the Jews,
it was the rabbi who was detained by the authorities or ransomed as a punishment.[29]
The calling of rabbi stayed in certain families for generations through the right of *serarah*, or patrilineal inheritance, lending great prestige (*yahas*) to their name.[30] The community as a whole acquired status through the good reputation of its rabbis, by paying
the obligatory taxes on time, by offering gifts to the ruling power on special occasions,
and through the mediation provided by those among them who directly served the sultan. Through these mechanisms, the Jewish community maintained a foothold in the
body politic, even if it was sometimes a precarious one.[31]

In the mid-nineteenth century, the fortunes of the Jews of Fez took a dramatic turn
for the better. The "opening" of Morocco to Europe placed a handful of Jewish merchants with international connections at the center of a revitalized network of overseas trade, and led them to cautiously abandon some of their habitual submissiveness.
Tastes evolved, stimulated by contact with Europeans and with the more urbane Jewish
communities of the coast. Relations with their Muslim counterparts also developed;
the expansive lifestyle of the Fâsî *tâjir*, or wealthy merchant, represented for their
Jewish counterparts the epitome of good taste.[32] Rich Jews built splendid residences

inside the *mallâh*, taking as their point of reference the elaborate palaces of the Muslim elite going up on the outskirts of the *madîna* at the same time.[33] They patronized the same skilled artisans, adopted the same materials and motifs, and aspired to the same standard of luxury. The results are visible in the lavish interior décor of the homes of the High Street (*darb al-fûqî*) of the *mallâh*.

A TOUR OF THE GREAT HOUSES OF THE MALLÂH

The *mallâh* house (*dâr*) is an organism made up of both collaborating and hierarchical elements. It cannot be described by simply dissecting its components, but must be understood as a whole with its complex structure of relations.[34] From the exterior, the house is blind, its external walls showing only minimal openings. Very few of the windows are covered with the openwork wooden screen (*mashrabîya*). The practice of opening windows on the street side is a relatively recent one, adopted under the influ-

Axonometric view of Dar Ben Simhoun, Darb al-Fûqî

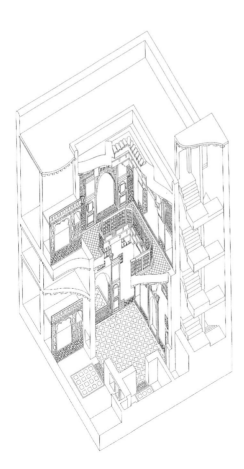

ence of Western building styles. Access to the house is usually through a room or a corridor (*saqîfa*) that mediates between the street and the interior, protecting the privacy of the courtyard. In the houses of the *madîna,* the entryway takes the shape of a dog-leg, while in the houses of the *mallâh*, it is usually a straight corridor with a door at each end. This passage leads directly into the courtyard or patio, the symbolic and functional core of the house. Its rigorous orthogonal geometry, the presence of a central fountain, the intricate woodwork, and the structural wooden beams that support the balconies above accentuate the regularity of the plan.

The life of the family revolves around the courtyard, and the surrounding rooms receive light and air from this central space. The elementary cell of the Moroccan house is the *bayt*, a room measuring about 2.5 X 7 meters. These aggregate around the circumference of the house in a parquet-like pattern. In the Moroccan house, the *bayt* is formally secondary to the courtyard, unlike the European house, where the room takes precedence over other elements. As a result, the *bayt* is often deformed under the pressure of the irregularities of the external urban morphology, and the orthogonal quality of the room is often more perceptual than real. One side of the courtyard is made up of small functional rooms and the stair leading to the upper floors in the corner. Most houses have at least two floors, the upper one being identical in plan to the lower, although many of the houses on High Street have three or more stories.

The roof terrace played an important social and functional role in the life of the house. During the day, it was a workshop of domestic activity, used for preparing food or drying laundry, while on the warmest nights the family used it for socializing and sleeping. Writing in 1902, Aubin called it "the chief pleasure-ground" of the *mallâh*, where in feast days the "gilded Jewish youth disports itself in silk kaftans of the most alluring shades, and *djellabas* in which the imagination has been given full scope."[35] At the Jewish Feast of Tabernacles (*Sukkoth*),[36] the family would erect a small booth of reeds on the roof, decorate it with wall hangings and symbols of the harvest season, and dine in this rustic enclosure. After the holiday, the booth was disassembled and the material lowered to the street to provide fuel for the local bread oven.[37] Another use of the roof was less convivial. When the street below became dangerous, it was a means of communication between the houses, and in 1703, when disorderly troops pillaged the *mallâh*, the Jews fled their quarter via the rooftops.[38] Another feature of the *mallâh* house was the cellar, frequently divided into rooms and storage areas, and in some cases, having a door that gave access to the street by a hidden stair. One can only conjecture about the use of these underground spaces: to stock foodstuffs, to give shelter in times of trouble, to provide an escape route.

In reality, no one house in the *mallâh* corresponds to this simple model. Processes of transformation, such as the acquisition or loss of one or more *bayt*s and their subdivision, have in some cases reduced the courtyard to an airshaft. In other cases, the spaces around the courtyard have been transformed into labyrinths of small rooms leading to half-levels and hidden stairways to the upper floors. Access to the hidden spaces was often found in a cupboard, so that it was often difficult to tell without close inspection that the stairway in fact existed. In the angles of courtyard beneath

83 FEZ. — Intérieur de Maison Israélite. — LL

Interior of a luxurious *mallāh* house

the stair were located the toilet facilities, equipped with running water, drawing on Fez's abundant subterranean supply.[39] Although the dimensions of the rooms and the courtyard differed slightly from house to house, the use of the elementary cell meant that the total width of each house was between 11 and 12 meters, giving the fabric as a whole a certain regularity.

From a formal perspective, Jewish houses of the *mallâh* differ little from their Muslim counterparts in the *madîna*. Building forms and methods used in the Jewish house were the same as those used in Muslim houses.[40] Muslim master builders supervised building projects in the *mallâh*, and Muslim craftsmen executed the finer decorative handiwork. "Carpenters and construction workers" is listed as a Jewish occupation in a census of the *mallâh* made in 1879, while "tilemakers" was specifically signaled as a non-Jewish profession, indicating that Muslims carried out the finer decorative work.[41] This tendency to integrate Jewish with Muslim building traditions seems to have been pervasive throughout in the Islamic world.

The furnishings of the household were very simple before the twentieth century, even in the houses of the wealthy. When the Jews were exiled from the *mallâh* in 1790, they took with them as many of their possessions as they could, including "armoires, tables, large and small cooking vessels, dishes, and special plates, pots and pans for Passover."[42] Often found among the furnishings of the *bayt* was an elaborate matrimonial bed made of carved wood, as well as small wooden cabinets built in the wall for storing objects. In terms of basic accoutrements of the room, there was little to distinguish a Jewish house from a Muslim one of the same class. However, it seems that Western-style furnishings were introduced into the *mallâh* earlier than into the

Bridal bed in a *mallâh* house

Hebrew inscription on wall tiles: "Blessings upon you on leaving"

madîna, and one European traveler speaks of "a considerable number of European comforts" in the richest Jewish houses.[43]

There were other reminders that this was Jewish space. Hebrew phrases of benediction were often used as elements of decoration at the entry to a room, and the amulets known as *mezuzot* were ritually required to be placed on the right side of the outside front door on the street. The small rectangle niche carved into the doorpost that once held the *mezuzah* can sometimes still be seen. The outside window frames of Jewish houses were painted in vivid colors—blue, yellow, rose, and bright red—contrasting sharply with the sober exteriors of the *madîna*.[44] The only real typological deviation from the Muslim model is the entryway, straight as opposed to dogleg, suggesting that Jews were less sensitive about maintaining the strict privacy of the interior than were Muslims.

In the Mediterranean region, the most important indicator distinguishing the fabric of the Jewish quarter from its non-Jewish counterpart is its greater density. Limitations on building space meant that transformations, subdivisions, and vertical additions often reached pathological levels in places such as Venice, where the houses are built one on top of the other. But in Fez this difference was less apparent.[45] Historic densities in the *mallâh* are hard to determine, but some generalizations are possible. The documentation indicates that periodic famine and disease frequently killed off large percentages of the population of both the *mallâh* and the *madîna*, relieving pressure on living space. As late as 1901, an epidemic of malaria reduced the population of the *mallâh* by one-third.[46] The entire city, *mallâh* and *madîna*, was overwhelmed by a flood of migrants from the countryside from the mid-nineteenth century onward, raising densities everywhere and giving rise to a large "floating population" of indeterminate size. René-Leclerc remarked in 1904 that "the *mallâh* is as dirty and as badly maintained as is the rest of Fez," suggesting that densities and health conditions there may not have been any worse than elsewhere in the *madîna*.[47]

This long, straight street commences at the monumental *burj*,[48] or main gate of the *mallâh*, marking the separation between the Jewish quarter and the rest of the Muslim city. From there it makes a gentle turn to conform to the shape of the Royal Palace in New Fez and the adjoining gardens of Lalla Mina, before it ends in a blind wall. Practically speaking, the street (*darb*) is a segment between two blind walls. It forms the backbone of the neighborhood unit. From this main street several perpendicular streets branch out, leading to the market (*sûq*) at the center of the *mallâh*. The hierarchy of the street pattern is simple and based on two elements: 1) the street itself, acting as the matrix onto which the doors of the most important houses open, and 2) the side streets running perpendicular to the street that provide the structure for a secondary settlement of lesser houses. Many streets, including the High Street, end in a tunnel darkened overhead by an extension covering the street (*sabât*). The tradition of the *sabât* is deeply rooted in Arab urban culture. If a homeowner wanted to add a room to an upper floor of his house by using the opposite wall as support, he only had to get the consent of his neighbor. Urban growth was the result of private negotiation between the parties and was not controlled by the rules and regulations of the municipality.[49]

The building fabric varies in depth and quality depending on its location. Most interesting is the block between the High Street and the exterior wall of the *mallâh* on the northern side, shielding the elaborate houses that are the real jewels of the *mallâh*. The great houses appear to be aligned to the outer wall, and the uniformity of their basic dimensions indicates that they were probably planned at the same time. Indeed, it appears that this block is a series of old mansions, originally built at the rear of the plot and attached to the thick outer wall of the *mallâh* overlooking the palace gardens, giving them access to both light and air. Each house has progressively encroached on the front edge of its plot by adding on rooms that are dependencies of it, so that the public space of the *darb* eventually became invaded. The original street was no doubt much wider, but it lost area over time to the homeowners along the street. These encroachments explain the long, dark internal corridor the visitor must traverse before reaching the courtyard of the house.

The High Street is mainly a residential street with a few amenities, the most important being the local bread oven. Traditionally, the bakers in the *mallâh* were Muslim, one of the few categories of employment not filled by Jews, as the bread oven had to function on the Sabbath.[50] Nowadays, business in the street is confined to a few small-scale entrepreneurs who display their wares on outdoor tables in a tentative effort at commercialization. The inhabitants of the *darb* usually walk the short distance to the main *suq* for their shopping.

The Gozlan and the Mansano synagogues face each other midway along High Street, constituting an urban node. The Gozlan synagogue is nothing more than an annex to the house next door, but the Mansano synagogue projects an important influence that goes beyond the limits of the *darb*. At the end of the nineteenth century, according to the manuscript *Yahas Fâs*, there were fifteen synagogues in the *mallâh*

7. - FEZ. - Une Rue
dans le Quartier du Mellah

A. Pleux, éditeur, Fez

Darb al-Fûqî in the 1920s

Sabât on Darb al-Fûqî

scattered around the quarter. Residents were always at most just a few steps away from a place of prayer. Most of these houses of worship were built in pre-existing rooms within private houses and furnished very simply. However, several were richly ornamented with stucco and mosaic tile and used Islamic architectural motifs such as arches, painted wooden ceilings, and carved wooden screens to clarify the functions of their various parts.[51] The smaller synagogues belonged to individuals and were supported by donations from members, while the larger ones were the property of the community. The *Yahas Fâs* notes that the only synagogue supported out of public funds in 1879 was the *Slât al-Fajr* (Synagogue of the Dawn), where early risers prayed. The text points out that all the synagogues of Fez are relatively recent, because the ancient ones were destroyed "in bad times" and were "forgotten," an apparent reference to the pillages of 1646 and 1790. The claim by Fâsî Jews that certain synagogues (such as the recently renovated Ibn Danân) date back to the seventeenth century can be explained as follows: although a synagogue may have been destroyed by the periodic violence that struck the *mallâh*, Jews continued to pray in its ruins, rebuilding it as soon as possible. Thus it may make more sense to speak of a continuity of sites rather than of actual structures.[52]

Another feature of the street is the presence of workshops at the lower level of the houses, two or three steps below street level. The *mallâh* of Fez in the nineteenth century was a beehive of activity, with many small ateliers devoted to the production of fine handicrafts, and especially the working of precious metals, which was a Jewish specialty. The *Yahas Fâs* tells us that the most important single craft practiced in the *mallâh* was the production of *sqalli*, a metallic thread used for decorating cloth and other objects. More than 300 men and women of the *mallâh* were employed at this trade in 1879, making it the most important single Jewish occupation in terms of both the number of craftspeople and the value of the goods produced.[53] It was closely associated with a variety of other luxury crafts, such as the manufacture of wall hangings, handbags, saddles, harnesses, belts, and slippers. The work of twisting the metal and silk together to form a braid was the responsibility of women and took place in the home, allowing them to alternate this work with other domestic chores.[54] Other trades practiced in the *mallâh* in 1879 included tailoring, especially of military uniforms and of fine imported fabrics for the palace household; the manufacture of harnesses for the royal cavalry; and the working of copper, silver, and gold into a variety of objects ranging from simple hardware to exquisite bracelets, earrings, and heavy gold belts.[55]

Much commercial activity took place in the street, without benefit of a permanent shelter. Tribesmen from the surrounding Middle Atlas Mountains brought in chickens and eggs, while fruits and vegetables were supplied by the Jews of nearby Sefrou, an important agricultural community. They would arrive in the *mallâh* on Thursday afternoon, spend the night under the arches of the main gate, and sell their merchandise at the busy Friday morning market, returning home before the start of the Sabbath. They carried home manufactured goods to be resold at rural markets, thus circulating Fâsî products throughout the hinterland.[56]

Interior of Ibn Danan synagogue, early twentieth century

Although the High Street contains the most beautiful houses, it covers only a small portion of the *mallâh*. The fabric changes as we move into other parts of the quarter. The neighborhood south of the *sûq* is far older and offers a more interesting layout consisting of two streets running parallel to the *sûq* and a series of shorter perpendicular streets in the north-south direction. The original alignment of the central lane of this neighborhood has been lost over time, and the street changes direction often. We can reconstruct the original path by paying attention to the marks left by the walls in the fabric. The blocks were quadrangles of 25 to 30 meters on a side, but today they are completely transformed due to a process of subdivision, subtraction, and addition. This phenomenon also tends to convert homes having a single courtyard into multi-family dwellings by reducing the house to a few rooms stacked one on top of the other. Frequently, one cell of the house is converted into a shop due to the commercial influence radiating from the nearby *sûq*. Streets that are completely occulted in the fabric can still be traced in the plan, while others that are in the process of disappearing are visible as impasses.

The impasse or cul-de-sac (*darîba*) is a common feature in both *madîna* and *mallâh*, consisting of a dead-end street closed off by a door giving access onto a micro-neighborhood of a few houses or a single large house inhabited by an extended family.[57] It is a version of the courtyard fabric inscribed on the street pattern, and it gives access to houses that are in the deepest part of the block. Impasses are present most often in fragmented blocks where the number of units and dwellings has multiplied. The function of the impasse is to increase the security of the group and its sense of mutual identity while mediating the transition from private to public space. It is a sort of entryway at the urban level. The maturity of this lower neighborhood is underscored by the presence of a number of synagogues in close association. Here are found the recently restored Ibn Danân synagogue and the Slat al-Fâsiyyîn, reportedly the oldest synagogue in Fez, laid out on a basilica plan.[58]

The few open spaces in the *mallâh* consist of the formalization of leftover areas. These spaces were not plazas or squares left open for the purpose of staging public events, but rather are simple openings in the street plan that became the setting for public manifestations. One such ceremony was the public procession associated with the *bar mitzvah*, the ceremony marking the passage of the Jewish male to adulthood. On the day of his *bar mitzvah*, the young man was marched through the streets of the *mallâh* led by his rabbi-teacher and his relatives. After the reading of the Torah in the synagogue, he was carried back through streets on a chair like a bride.[59]

Public ceremonies took place on other occasions as well. In times of distress such as a famine or a drought, the rabbis would organize public prayers in which the Scrolls of Law would be carried about in the streets accompanied by the lamentations of the worshippers.[60] This appropriation of the street reinforced the sense of the *mallâh* as specifically Jewish space, where little distinction was drawn between "private" and "public" in terms of ceremonial life.

Unlike the other major *mallâh*s of Morocco, such as Tetuan, Rabat, and even Marrakesh, the *mallâh* of Fez has a complex morphology that reveals its incremental growth over time. This is confirmed by the position of the main gate, which is oriented on a north-south axis. Its orientation is incongruent with the main street, which must turn slightly in order to enter into it. We conjecture that the two sections of the *mallâh* that are the oldest were probably laid out concurrently; first, the triangle formed between the High Street and the main street, and second, the area south of the *sûq* that appears on the map as three blocks of regular size divided by an impasse. The greater age of the area close to the main gate is confirmed by the presence of the synagogue of the Fâsiyyîn, the most ancient and important of the communal synagogues.[61]

Originally, the market area located along the main street must have been a large, irregular, and open space, because the plan shows traces of commercial encroachment on both sides of the street. It is not difficult to imagine how the original temporary wooden shop fronts eventually became fixed in space. René-Leclerc, writing at the turn of the century, called this area "a *qaysarîya* (great market) in miniature," filled with the shops of grocers and sellers of products of European manufacture unavailable in the *madîna,* such as shoe polish, cooking pots, colanders and knives.[62] Some of these shops also sold wine and fig brandy (*mahiya*), a specialty product of the Jews, forbidden for sale in the Muslim quarters.[63] The shops and markets of the *mallâh*, according to Le Tourneau, were supervised by the *muhtasib* of New Fez, an official of the municipality who inspected weights and measures and generally enforced standards of cleanliness and honesty in the conduct of commercial affairs.

Moving down the main street (*darb as-sûq*) toward the Place du Commerce, the fabric changes to one that is more recent. The Nawâwil quarter to the south of the *mallâh* probably dates from the end of the nineteenth century, although it aligns with the original tissue around the synagogue of the Fâsiyyîn. The toponym of this quarter refers to a type of structure—the straw huts (*nawâwil*) erected by country people as temporary shelter. The name suggests that migrants from the rural areas around Fez originally inhabited the quarter.

Unlike the rest of Fez, the *mallâh* contains few important landmarks other than the *burj* and the cemetery. The *burj* itself was a kind of cemetery, serving as the crypt for martyrs who died in a riot in the *mallâh* in 1465. The cemetery outside the *mallâh* migrated several times over the centuries. The site of the present cemetery is relatively new, dating from the early part of the nineteenth century. As one of the few open spaces in the environs of the *mallâh*, the cemetery was used for a variety of outdoor activities, not all of them licit. It was also the scene of the nightly vigils held at the tombs of venerated rabbis considered to have miraculous properties of healing and intercession.

Main street of *mallâh*, 1920s

Main street of *mallâh,* 2007

The *mallâh* extends over a plateau overlooking the Wâd al-Zaytûn that gently slopes down to the Jewish cemetery. To understand the morphology of the site, it must be seen in relation to New Fez, whose plan is very clear and serial. It is a sequence of separate nodes, first in the form of gates reinforced by a mosque, as seen at Bâb Dkâkin; the huge monumental esplanade (*mashwâr*) encircled by high walls; and three rectilinear *sûqs*, each of which forms the backbone of a settlement. Each settlement is enclosed by walls and communicates with the exterior through the single monumental gate. The palace both overshadows and protects the ensemble. The palace is a quarter unto itself, having a single main entrance at Bâb Dkâkin, which is the real pole of New Fez. Routes leading to it could be controlled by opening and closing the gates, making the spaces between into something like the watertight compartments of a submarine. In case of an insurrection, it was possible to isolate the palace or any one part of New Fez.

In the nineteenth century, the Jews of the *mallâh* had three possibilities when emerging from their quarter. They could head south toward the river valley, passing through a gate near the Bâb Sammarîn that is now demolished; they could go out the west, exiting via the present Place du Commerce; and they could go to Old Fez, traversing New Fez via the main axis of its *sûq*. If they chose this last route, they first had to cross an area between the *mallâh* and New Fez that was called the Sikkâkîn, or the place for the minting of coins. This was a transitional area where Jewish and Muslim shops were intermingled and space was shared.[64]

Outside the *mallâh*, Muslims easily recognized Jews because of their distinctive dress. A handful of Jews had their shops in the *madîna*, and others were required to go there on a daily basis to conduct their affairs. Adherence to a strict code of behavior usually allowed the Jew to pass unmolested, but it was a passage fraught with tension. Muslims, for their part, entered the *mallâh* at will. When a Muslim became sick in the pre-Protectorate era, he went to the *mallâh* to seek treatment and medicine. If he needed a letter written in a foreign language, or wanted to read a foreign newspaper, he had to consult a Jew.[65] If he wished to engage in activities not permitted in the *madîna*, such as drinking alcohol or gambling, he would have to enter the *mallâh*. But on the whole, actual mixing between the two groups was kept to well-defined situations and locations.

Although the two groups kept physically apart, they shared a distinctive set of common values. Whether Jew or Muslim, the Fâsî was known for his acute moral sensibility, his respect for the models of the past, his serene awareness of his aristocratic antecedents. A precarious balance between the similarities and differences that defined Muslim and Jew in pre-modern Fez gave special meaning to the physical barriers that kept the two groups apart. The walls surrounding the *mallâh* constituted a metaphorical as well as physical divide, separating two communities that agreed to cohabit but not assimilate. This understanding was elaborated by a complex array of emotions that included wariness as well as acceptance, attraction as well as repulsion, tolerance as well as ill-will. These emotions formed the substratum of an unwritten social contract that allowed Jews to survive and even flourish in the Moroccan milieu.

The coming of the French Protectorate in 1912 was the watershed event that marked the beginning of the end of the *mallâh* as a Jewish quarter. The French occupation of Fez in April 1912 was accompanied by an artillery attack that caused great damage to its physical structure. This attack was followed by a pillage that lasted several days.[66] The Jewish population fled the quarter for the relative safety of the palace grounds and took shelter in the empty lion cages of the sultan's menagerie. The rebuilding of the *mallâh* was a slow and painful process that took several years. The fronts of many buildings were altered to accommodate more modern building styles, windows and balconies were added, and the face of the *mallâh* changed radically. Soon wealthy Jews began abandoning the confinement of the *mallâh* for villas and apartments in the new town, leaving the poorer Jews behind. As the *mallâh* declined as a center of Jewish life, so did the distinct corporate identity of Jews in the Muslim imagination. Atomized and to a large extent secularized, Jews were gradually absorbed into the wider city. The *mallâh* was not only abandoned to decay but became a negative space for Jews, particularly after the noxious edicts of the Vichy regime during World War II that attempted to coerce all Jews to return to what they now regarded as a purgatory. Eventually, all Jews left the *mallâh* during the massive exodus surrounding the creation of the State of Israel in 1948 and the rise of an independent Morocco in 1956.

Today the houses of the quarter have found a new life as the dwelling places of Muslims. Only a few signs of the former Jewish presence are still evident, such as the restored Ibn Danân synagogue and the whitewashed tombs of the carefully tended cemetery. What is the historic and intellectual significance of the 500-year-old architectural heritage of the *mallâh* of Fez? To draw far-reaching conclusions based on a single study is hardly possible. However, certain points emerge that may help us to understand the evolution of the Jewish quarter in Morocco and in the Muslim Mediterranean city more generally.

An adherence to past models was as important to Jews as it was to Muslims, and the continuity of building types such as the courtyard house within the quarter reflects a conservatism that prevailed in other spheres of cultural production as well. Unfortunately, we do not have the benefit of archeological studies to confirm the general impression that much of the standing architecture of the *mallâh* does not predate the beginning of the nineteenth century. Nevertheless, the existing structures conform to typologies having roots deep in the Mediterranean past. The repeated destruction of the Jewish quarter documented in the chronicles supports a scenario of continuous rebuilding on old foundations, especially in the case of the synagogues, that suffered most from the periodic devastation.[67] We must look to buildings constructed in the Protectorate period to find any significant deviation from the typologies we have described.

The *mallâh* was tied to the larger city through many dependencies, both seen and unseen. The ability of Jewish architecture to absorb influences from its surroundings through a process of creative mimesis is not particular to Fez. It exists at every time and place of Jewish habitation in the Diaspora. It is not surprising that the fabric and feeling of the *mallâh* replicate that of the *madîna*, although on a smaller scale: the impasse, the *sabât,* and the *saqîfa* are only a few examples of appropriated building forms. Nor are

EZ. – Rue du Mellah après les événements d...17 av...

The *mallâh* after the bombardment and pillaging of April 1912

the sensations when walking through the *mallâh* dissimilar from those felt when walking through the *madîna*: the echo of voices behind closed doors, the shouting of children at play in the narrow streets, the deep silences of the night. Other aspects of the urban form joined the *mallâh* and the rest of the city; for example, the underground water system of the *mallâh* was part of the canalization that fed Fâs al-Jadîd.[68]

Finally, it should be noted that, unlike the Jewish quarters of Rabat, Tetuan, and Marrakesh, planned and settled at one time, the *mallâh* of Fez grew slowly, expanding from a small central core of settlement to one that was larger and more differentiated. The irregularity of the street plan and the variety of building types found within the walls of the quarter support the notion of a slow process of organic growth. Evidence from the physical data explains why two different dates are often given for the founding of the *mallâh*: one corresponding with the founding of New Fez in 1276, and the other coinciding with the expulsion of the Jews from Old Fez in 1438. Both dates mark moments in the historical process of the *mallâh*'s expansion. It is possible to imagine a small Jewish settlement outside the walls of New Fez at the end of the thirteenth century, coinciding with the founding of New Fez and providing a home to Jews associated with the palace service. Another spurt of growth came in the fifteenth century, when the Jewish population was expelled from Old Fez *en masse*. This relocation of the entire

Café next to the *mallâh* gate, c. 1921

community, including its rabbis, established the long-term viability of the quarter. Now the *mallâh* became the spiritual as well as physical center of Jewish Fez. Yet another jump occurred sixty years later in 1492, with the arrival of the exiles from Spain who helped crystallize already existing social groupings. In other words, as in other parts of the city, the *mallâh* was an organic structure, expanding and contracting at various stages of its life cycle, usually as a result of events taking place far beyond its walls.

Moroccan Jews in the Diaspora and Israel continue to maintain a strong connection to their roots, reenacting special ceremonies tied to their place of origin, returning periodically to visit their former homes, and surrounding themselves with symbols that act as reminders of the past.[69] Outsiders often wonder how Moroccan Jews in Israel, Canada, France, or Venezuela manage to hold fast to their former identities, while appropriating new identities with an alacrity that defies explanation. Central to this attachment, at least for the generation that still retains a first-hand memory of Fez, is a nostalgic connection to place. That place, for better or worse, is most often the *mallâh*. Mystical, paradoxical, and elusive, this attachment becomes better defined if we recall the historical and architectural reality from which it is derived. The *mallâh* was a complex spatial construct that enforced separation but at the same time allowed for a convergence of mentalities that made Jewish and Muslim Moroccans into mirror images of each other.

Notes

1. Written in Hebrew and the dialect of Judeo-Arabic spoken in Fez, the entire work was translated to French, edited and chronologically rearranged by the French scholar Georges Vajda. The Diaspora Research Institute at Tel Aviv University published a Hebrew version in 1993, and recently an Arabic version was edited by Moroccan scholar of Hebrew `Abd al-`Azîz Shahbâr. Georges Vajda, "Un Recueil de textes historiques judéo-marocains," *Hesperis* 35–36 (1948–1949): 35 (1948): 311–358 and 36 (1949): 139–188; `A. Shahbâr , ed., *al-Kitâb al-tawârîkh aw tarîkh fâs* (Tetuan: Association Tetuan Asmir, 2002); Meir Benayahu, ed., *History of Fez: Misfortunes and Events of Moroccan Jewry as Recorded by Ibn Danan's Family and Descendents*; in Hebrew, *Divre Ha-Yamim shel Fas* (Tel Aviv: Diaspora Research Institute, 1993).

2. Published in several editions, perhaps the most accessible being `Alî ibn `Abd Allâh Ibn Abî Zar' al-Fâsî, *Anîs al-muṭrib bi-rawd al-qirṭâs fî akhbâr mulûk al-Maghrib wa-târîkh madînat Fâs* (Rabat: Dâr al-Manṣûr, 1972).

3. Muhammad ibn al-Tayyib al-Qâdirî, *Nashr al-mathâni li-ahl al-qarn al-hâdî ashar wa-al-thânî*, 4 vols. (Rabat: Maktabat al-Tâlib, 1977–86). A fine abridged English edition is Norman Cigar ed., *Muhammad al-Qadiri's Nashr al-mathani: The Chronicles* (Oxford: Oxford University Press, 1981).

4. Several of these sources are mentioned in Mercedes García-Arenal, "Les Bildiyyîn de Fès, un groupe de néo-musulmans d'origine juive," *Studia Islamica* LXVI (1987): 115–116.

5. Ibn 'Âbi Zar', *Anîs al-Mutrib*, 8 and 322.

6. Roger Le Tourneau, *Fès avant le Protectorat* (Rabat: Ed. La Porte, 1987), 66–67. According to the *Yahas Fas*, Maimonides came to Fez "at a very young age" and lived in a house in the Old City that was "well-known." It had thirteen windows and under each window was a bell (*cloche*). "Tourists came to visit it," and Jewish women made it a goal of pilgrimage, according to Y.D. Semach, "Une Chronique juive de Fès: Le "Yahas Fès" de Ribbi Abner Hassarfaty," *Hesperis* 19 (1934): 83. The *Yahas Fâs* (The Lineage of Fez) is an unpaged manuscript in Hebrew and Judeo-Arabic found at the Library of the Alliance Israélite Universelle (AIU) in Paris, MS #84. The *Yahas* was written in 1879 in response to a series of questions sent to the rabbis of Fez by the directorship of the AIU regarding the status of their community. My thanks to Jean-Claude Kuperminc, Conservator of the AIU archives, who gave me permission to photocopy this document.

7. Leo Africanus, *The History and Description of Africa*, 3 vols. (New York: Burt Franklin, 1967), 2:477.

8. Semach, "Chronique juive de Fès," 79–80.

9. David Corcos, "Les juifs du Maroc et leurs Mellahs," in Abraham Elmaleh and Joachim Wilhelm Hirschberg, *Zekhor le-Avraham: kovets ma amarim le-zekher Avraham Almalia: hamesh shanim li-fetirato* (Jerusalem: Va`ad` adat ha-Ma`aravim, 1972). The disparity between 1437 and 1438 is perhaps due

to the fact that the Hebrew year 5198 covers portions of both years in the Gregorian calendar. Without knowing the specific day and month in the Hebrew year, it is impossible to compute its exact equivalent.

10. On Jewish traders in the Mediterranean in the medieval period, see S.D. Goitein, *A Mediterranean Society: The Jewish Communities of the Arab World as Portrayed in the Documents of the Cairo Geniza*, 5 vols. (Berkeley: University of California Press, 1967–1988).

11. According to Le Tourneau, quoting the *Rawd al-Qirtâs*. The *funduq al-yahûd* was located on the left bank of the Wad Fâs, just north of the quarter of al-`Aliya, the nuclear town founded by Idrîs II. The Jews inhabiting this quarter were the *toshavim*, the autochthonous Jews of Morocco, as opposed to the *megorashim*, or refugees from Spain. Even in the very early years of the settlement of Fez, the Jews contributed handsomely to the royal treasury in the amount of 30,000 dinars of gold in taxes each year. *Fès*, 44.

12. Leo Africanus, *History*, 2: 475 – 478.

13. H.Z. Hirschberg, *A History of the Jews in North Africa*, 2 vols. (Leiden: E.J. Brill, 1974), 1: 346–347.

14. Semach, "Chronique juive de Fès," 83. See note 6.

15. Simon Levy. "Fès et ses synagogues: Une restauration pour le souvenir et l'avenir," unpublished text. Levy cites 'Abd al-Wahîd al-Marrâkûshî, *Mu'jib fi talkhis akhbar al-Maghrib* (The Admirable in the Summary of Information about Maghrib) (Casablanca: 1978), 434–435 as the source of the quote. See also Jacqueline Hadziiossif, "Les conversions des juifs à l'islam et au christianisme en Méditerranée XIe-XVe siècles," in *Mutations d'identités en Méditerranée: Moyen Age et époque contemporaine*, eds. Christiane Veauvy, Eliane Dupuy and Henri Bresc (Saint-Denis: Bouchène, 2000), 159–173.

16. Le Tourneau, *Fès*, 66.

17. Among the major cities of Morocco, the *mallâh* of Marrakesh was built in the sixteenth century under the Sa'di dynasty; the *mallâh* of Meknes was built in the seventeenth century under the Alawi sultan Isma'il; and the *mallâh*s of Rabat, Salé, and Tetuan were built early in the nineteenth century.

18. Levy, "Hara et *Mallâh*: Les Mots, l'Histoire et l'Institution," in *Histoire et Linguistique*, ed. Abdelahad Sebti (Rabat: Université Mohammed V, 1992, 46; on factional infighting within Fâsî society at the time, see Mercedes García-Arenal, "The Revolution of Fâs in 869/1465 and the Death of Sultan 'Abd al-Haqq al-Marini," *Bulletin of the School of Oriental and African Studies*, 41, part 1 (1978): 43–66, and especially 44–45.

19. Georges Salmon, "Le culte de Muley Idrîs et la Mosquée des Chorfa à Fès," *Archives marocaines* III (1905), 415. Nahum Slousch(z) avoids altogether mentioning the founding of the Fez *mallâh* in "Études sur l'Histoire des Juifs au Maroc," *Archives marocaines* VI (1906).

20. Quoted in Louis Brunot and Elie Malka, *Textes judéo-arabes de Fès: Textes, transcription, traduction annotée* (Rabat: Ecole du Livre, 1939), 197.

21. Mercedes García-Arenal, "Jewish Converts to Islam in the Muslim West," in *Dhimmis and Others: Jews and Christians and the World of Classical Islam,* eds. Uri Rubin and David Wasserstein (Winona Lake, Indiana: Eisenbrauns, 1997), 243.

22. Roger Le Tourneau, "Notes sur les lettres latines de Nicolas Clénard relatant son séjour dans le royaume de Fès (1540–41)," *Hespéris* 19 (1934): 51–53; see also Jane Gerber, *Jewish Society in Fez 1450–1700: Studies in Communal and Economic Life* (Leiden: 1980), 47–48.

23. On the legacy of Sephardic culture in the Middle East, see the collection edited by Harvey Goldberg, *Sephardi and Middle Eastern Jewries: History and Culture in the Modern Era* (Bloomington: Indiana University Press, 1996).

24. *Descripción general de África* (Malaga, 1599), quoted in Mercedes García-Arenal and Gerard Wiegers, *Entre el Islam y Occidente: Vida de Samuel Pallache, judío de Fez,* (Madrid: Sigloveintiuno de españa editores, 1999), 40–41.

25. See Simón Levy, "Arabófonos e hispanófonos (bildiyin y 'azmiyin) en la judería de Fez, dos siglos después de la expulsión," in *El siglo XVII Hispanomarroqui,* ed. Mohammed Salhi (Rabat, 1997), 333–351.

26. Norman Cigar, "Société et vie politique à Fès sous les premiers 'Alaouites (c. 1660/1830)," *Hespéris-Tamuda* 18 (1978–1979): 99.

27. Vajda, "Recueil," 36 (1949): 161–162.

28. Ibid., 36 (1949): 170 –181.

29. Ibid., 35 (1948): 333, 337–338, 344; 36 (1949):144, 146–147.

30. Shlomo Deshen, *The Mellah Society: Jewish Community Life in Sherifian Morocco* (Chicago: University of Chicago Press, 1989), 71–74.

31. In addition to the *jizya*, or poll tax, Jews were subject to other special taxes imposed when the sultan was in need of ready cash. The coming to power of a new sultan was also time for a payment of the *hadîya*, or a "gift," handed over by various social groups, including the Jews. See Vajda, "Recueil" 35 (1948): 318, 321, 331. Also Rahma Bourqia, "Don et théatralité: Réflexion sur le rituel du don *(hadîya)* offert au sultan au xixe siècle," *Hespéris-Tamuda* 31 (1993): 61–75.

32. Finding lodgings in the *madîna* was "nearly impossible" for foreigners in the nineteenth century, so most stayed in the *mallâh* in the houses of the wealthy (Le Tourneau, *Fès*, 173). Contemporary travel accounts give colorful first-hand glimpses into *mallâh* life. Charles de Foucauld, who traveled in Jewish disguise, was lodged in the house of Samuel Ben Simhoun on Darb al-Fûqî in 1883, where he received "le meilleur accueil." *Reconnaissance au Maroc: Journal de route* (Paris: Société d'editions, 1939), 78.

33. Jean-Louis Miège, *Le Maroc et L'Europe (1830–1894),* 4 vols. (Rabat: Éditions La Porte, 1989), 2: 560–573.

The *Yahas Fâs* (1879) says "the definition of someone who is rich in our town is someone who has ten to twenty thousand *duros* [equivalent to two to four thousand U.S. dollars in 1900] and engages in commerce overseas. They are only ten in number. They have to go every day to the part of the city where the gentiles live, which takes at least half an hour, and they must go barelegged and barefoot in days of extreme heat and cold. Nevertheless, they are rich, and the majority of them are moneylenders."

34. These observations were made in the summer of 1998. At that time, many of the houses of the nineteenth-century Jewish merchants were still standing, although in various states of conservation. With the permission of the municipal authorities, the inhabitants allowed researchers to enter and survey their interiors.

35. Eugène Aubin, *Morocco of Today* (London: J.M. Dent, 1906), 299.

36. This feast commences on the fifteenth of the Hebrew month of Tishri, corresponding with late September.

37. Brunot and Malka, *Textes*, 282–283 and 284, note 1.

38. Vajda, "Recueil" 36 (1949): 150, 157.

39. This space could also enclose a small private bath. See Ali Amahan and Catherine Cambazard-Amahan, *Arrêts sur site: Le patrimoine culturel marocain* (Casablanca: Le Fennec, 1999), 106.

40. The most important study of domestic architecture in Fez is Jacques Revault et al., *Palais et demeures de Fès*, 3 vols. (Paris:CNRS, 1985–1992). See also Amahan and Cambazard-Amahan, *Arrêts*, 99–130.

41. *Yahas Fâs*, n.p. Brunot and Malka assert there were no Jewish builders in the Fez *mallâh* (without reference to date) but there were "a few Jewish masons" who could make simple repairs. *Textes*, 205, note 25.

42. Vajda, "Recueil" 36 (1949), 170.

43. Aubin, *Morocco*, 288.

44. Ibid., 299.

45. In response to the question of how many Jews lived in Fez in 1879, the author of the *Yahas Fâs* explains that the *mallâh* has 235 "courtyards" (*hatzerim*), or apartment buildings each having rooms (*bayts*) inhabited by individual households. The total number of Jewish households, according to the *Yahas*, was 1461, an average of 6.2 households per building. If we multiply the number of households by 6 (members), we reach a total Jewish population of 8,766, an average of 37.3 people per building, a very high density indeed. There is no comparable data for the *madîna* at that time, although de Foucauld, writing in 1883, says that the Muslim population was 70,000, with 3,000 Jews (*Reconnaissance*, 80). For purposes of comparison, officials at the ADER, or Agency for the Development of Fez, record the population of the "old *mallâh*" in 1998 (not including the adjacent quarter of Nawâwil, which did not exist in the late nineteenth century) as 5,485, consisting of 1,219 households distributed among 322 buildings, or an average of 3.7 households per building, with an average density of 17 people per building.

46. M. Nahon, "Les Israélites du Maroc," *Revue des études ethnographiques et sociologiques* (1909), 258–279. For more on epidemics, see Vajda, "Recueil," 35 (1948): 319, 326; 36 (1949): 161–62, 188.

47. Charles René-Leclerc, *Le Maroc septentrional: souvenirs et impressions (été 1904)* (Algiers: Imp. Algérienne, 1905), 149.

48. The *burj* is one of the few structures in the *mallâh* having pretensions to monumentality. More than a gate, it is also a shrine and burial place of martyrs who died in an attack on the *mallâh* in 1465. Gravestones marking the burial places were visible in the walls of the rooms inside the bastion, according to Brunot and Malka, *Textes*, 202, note 8.

49. Leonor Fernandes, "Habitat et prescriptions légales," *in L'Habitat traditionnel dans les pays musulmans autour de la Mediterranee: Rencontre d'Aix-en-Provence (6–8 juin 1984)*, 3 vols. (Cairo, 1984): II, 419-426. General principles influencing Islamic urban form are the following: (1) it is forbidden to invade the privacy of others or to look into their homes, which affects the height of buildings and the location of entrances; (2) neighbors and their relatives have the right to buy adjacent property; (3) vertical extension is permitted, even if it blocks light and air, so long as it does not invade privacy; and (4) the *fina'*, or frontage, belongs to the house but does not entail the right to build.

50. Brunot and Malka, *Textes*, 203. The traditional Sabbath midday meal included the *sakhîna*, a hearty dish similar to a *cassoulet*. It baked in the community oven all Friday night and was conveyed to the Jewish household Saturday at midday.

51. Some of the synagogues of Fez are described in Joel Zack, *The Synagogues of Morocco: An Architectural and Preservation Survey*, 2nd ed. (New York: World Monuments Fund, 1995).

52. See Vajda, "Recueil," 36 (1949), 144.

53. *Yahas Fâs*, n.p.

54. On the production of *sqalli*, see two articles by Roger Le Tourneau and M. Vicaire: "La Fabrication du fil d'or à Fès," *Hespéris* 2, 1–2 (1937): 67–88 and "L'Industrie du fil d'or au *mellah* de Fès," *Bulletin économique et social du Maroc* 3, 13 (1936): 185–190. They describe how the 700 workers engaged in this craft in 1930 were suddenly thrown out of work by the introduction of machinery imported from France. The *sqalli* workers organized public prayers, made appeals at the tombs of venerated saints, and protested to the governor (*pasha*), to no avail. Le Tourneau and Vicaire, "L'industrie," 188.

55. On the commerce of the *mallâh*, see Le Tourneau, *Fès*, 350–352.

56. Le Tourneau, *Fès*, 390, 423. For a stimulating discussion of the Jews of Sefrou and their social and commercial relations with Muslims, see Lawrence Rosen, *Bargaining for Reality: The Construction of Social Relations in a Muslim Community* (Chicago: University of Chicago Press, 1984), 148–164.

57. The impasse is not a feature produced by Islamic culture per se, but is the logical conclusion of a process of growth when the urban fabric is made up of courtyard houses. We see this feature in Palermo, Italy (where it may be an Arab import), as well as in the ancient Sumerian city of Ur.

58. The synagogue of Shlomo Ibn Danan, also known as the Synagogue Boussidan, was constructed at the end of the seventeenth century, according to Simon Levy, "La synagogue Danan restaurée" (Casablanca: Fondation du Patrimoine Culturel Judéo-marocain, n.d.). It served as the synagogue of the Danan family of rabbis from 1812 until its closure in the 1960s. Members of this family were the authors of the manuscript *Dibre ha-Yamim*. The synagogue was named after Rabbi Shlomo Danan (1848–1928), who officiated there at the beginning of the twentieth century. The building is attached to the ancient wall of the *mallâh* on its east side. Another interesting aspect of its construction discovered during the recent restoration was a sealed door leading to a subterranean ritual bath (*mikveh*).

59. Le Tourneau, *Fès*, 576.

60. Vajda, "Recueil," 36 (1949), 330.

61. The Slat al-Fâsiyyîn, or synagogue of the Fâsîs, is the synagogue of the *toshavim*, the original inhabitants of the *mallâh*. The ritual followed in this synagogue until its closing in 1970 included prayers that were not part of the regular Sephardic liturgy, suggesting that its founding predated the arrival of the Spanish exiles in 1492. Today it serves as a boxing club for the *mallâh* youth.

62. Charles René-Leclerc, "Le commerce et l'industrie à Fès," *Renseignements coloniaux* (1905), 319. The *qaysarîya* was the principal *sûq* of the Fez *madîna* adjacent to the Qarawîyin mosque.

63. The availability of such products enhanced Muslim perceptions of the Jewish quarter as a place of transgression, and the idea of the *mallâh* as liminal space was deeply rooted in the Muslim imaginary. Jewish sources hint at prostitution in the *mallâh*, as well as the presence of "tavernas" that were frequented by Muslims. (Vajda, "Recueil," 35 (1948), 344, 350; Le Tourneau, *Fès*, 579). Another popular vice was gambling, which took place in the Jewish cemetery (Le Tourneau, *Fès*, 580).

64. Le Tourneau, *Fès*, 101; according to him, here Jewish moneylenders plied their trade in shops that fronted on a Muslim market where oil, soap and candles were sold. But the original meaning of the term is derived from the Arabic root meaning the minting of coins, a specifically Jewish trade in the sixteenth century, according to Leo Africanus, *History*, 2, 476–77.

65. Nahon, "Les Israélites," 268.

66. For an account of the event from a woman's perspective, see Brunot and Malka, *Textes*, 206–209. Also Jacques Hubert, *Les journees sanglantes de Fez, 17–18–19 avril 1912: les massacres, recits militaires, responsabilities* (Paris: Librairie Chapelot, 1913), 67–73.

67. The author of the "Dibre ha-Yamim" tells us the Jews returned to the *mallâh* after the exile of 1792 to find their quarter totally devastated. Pillagers had not only carried off the contents of the houses but also removed "the doors, the rafters, the coffers, in short, anything that could be called wood." Vajda, "Recueil," 36 (1949): 180.

68. The *mallâh*'s water supply, according to Le Tourneau, came from a source first introduced to Fâs al-Jadîd in the Marinid period called `Ayn Bû Amîr. (*Fès*, 267, 270). Many of the *mallâh* houses also had their own wells (Ibid., 270).

69. On the phenomenon of return, see André Levy, "To Morocco and Back: Tourism and Pilgrimage among Moroccan-Born Israelis" in *Grasping Land: Space and Place in Contemporary Israeli Discourse and Experience*, ed. E. Ben-Ari and Y. Bilu (Albany, NY: State University of New York Press, 1997), 25–46.

EMILY R. GOTTREICH

4

THE *MALLĀH* OF MARRAKESH: EPICENTER OF A DESERT ECONOMY

THE CITY AS *SÛQ*

The southern Moroccan capital of Marrakesh was, and to some extent still is, one huge marketplace. As nineteenth-century French scholar Paul Odinot remarked, "[Marrakesh] is not an intellectual city, it is not a city that one loves; it is a city where one sells, where one lives, to which one goes and from which one returns."[1] Certainly, this characterization gives short shrift to the other forms of creativity for which Marrakesh is known, such as its monumental architecture and its centrality to the reinvigoration of Moroccan Sufism. Yet it is nonetheless undeniable that the city's dynamism is derived primarily from its historical role as one of North Africa's great trade emporiums. Though it was originally built as a military encampment, Marrakesh soon grew to extraordinary prosperity as a result of commerce, not conquest. With direct access to all the major trade routes of the Maghrib, soon after its founding it became the major redistribution center for the entire region, a position its inhabitants exploited equally well whether in the pre-modern trans-Saharan caravan trade or in a colonial mercantile economy.

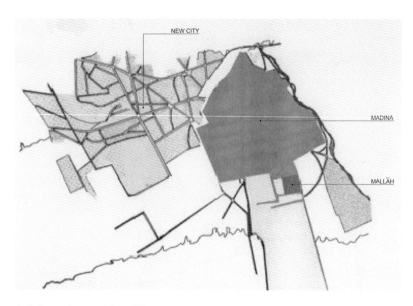

Map of Marrakesh showing location of the *mallāh*

As the "crossroads of all the Moroccan world,"[2] Marrakesh and its markets over-flowed with an abundance of goods. From south of the Sahara came tropical fruits, ostrich feathers, animal hides, and slaves; human goods were auctioned off three times weekly in the place that also served as the market for wool.[3] Regional products such as cereals, goatskins, and wax were regularly brought into the city from the Atlas Mountains and pre-Saharan oases beyond. Products not consumed locally were sent north to Fez or to coastal towns like Essaouira and Tangier for export to more distant lands. Marrakesh was not simply an entrepôt, for some of Morocco's most sought-after products were manufactured in the city. Refined sugar, embroidered slippers (*bâbûj*), and olive oil were just a few of the local specialties.

Sustaining all of this economic activity, and sustained by it, was a populace of tremendous vitality. On the eve of the French Protectorate in 1912, nearly 90 percent of all Moroccans lived in rural areas, with the vast majority concentrated in the south, the *sud-marocain* of colonial parlance.[4] As the undisputed capital of this vast area, Marrakesh was a natural magnet for the rural population. The flow of people into Marrakesh increased dramatically in the second half of the nineteenth century, when natural and human forces combined to stimulate a major demographic shift toward the cities. A seemingly endless cycle of tribal infighting, epidemics, and droughts in the region around Marrakesh during this period induced large numbers of rural inhab-itants to flee their homes for the relative security of the capital. During the famine of 1878-1879, for example, more than 100 refugees arrived in Marrakesh each day.[5] At the same time, the impact of European economic and political encroachment was begin-ning to wreak havoc on the countryside. Many of the refugees arriving in Marrakesh must also be considered economic migrants struggling to adapt to the disruption of longstanding patterns of exchange, and to find new opportunities available in the urban centers. Ahmad b. Khâlid an-Nâsirî, Morocco's pre-eminent historian of the period, observed:

> We must note that the situation of the present generation is entirely different from that of the previous generation. Everywhere the habits of the people have been turned upside down. The customs and practices of merchants and crafts-people have been altered in all ways, including the way they do business, earn and handle money, price goods and manage other types of expenses. The primary cause of this state of affairs is the meddling of the French and other foreigners with the population. Their habits collide violently with ours, and in the clash their ways defeat and absorb ours.[6]

After 1830, Marrakesh increased its population size by an average of 50 percent every thirty years. This figure did not include a large floating population consisting of itiner-ant merchants, pilgrims, and members of the sultan's seasonal entourage that had no fixed residence in the city. There were periods in the nineteenth century when the float-ing population of Marrakesh was in fact equal to the permanent one. Thanks in large part to this rural influx, Marrakesh was one of Morocco's only traditional inland centers actually to expand rather than contract during the pre- and early Protectorate period.[7]

URBAN-RURAL CONNECTIONS

Marrakesh was home to the country's largest Jewish community, comprising up to one-third of the city's total population at certain times.[8] Rural communities throughout the vast south of Morocco included some of the oldest Jewish settlements in the region, dating from the destruction of the First Temple of Jerusalem in the sixth century BCE, many centuries before the introduction of Islam into North Africa. Small towns and vil-lages such as Demnat, Qal'a, Intifa, Aït Adrar, Aghmat, Asni, Zagora, and Taroudant con-tained dozens, if not hundreds in some cases, of Jewish families. In the late nineteenth century, these outlying communities were officially linked to Marrakesh Jewry through their mutual submission to the pasha of the *qasba* (citadel) of Marrakesh.[9] Unofficially, they looked to the Jews of the city to supply them with food and shelter in times of trouble, advanced educational opportunities, and a large pool of potential spouses.[10] But above all else, they looked to the capital to do business, the great Moroccan game of *shirâ' wa- bay`a* (buying and selling). An 1888 article in the *Times of Morocco* noted: "Being close to the Atlas, very many Soosis, and mountaineers, both Berbers and Jews are to be met in the streets [of Marrakesh], in their strangely marked clothes."[11] Jews from Intifa, Asni, and Aït Adrar were especially frequent visitors to Marrakesh, where they bought tobacco, textiles, and coffee, all items not easily found in the small *sûqs* of the interior.

The relationship between urban and rural Jews in the south was not one-sided, however, and Jewish merchants from Marrakesh counted on these satellite communi-

View of the *mallâh* from the north in 2007

ties for practical support during their forays into the countryside, where they sold the products of the city and bought local goods to resell in Marrakesh. Some of these traders were members of the *tujjâr as-sultân,* the elite corps of official merchants of the Moroccan sultan. The *tujjâr* were accorded many advantages to facilitate their activities. They were granted monopolies over certain commodities, exempted from customs duties, and extended credit by the royal treasury in order to conduct trade. In return, the Moroccan government relied heavily on them to verify the weights and measures for the royal treasury, to resolve complicated financial matters, and to represent the *makhzan* (government) in dealings with the Christian powers.

Influential as the *tujjâr* were, the vast majority of merchants of Marrakesh were simple itinerant traders who roamed the countryside for months at a time buying and selling their wares. The influence of Jewish traders among this group was considerable. In the long periods of rural unrest around the turn of the last century, Jews were often the only outsiders allowed to travel through remote areas.[12] Jews lacked any fixed tribal allegiances and were considered too politically inconsequential to foment insurrection. They would simply buy temporary protection from the local *qâ`ids* (tribal chiefs) whose territories they traversed. As a result of their relative mobility, it was Jewish traders from Marrakesh who were largely responsible for introducing goods of foreign origin, such as tea, into remote areas of the south.[13]

Within the city, Jews were active in the full range of commercial exchanges with the exception of the slave trade, from which they were officially banned.[14] Local Jewish merchants dealt mainly in sulfur, almonds, apricot kernels, cotton, barley, and wax. Not all Jews were merchants, however; some contributed to the economy as artisans, craftsmen, and service providers of all types. Jewish women were an important part of the local labor force, working outside the home as water-carriers or seamstresses.

Finally, as the only indigenous religious minority, Jews dominated those occupations that were shunned by Muslims or forbidden by Islamic law, such as the manufacture and sale of alcohol, lending money at interest, and metalwork. Indeed, the Jews of Marrakesh were known to be master craftsmen in this area, with the silver- and gold-smiths considered the "aristocracy" among them. This reputation was derived not only from the steady income and strong tradition of father-to-son succession that distinguished the profession, but also from the amazingly varied repertoire of its practitioners. Precious stones, coral, pearls, and Italian sequins were commonly worked into their creations, which included jewelry, talismans, stirrups, tobacco boxes, and cases for the Koran. The last item in particular tells us that the Jewish jewelers of Marrakesh had a large Muslim clientele that included important *shaykh*s and *qâ`id*-s. To better accommodate this Muslim clientele, in the mid-1890s the jewelers' workshops were moved out of the quarter and relocated to a separate *sûq* for metalworkers in a quadrant east of the palace. The metalworkers' *sûq* continues to occupy this same area today.[15]

A BEEHIVE OF ACTIVITY

Although the economic reach of the Jews of Marrakesh, enhanced by family networks, mobility, and language skills, was widespread over the region, its center was clearly defined: the *mallâh*.[16] For nearly four centuries, all the Jews of Marrakesh were required to live within its walls, and no Muslim was allowed to spend even a single night there.[17] This arrangement was consistent with the clear hierarchy of space that in theory prevailed in Marrakesh: the *qasba* for the ruling class, the *madîna* for the Muslim masses, and the *mallâh* for the Jews. Yet the walls that separated these three entities were in reality quite porous. A steady daily traffic of Muslims coming into the *mallâh* and Jews leaving for other parts of the city was an indicator of the extensive relations that developed between the two communities. Their exchanges, primarily economic but having important social and even religious components, had a lasting impact on the identities of both populations, mutually reinforcing what the Moroccan urbanist Mohammed Naciri has called "*madanîya*," the sense of being both "in" and "of" a city.[18] The signatures of some of the city's more prominent Jewish merchants, who made it a point to append the suffix *al-Marrâkushî* ["from Marrakesh"] to their names, bear witness to this particular sentiment.[19]

Specialties of the region and manufactured goods imported by Jewish merchants were made available for purchase in the *mallâh* well in advance of their appearance in other parts of the city. Muslims were naturally attracted to these goods, and Muslims were noticeably present alongside Jewish shoppers on Friday mornings when the *mallâh*'s main *sûq* was stocked for the Jewish Sabbath. Because kosher meat is generally acceptable for consumption under Islamic law, Muslims came to the *mallâh* to patronize the Jewish butchers, whose prices were often lower than those of the *madîna*.[20]

Alcohol could also be purchased in the *mallâh*, though it was forbidden elsewhere in the city. Especially popular among Muslim and Jewish clients alike was *mahiya*, a strong brandy-like concoction composed of figs, dates, and grapes, traditionally made

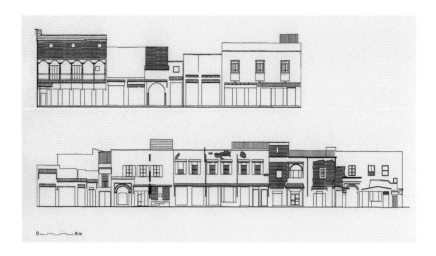

Survey of the main commercial street. Shops are below, living space above.

by Moroccan Jews. *Mahiya* was sold by the glass in small bars on the *mallâh*'s periphery along the *rue du Cimitière* leading to the Jewish cemetery. During the Protectorate era, many of these bars migrated to an area bordering the Berrima quarter where the French *Administration des domaines* had granted a building to the French Jewish educational organization, the *Alliance Israélite Universelle* [A.I.U.] for use as a school. The A.I.U. administrators were constantly complaining about the "*gens mal famés*" who gathered on the terrace at night, drunk on alcohol purchased from the bars in the street below.[21]

Cotton was another specialty item in the *mallâh*, where it was initially auctioned off before being resold in the *madîna* at a higher price. Harry Maclean, a British consul in Marrakesh early in the Protectorate period, describes this trade:

> I find that cotton goods are cheaper here than in Gibraltar. I could not understand why until the other day a Jew told me that the merchants on the coast send cotton goods to the Jews in Marrakesh, and that the merchants have very little or no money and do all their business by bills. When they get hard pressed for funds,

the merchants send word to their agents that they must have so many dollars by such time. The Jews then sell the cotton goods by auction in the Jews' town taking care to buy the goods among themselves and then resell it to the Moores.[22]

Among the principal *sûq*s of the *mallâh* was the *al-'attârîn*, or spice market. It was (and still is) located on one of the main north-south thoroughfares of the *mallâh* leading to the main well, on a street anchored by synagogues at both ends. Most of the buildings that line this street are two-storied, the street level housing the shops, the upper levels reserved for living space.

As importers and exporters, producers and consumers, buyers and sellers par excellence, the Jews of the *mallâh* formed the economic backbone of Marrakesh. Indeed, it was unlikely that the city could have functioned properly without their participation. Insofar as Marrakesh was the capital of the south, the *mallâh* was clearly the "*capital juive*," a role it had assumed from the moment of its founding in the mid-sixteenth century.[23]

ORIGINS AND EARLY DEVELOPMENT

Most great Islamic cities were built on the ruins of earlier settlements: Roman, Punic, or Berber in North Africa, Byzantine and Persian in the East.[24] By contrast, the "Red City" of Marrakesh seemingly arose out of dust and scorching air, in the middle of nowhere, in the hot plains of the Hawz. At its foundation lay not ruins but an idea—eventually a doctrine—having to do with the sovereignty of an emerging Berber Islam.[25] This idea was first articulated in spatial terms by the Almoravids (reigned 1056-1147) who founded Marrakesh in 1070; it was then developed further by the Almohads (reigned 1130-1269).[26] Prior to the founding of Marrakesh, a sizable Jewish settlement already existed in the nearby village of Aghmat Aylan, later to emerge as the capital of the Rahamna tribe, Arabic-speaking Muslim nomads originally from north of the Senegal River who established themselves in the plains around Marrakesh in the sixteenth century. They entered Morocco as recruits to fight in the *jihâd* against the Portuguese and Spanish Christians harassing the Moroccan Atlantic coast, but never fully submitted to the *makhzan*'s rule.[27] The first Jewish inhabitants of Marrakesh probably came from Aghmat and other villages in the region, though it is unclear when they were allowed to settle in the city permanently, or whether they were banished or even destroyed as a community by the Almohads, who waged a campaign of oppression against them.[28]

By the Sa'dian era (1523-1660), Jews were well-established residents of Marrakesh. Their homes numbered in the thousands and were concentrated in two neighborhoods: the Muwassin quarter, where most of them lived, and an area known at the time as Aswâl.[29] Individual Jewish families also lived scattered among the Muslim population elsewhere in the *madîna*. But the future of these neighborhoods became unclear as the Jews of Marrakesh were drawn into the power politics swirling around the question of Sa'dian legitimacy, relentlessly challenged by the powerful `*ulamâ*' of Fez. Although Fez was finally conquered by the Sa'dians in 1554, the resulting loss of life and property left a sense of bitterness and rivalry between the two cities that endured over time. Rebuffed from the northern capital, the Sa'dians turned their backs on Fez and headed south to build an even more glorious capital for themselves in Marrakesh. Indeed, a sixteenth-century visitor found Marrakesh to be more worthy of the title "city" than his hometown of Paris.[30]

One of the first urban institutions created by the new rulers was the *mallâh*. In scholarship on Moroccan Jewish history, explanations for the creation of a *mallâh* are either overly reliant on apocryphal accounts or offer a single cause, when the question of the origins of Morocco's Jewish quarters usually has multiple and overlapping answers, depending on place, time, and historical circumstances. The immediate impetus for building a new Jewish quarter in the southern capital was religious; namely, the construction of a major mosque complex for the Muwassin quarter.[31] Jews living in the Muwassin neighborhood had to be relocated to accommodate the new mosque, for it was considered inappropriate for non-Muslims to be the first to hear the call to prayer. Originally known as the *jâmi` al-shurafâ'* [the mosque of the *sharîf*s, or descendents of the Prophet], the Muwassin mosque was completed in 1562, and included a *madrasa* and a monumental fountain. The forcible transfer of the Jews of Muwassin quarter and the rest of the city's Jews, who lived in other neighborhoods as well, to the new Jewish quarter occurred sometime around 1557.

However, religious concerns were not necessarily separate from political considerations. Appeasing the *`ulamâ'* by segregating the Jews provided the Sa'dians with a means to solve other problems, such as absorbing the restive post–1492 Jewish and Muslim *expulsados* arrived from Spain, answering challenges to their religious legitimacy, and reinforcing their right to rule by asserting their dominance over minority populations. The transfer also freed up space in a central part of the *madîna*, making it available for redistribution to allies and supporters of the *makhzan*.[32]

The area chosen for the new Jewish quarter lay in the southeastern quadrant of the city, just east of the *qasba*. Considered remote by some observers, this area nonetheless held the distinct advantage of being close to both the seat of royal authority and the main north-south trade route to Fez.[33] Because the area had previously served as the royal stables, all infrastructure for human habitation such as houses, fountains, and communal ovens, not to mention structures to maintain religious and ritual life such as synagogues, ritual baths, and schools, had to be built. The choice of this site highlights an important similarity with the Fez *mallâh*: in both cities the *mallâh* was built adjacent to the royal compound. In Fez the *mallâh* was built several miles away from the *madîna* next to a newly constructed royal city, Fâs al-Jadîd, while in Marrakesh the *mallâh* was built within the existing city walls, contiguous with Muslim residential space. The single entry gate to the Marrakesh *mallâh* faced the *qasba*. To reach the *madîna*, one had first to pass through the *qasba*. As the *madîna* expanded and new neighborhoods such as Riyâdh al-Zaytûn were incorporated into the urban plan, Jewish and Muslim residential space drew even closer together, which in turn facilitated greater integration of each settlement into the daily life of the other.

The *mallâh*'s dimensions were roughly rectangular, measuring 700 meters by 250 meters, with a surface area of eighteen hectares, more than three times larger than the Fez *mallâh*. Eight additional hectares were added later for a cemetery; this space was kept as a garden until 1594, because Jews continued to use the old cemetery in the *madîna* for several decades after the *mallâh* was created. The most striking topographic feature of the *mallâh* was its grid pattern, with four distinct quadrants. The intention behind the use of this form, unusual in the North African city, may have something to do with the fact that the *mallâh* was planned and built *de novo*, on previously unoccupied ground. We see the grid in other *mallâh*s of Morocco, such as of Tetuan and Salé, also built on empty terrain but at a much later date. The advantages of the grid for both defense and surveillance are well known. Judging from the location of the *mallâh*'s main well at the junction of the four quadrants, the system of water delivery may have also determined this plan. Murdukhai ben Attar, the *mallâh*'s first *shaykh al-yahûd* (lit. *shaykh* of the Jews, the Jewish community's representative to the Muslim authority) was charged with the task of building the *mallâh* and allotted the funds to create this first example of Jewish urban planning in Morocco. The result was an urban form totally unlike that of any other part of the city.[34]

The *mallâh* was surrounded by walls. The eastern wall of the *qasba* marked the *mallâh*'s western limit. Sixteenth-century sources indicate the existence of a southern wall extending from the southeast corner of the *qasba* to the northern limit of the Jinân al-`Afiya, the royal gardens located near the Jewish cemetery. Only part of the eastern wall built by the Sa'dians is visible today; originally, this wall met the northern rampart of the *mallâh*. The most likely explanation for the disappearance of such a large segment of the wall is severe flooding that struck the *mallâh* during the late sixteenth cen-

Plan of the *mallâh* of Marrakesh

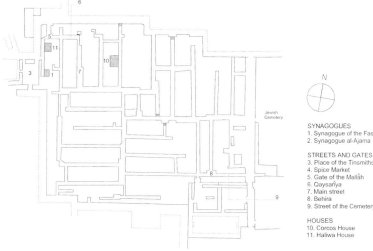

Jewish
Cemetery

N

SYNAGOGUES
1. Synagogue of the Fasiyyin
2. Synagogue al-Ajama

STREETS AND GATES
3. Place of the Tinsmiths
4. Spice Market
5. Gate of the Mallâh
6. Qaysariya
7. Main street
8. Behira
9. Street of the Cemetery

HOUSES
10. Corcos House
11. Haliwa House

tury. The northern wall of the *mallâh*, of Almoravid construction, is likewise only partially visible. In addition to the walls, the main gate and the cemetery deserve further notice, given their durability and monumentality.[35]

THE GATE OF THE *MALLÂH*

The chief monument of the Sa'dian *mallâh* is the main gate, known as *bâb al-mallâh*, located at the northwestern corner, and leading directly into what is now known as the *qaysârîya al-qadîma*, or the main market of the *mallâh*. For most of the *mallâh*'s history, it was the only gate in or out of the Jewish quarter. The gate stands approximately twelve feet high at its apex, and is closed from the inside by two massive wooden doors. It is treated as sanctified space in Jewish memory. Its *baraka* (divine beneficence) stems from the belief that a heroic deed was performed there by Murdukhai ben Attar, the first *shaykh al-yahûd* of the *mallâh*.[36] According to local lore, a group of tribesmen from the surrounding countryside laid siege to the city. In a pattern that was often repeated, the Jewish quarter was a special target of the siege, as the invaders believed that great riches would be found there.[37] It so happened that Ben Attar was inside the *mallâh*'s gate when the tribesmen approached. Hearing the tumult, he fervently prayed for divine intervention, made manifest when the stick he was holding burst into flames. The fire created a barrier that blocked entry to the *mallâh*, thus saving its inhabitants. Upon his death, Ben Attar was revered by the Jews as a saint. Meanwhile, his *baraka* was transmitted to the *mallâh*'s gate through a relic buried in it, perhaps his *talîth* (prayer shawl), a piece of parchment with a prayer written on it, or the stick that self-ignited to save the *mallâh*. Jews kissed the gate each time they passed through in recognition of its sanctity.[38]

THE JEWISH CEMETERY

A similar story of meeting between the mundane and the sacred can be found in connection to the Jewish cemetery, a site also dating from the Sa'dian period. Known in the contemporary period as al-Miyâra, the Jewish cemetery is located in the eastern corner of the *mallâh*, within the walls and next to a Muslim cemetery. The cemetery exists in several layers, with the oldest graves buried deep below the surface. Women and men are buried in the same areas, though a special section for children is located in one corner. The children's section may have been created as the result of a smallpox epidemic in the late 1880s, in which 1,600 Jews, many of them children, were reported to have lost their lives.[39]

The religious significance of the cemetery derives from the fact that several saints are buried there. Known collectively as *saddiqim*, the saints venerated by the Jews of Marrakesh achieved their status by dint of heroic acts that involved intervention with the divine to save the community. Moreover, the tombs of the *saddiqim* were reputed for their healing powers. Indeed, so many sick people visited the Jewish cemetery of Marrakesh that a teacher at the A.I.U. school cautioned visitors against touching the

A portion of the Jewish cemetery

commemorative stones placed upon the saints' tombs, warning that those who did were "sure to catch a disease."[40]

The cross-veneration of saints, an important phenomenon in Jewish-Muslim relations in Morocco, found its fullest expression in Marrakesh. However, there is considerable debate about the "true" identity of such saints, whether they were Muslims or Jews, a reminder of how deeply interwoven were Jewish and Muslim lives.[41] The phenomenon of saint veneration and its position within Moroccan Muslim and Jewish religious practice has received considerable attention from scholars.[42] Marrakesh was an important pilgrimage destination, accounting for a part of the floating Jewish population. Jews making a *ziyâra* (pilgrimage) were expected to first pay their respects to Hananiya ha-Kohen, known as "the lion of Marrakesh." While local Jews visited his grave regularly, often on Saturday nights—one woman recalled how she and her friends left the cemetery "as if leaving the cinema after a film"—those who came on an organized pilgrimage from elsewhere stayed for a full seven days.[43] They lit candles, prayed, sang, and, especially in the case of the sick, waited for saintly intervention. One pilgrim remembered "the entire world gathered together at the tomb of Rabbi Hananiya."[44] This world included Muslims, who also venerated this particular saint.

Like Ben Attar, Kohen's saintliness resulted from his having thwarted an attack on the *mallâh* from hostile tribes. He succeeded in this by summoning cannon-shooting phantoms and a swarm of wasps to ward off the invaders. His tomb is believed to date from the mid-seventeenth century.[45] A mausoleum was recently erected on the site to replace the small edifice that had stood there previously. Other important pilgrimages in the Jewish cemetery of Marrakesh include the tombs of Shlomo ben Tameshut from 1832, and the more recent tomb of Pinhas Kohen, the *shaykh al-yahûd* of Taroudant, dating from 1952. A female saint by the name of Lalla Rivka is also associated with Marrakesh Jewry.[46]

CHRISTIANS IN THE *MALLÂH*

Christian space overlapped with Jewish space in the *mallâh*. Christians inhabited Marrakesh from at least the thirteenth century, maintaining their own missions, *funduqs* (warehouses), and prisons, mostly concentrated around the area of the *qasba*. With the creation of the *mallâh* in the sixteenth century, the Sa'dians required all foreign non-Muslim visitors to move to the *mallâh* for the extent of their stay in the city. Even without such pressure from the *makhzan*, all those who could afford to escape the horrors of sleeping in the European *funduq* did not hesitate to do so. The Barbary Company's factor, Henry Roberts, conducted a lively trade in armaments from his home in the *mallâh* in the late sixteenth century.[47] Ambassadors and foreign princes typically lodged in the Jewish quarter.[48] Iberian Catholics, mostly captives, were a significant enough presence in the *mallâh* to warrant their own neighborhood, known as Amît, according to the memoirs of one captive. In 1660, the Franciscan church was definitively relocated to the *mallâh*. Once established, the Franciscans occupied the "most beautiful" houses the *mallâh* had to offer.[49] That upper-class foreigners preferred to reside there indicates that the *mallâh* was a desirable abode. And that Christians as well as the Muslims maintained a continual presence in the Jewish quarter throughout its history suggests an entity very unlike the European ghetto, the urban institution to which the Moroccan *mallâh* is so frequently (and erroneously) compared.

EXTREME DENSIFICATION AND ITS CONSEQUENCES

In the first three centuries of its existence, the *mallâh*, like the rest of Marrakesh, retained a sense of great spaciousness. Whole areas on the perimeter of the quarter remained empty, and population growth was kept in check by frequent epidemics, including a very serious one in the sixteenth century that killed more than half the city's Jews.[50] The situation changed dramatically in the second half of the nineteenth century with a region-wide population boom and the influx of rural migration. While the spacious *madîna* was able to provide housing for the city's steadily increasing Muslim population without much difficulty, the *mallâh*, with its sharply defined perimeter, was unable to accommodate the growing number of Jews seeking refuge within its walls. Not surprisingly, this led to the extreme densification of the existing fabric. The ill effects of crowding were already apparent in the 1860s, and intensified greatly in the following decades.[51] By 1900, as many as 15,000 inhabitants lived in an area originally designed to hold only a few thousand, and just one out of every six houses in the *mallâh* was occupied by a single family. The rest lived anywhere from eight to ten families to a house, with up to sixty-one individuals inhabiting a single residence. In these circumstances, even the richest families in the *mallâh* had at most two rooms within a house to themselves.[52]

The overwhelming density of the *mallâh* turned a visit into a gut-wrenching ordeal.[53] José Bénech, the director of the Marrakesh branch of the Banque

Commerciale du Maroc during the 1930s and the main observer of Jewish life in the city under the French Protectorate, compared passing through the *mallâh*'s main gate to descending into the Paris metro, with the attendant sensation of "suddenly breathing air polluted by the abnormal density of the population."[54] A less generous observer consigned it to one of the circles in Dante's vision of hell.[55] Even the teachers of the A.I.U, whose mission was to "regenerate" Jews of the East, complained bitterly when sent to Marrakesh, and at least one requested extra pay to compensate for the hardship of the assignment.[56]

Crowding in the *mallâh* was temporarily alleviated in 1891 when the Jewish quarter was enlarged along its northwestern and southern peripheries, in the areas known respectively as *mallâh al-jadîd* (or the "new" *mallâh*, though it was an extension of the old) and al-Bahîra, soon to become the poorest section of the *mallâh*. The enlargement was the result of a partnership. The land and some materials were provided by the *makhzan*, while private Jewish investors living within the *mallâh* built the houses. What accounts for the *makhzan*'s willingness to cede valuable land to the *mallâh*? European pressure on the Sultan to improve the living conditions of Moroccan Jews had been steadily mounting since the visit by the Anglo-Jewish philanthropist Sir Moses Monte fiore in the early 1860s.[57] However, it would be wrong to understand the *makhzan*'s decision to enlarge the Marrakesh *mallâh* simply as a concession to European concerns or the result of sympathy for the situation of the Jews. Rather, it grew directly out of the Moroccan government's long-held view of the *mallâh* as a cash resource; in this case, taking advantage of the overcrowding by creating new income properties. This is borne out by how quickly the *makhzan* decided to raise rents as high as the market would bear without "frightening the inhabitants." [58] Jewish investors understood that the *makhzan*'s motivation was financial. When a municipal official tried to block the transfer of land, two wealthy Jewish investors called for the sultan's intervention, reminding him that the sooner they began building, the sooner the royal treasury would start collecting rent.[59]

Population increases were behind other spatial changes during this period. The *mallâh*'s main *funduq* was renovated in December of 1879, and a new *qaysariya* was built in an interstitial space at the entryway to the *mallâh* in 1891, financed by Yeshu'a Corcos and Eliyahu Ben Sussan, two of the *mallâh*'s wealthiest businessmen.[60] The building of a new covered market indicates that the *mallâh*'s economy was growing along with its population, bringing handsome profits to a few. Indeed, class stratification had become increasingly apparent in the *mallâh* as the century drew to a close. In an 1894 British consular report, the wealthy notables of the *mallâh* were accused of extortion and of lording their authority over poorer Jews.[61] The gap between the *tujjâr as-sultân* and the peddlers and small shop owners had grown wide. Even the pasha, usually not one to plead for clemency for Jews, urged the sultan not to punish severely those caught selling tobacco illegally, as they were "not members of the rich *tujjâr* but poor and of doubtful guilt."[62] Financial resources also allowed the rich to escape the city during periods of epidemic, famine, or siege, when the poor were left behind to suffer.[63]

TWO HOUSES IN THE *MALLÂH*

According to an 1890 census taken by the Moroccan authorities, the Jewish quarter of Marrakesh contained 210 houses, each with an average of 6.05 rooms.[64] The typical dimensions of a room were 2.5 x 1.8 meters, though the shape varied depending on their location in the house's general layout and its alignment with the street.[65] The houses themselves did not differ in their design or materials from *madîna* houses in any significant way. They were constructed of the same red clay (*tâbiya*) that distinguishes all buildings in Marrakesh. The courtyard type predominates, the advantages being the economical use of land, a guarantee of privacy, and adaptation to the hot, dry climate of Marrakesh.[66] Two main types of courtyard houses are represented in the *mallâh*: the *dâr*, with a small paved courtyard, and the larger *riyâdh*, with greenery and a water source in the central courtyard. Both dogleg and non-dogleg entryways are found, refuting the generalization that Jewish houses in Morocco do not have the dogleg entry. The *mallâh* also had several *funduq*s for storing goods and sheltering animals. Some of these were transformed into living quarters as the trans-Saharan trade diminished at the turn of the last century, while others functioned as workshops.

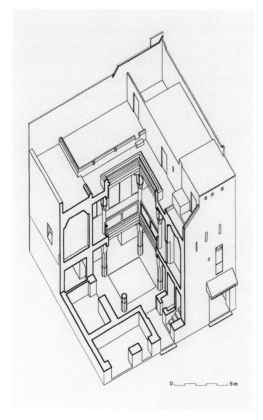

0 ⌐————⌐ 5 m

Left: Axonometric view of the Haliwa house

Opposite, top: First-floor plan, Haliwa house

Opposite, bottom: Interior of the Haliwa house

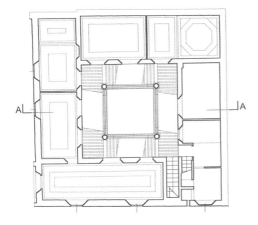

FIRST FLOOR   0 ⌐___⌐___⌐ 5 m

Haliwa family cloth merchants, father and son, with their Muslim employee (1990)

Density distinguishes residential space in the *mallâh* from the rest of the city. The heavy human burden is palpable in the streets. The streets are much narrower than the streets of the *madîna*, perhaps due to the gradual encroachment of houses onto the public way. The street level sometimes stands as much as a meter above the threshold to the house, due to centuries of accumulated detritus.[67] Other features peculiar to *mallâh* space are exterior balconies and the greater use of ornamental metalwork made by *mallâh* artisans, most likely innovations introduced after the coming of the Protectorate. The niches for *mezuzot* (amulets) and the representations of prophylactic religious symbols, such as the *menorah* (the seven-branched candlestick), occasionally appear on doorways and walls, but other than that, there is no external sign of a Jewish presence. Moreover, given the overwhelming poverty of most *mallâh* residents, little ornate decoration found its way inside the Jewish homes. Overall, an atmosphere of austerity ruled in the streets and interiors of the *mallâh*.

THE MERCHANT'S HOUSE

The Haliwa house is situated on the main street on the northwest periphery of the *mallâh* within the area of late nineteenth-century expansion. The Haliwa family migrated to Marrakesh during the Protectorate period from Zagora, a small oasis town about 350 kilometers to the southeast. This house exemplifies the pattern of mixed-use housing commonly found in the *mallâh*. The second and third floors of the house serve as living space for the extended family, consisting of three generations, containing a kitchen, bedrooms, and salons. The Haliwa home is one of the few in the *mallâh* with decoration on ceilings and walls. The ground floor is occupied by the family-owned textile business, and the individual rooms around the ground-floor courtyard are used for the storage of bolts of cloth, while transactions are carried out in the central space. S. L. Bensusan captured the animation of a Jewish mercantile household at the beginning of the last century:

> The courtyard is clean and wide, an enlarged edition of a patio, with big storerooms on either side, and stabling or a granary. Here, also, is a bureau, in which the master sits in receipt of custom, and deals in green tea that has come from India via England, and white sugar in big loaves, and coffee, and other merchandise. He is buyer and seller at once, now dealing with a native who is talking Shilha [Fr. Chleuh], the language of the Berbers, now the Maghrebbin [North African] Arabic of the Moors, and again debased Spanish or Hebrew, with his own brethren.[68]

In March 2007, this house was still occupied by the Haliwa family, who continued to ply the textile trade in their ground-floor shop. The shop was closed on Saturday, but a visit the next day found the place filled with Muslim customers, mainly from the countryside. Two Muslim clerks served the clientele, while Moushi Haliwa, now head of the family, surveyed the scene and took charge of the accounts.

THE RICH MAN'S HOUSE

The scion of Marrakesh Jewry in 1900 was Yeshu'a Corcos. His palatial house is located in the older part of the *mallâh* on a street today called *rue du Commerce*, formerly known simply as *darb Qurqûz,* named after its most important resident.[69] After Corcos's death in 1929, the house became Jewish communal property, serving first as a school and later as an *asile*, or home for the aged. In 2004, the kitchen was being used for ritual slaughtering (*shehita*) on Friday mornings, filling the room with feathers and the squawk of terrified chickens.

Jérome and Jean Tharaud, popular French belletrists of the 1920s, romanticized Corcos by calling him "the millionaire of the *mallâh*."[70] His wealth came from many sources, including real estate holdings. According to the 1890 census, he owned at least ten *mallâh* properties, and no doubt accrued more in the following decades. As the wealthiest individual in the *mallâh*, he was the obvious choice for the office of *shaykh al-yahûd*, a position he held for most of his adult life. Corcos's power in the *mallâh* was absolute; even the rabbis complained that they could do nothing without his approval.[71] The autocratic streak he exhibited in communal politics extended to economic affairs. In one instance, he obliged the *makhzan* to grant him a monopoly over the rural wax market by forcing out another Jewish bidder from the village of Tamlalet. There were no other bidders, for "not one Jew of Marrakesh could enter this

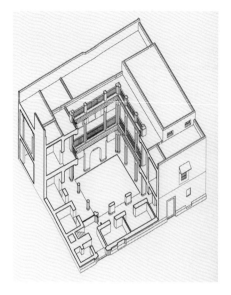

Left: Axonometric view of the Corcos house

Below: Courtyard of the Corcos house

Opposite, top: Section of the Corcos house

Opposite, below: Doorway to the ground-floor
reception room, Corcos house

market out of fear of Corcos."[72] He also maintained a monopoly over barley in partnership with another merchant named Rosillio.[73]

Despite repeated attempts by the representatives of the A.I.U. to win Corcos over to the aims of their project, he never abandoned his ties to the Moroccan authorities and remained firmly unaligned. This sometimes placed him in seemingly contradictory situations: he conducted trade with *makhzan* money while enjoying the special status of a French *protégé*; he maintained monopolies by intimidating his co-religionists, yet he also flexed his power as chief of the Jewish community by refusing to hand over to authorities a Jew forced to convert to Islam.[74] His complex and multifaceted responsibilities are reflected in the palatial family house. Consisting of two smaller houses joined together by an internal walkway, the house is centrally located close to the *mallâh*'s main market and gate and is by far the largest private residence in the quarter. Thomas Hodgkin, who accompanied Moses Montefiore during his visit to the Marrakesh *mallâh* in 1864, described it as follows:

> [Corcos's] house, though in a narrow lane, was of good size, as usual surrounding an inner court, and two, if not three, stories in height. We were assembled in the court, where members of the family, richly dressed, received us, and supplied us with tea in the Morocco style, and with abundance of sweet cakes. Whilst we were so engaged we were gazed upon from the upper windows by many well-dressed Jewish ladies; but it is probable that they were not all members of the family. The vessels were of glass, gilt, served upon chased brass salvers, such as we had seen manufactured at Mogador [Essaouira].[75]

In a large upstairs room, perhaps the very room from which the "well-dressed Jewish ladies" gazed down at Hodgkin, an ornately carved and decorated wooden ceiling similar to those found in very wealthy Muslim homes retains its original vibrant color. This sumptuous room was used for special gatherings of friends and family, and served as a setting for Sabbath and festive meals. Directly beneath this room on the ground floor is a similar large rectangular room, though less lavishly appointed, used for receiving clients and officials. Members of the Corcos family lived elsewhere in the *mallâh*, and an important branch made their home in Essaouira; but if size is any measure, the dimensions of this house announce that Yeshu'a was the head of the clan.

SYNAGOGUES AND RITUAL LIFE

Religion was central to both Jewish identity and daily life in the Marrakesh *mallâh*. While formal rites and rituals took place in the synagogue, the saints' tombs in the cemetery, certain alleyways inhabited by *jinns*, and various trees, wells, and other sites also had religious meaning. About twenty-four synagogues served the population of the *mallâh* at the turn of the twentieth century.[76] Although a few buildings were used exclusively for religious purposes, most were dedicated rooms inside private homes, usually belonging to well-to-do Jews.

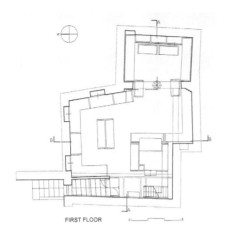

FIRST FLOOR

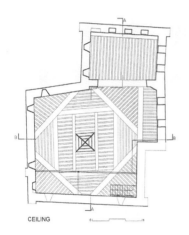

CEILING

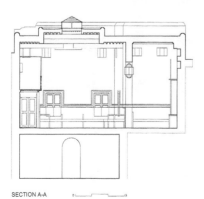

SECTION A-A

Above: Entryway to the Fâsî synagogue

Top, left: First-floor plan, Fâsî synagogue

Middle, left: Ceiling of the Fâsî synagogue

Below, left: Section of the Fâsî synagogue

Synagogues were the only setting for formal education until 1900, when the A.I.U. established the first "secular" school in the *mallâh*. The larger synagogues maintained a school where the youngest boys learned to read and recite the basic prayers, and a Talmud Torah for the older ones, where they learned more advanced texts, prayers, and rituals of Moroccan Judaism.[77] In 1876, Joseph Halevy was sent by the A.I.U. to make a survey of Marrakesh's synagogues and their educational facilities and found them ripe for "regeneration":

> One counts more than twenty synagogues in the *mallâh*, all constructed according to the same plan and distinguished by their narrow and dirty entranceways. The synagogue called Adjama is distinguished among all the others by its beautiful appearance. Eight or ten of these buildings serve also as religious schools or Talmud Torahs. The cramming together of children in these spaces that are inade-

A typical *mallâh* street in Marrakesh

quate and exposed to the sun is frightening. One can gain an idea [of this] when one considers that each of these schools contain at least 120 children of all ages. In one of them, I counted more than 150 children randomly seated on tattered mats. There they learn to read Hebrew and recite the Bible and the Talmud. The oldest learn to write and basic arithmetic. Despite the absence of any reasonable method, those engaged advance rather rapidly, thanks to their natural intelligence. What progress could be accomplished if one followed a scientific method and a teaching program better suited to our century![78]

In the summer of 2004, two synagogues within the *mallâh* were still Jewish communal property, but only one of them, the *Slât al-Adjama,* still functioned as a house of prayer.[79] A second synagogue that remains intact is the *Slât al-Fâsiyyîn*. Located in the northwest quadrant of the *mallâh*, it is named for the merchants from Fez who prayed there. The interior contains several rows of red leather benches just long enough for one person to lounge with his feet resting on the bench, said by Jews of Marrakesh to be "the Fâsî fashion" of prayer. The open interior indicates it was constructed specifically as a large meeting space. The *tevah,* or podium, is located in the northwest corner of the room, rather than in the middle, to maximize seating. The supporting pillars have been removed and replaced by reinforcement in the ceiling, resulting in a room of especially broad and tall dimensions. Small windows in the eastern wall let in light. A women's gallery was perhaps a later addition; initially, the Fâsî community in Marrakesh consisted only of men. The basement of the building contains a *mikveh*, a *genizah*, and storage space. The impressive scale of this building connotes the wealth and size of the Fez community in Marrakesh and its devotion to maintaining ties with its place of origin.

CONCLUSION: A MICROCOSM OF THE CITY

The continuity between city and countryside in Morocco has been amply documented in recent regional economic histories of Essaouira, the Sûs and the Sahara.[80] In the case of Marrakesh, Paul Pascon's work on the Hawz has similarly proven that the southern capital was anything but the "closed city of Islam," permanently separated from the hostile countryside by its walls, as was once suggested by the colonial historian of Marrakesh, Gaston Deverdun.[81] Rather, the linkages between Marrakesh and the surrounding countryside are so strong that the southern capital has sometimes been described as a city overwhelmed by its hinterland.[82] Marrakesh was watered by the melting snows of the nearby Atlas Mountains and nurtured by the rich grain fields of the Misfiwa region. Even in the sphere of politics, the countryside exerted influence on almost all the major events of the period.[83] But above all else, it was trade that bound Marrakesh to its hinterland, as well as to the wider Moroccan and Mediterranean worlds.

The Jewish quarter was a microcosm of the commercial activity that animated the city. It stood at the center of a series of concentric circles, held together by a network of ties that connected the local Jews to their Muslim neighbors in the *madîna*, the municipal authorities in the *qasba*, the rural populations of the countryside, the European firms and their fellow Jewish entrepreneurs on the coast, and finally, their contacts in the world at large. As traditional patterns of exchange evolved, so too did traditional patterns of habitation. The process of migration that had begun in the nineteenth century with an influx of rural Jews to the *mallâh* suddenly changed direction. During the Protectorate period (1912-1956), Jews began to move out of the *mallâh* and into the new European quarters of the city. From there they began to leave Marrakesh altogether, first moving to Casablanca and afterwards, during the tumultuous years of the independence, to France, Israel, other European destinations, the United States, and Canada. Today, only a few hundred Jews live in Marrakesh, and only three Jewish families still reside in the *mallâh*. Now officially known as *Hayy al-Salâm* (the Peaceful Quarter), the *mallâh* still is one of the city's most densely populated and poorest neighborhoods, with its houses subdivided into apartments, pool halls, workshops, and stores.

The great changes that have taken place in Marrakesh in the past fifteen years because of a boom in tourism have begun to affect the *mallâh,* neglected by the municipality for decades. In an effort to ease overcrowding, the authorities are embarking on various programs of urban renewal. Meanwhile, in the relentless search for investment opportunities, entrepreneurs have bought some of the grand old *mallâh* houses (at a fraction of the price of comparable houses in the *madîna*) and renovated them into guesthouses [*riyadh*s] or private homes. As this process of gentrification moves forward, the insistent yet unspoken questions are: What, if anything, of the 400-year-old story of the quarter's rich multicultural past will be preserved? How much, if anything, of this legacy will be retained in the popular imagination, and to what extent will the authorities try to incorporate it into narratives about the past?

Notes

1. Paul Odinot, quoted in Jean Gaignebet, "Marrakesh: Grand Carrefour des Routes Marocaines," *Revue de Geographie Marocaine* 7 (1928): 273–274.

2. Jean-Louis Miège, *Morocco*, transl. O.C. Warden (Paris: B. Arthaud, 1952), 179.

3. Jean-Louis Miège, *Le Maroc et l'Europe*, 4 vols. (Rabat: Editions La Porte, 1989) 3:57, 59–60, 85, 94–95. For first-hand observation of the slave trade in Marrakesh, see T. Zerbib, "Slave Caravans in Morocco," *Anti-Slavery Reporter* (May–June 1887), 98–99. For a general discussion of the slave trade in Morocco during this period, see Mohammed Ennaji, *Serving the Master: Slavery and Society in Nineteenth-Century Morocco*, transl. Seth Graebner (New York: St. Martin's Press, 1999).

4. Daniel Noin, *La population rurale du Maroc* (Paris: P.U.F., 1970), 42. Frances's Protectorate over Morocco began in 1912 and ended with Moroccan independence in 1956.

5. Miège *Le Maroc et l'Europe*, 3:387.

6. Ahmad b. Khâlid an-Nâsiri, "Kitâb al-Istiqsâ li-akhbâr duwwal al-maghrib al-aqsâ," *Archives Marocaines* 34 (1936): 381–382, as quoted in Mohammed Kenbib, "Changing Aspects of State and Society in Nineteenth Century Morocco," in *The Moroccan State in Historical Perspective, 1850–1985*, ed. Abdelali Doumou (Dakar: Codesria, 1990), 11.

7. Miège, *Le Maroc et l'Europe*, 3:16. In 1913, the floating population of Marrakesh was estimated at 30,000. Louis Botte, "Marrakech une année après la conquête," *L'Afrique française* 12 (1913) : 431. In 1926, it was estimated at 20,000–25,000, the equivalent of one-sixth of the city's permanent population of 149,263. *Encyclopedia of Islam*, 2nd ed., s.v. "Marrâkush."

8. Joseph Thomson, *Travels in the Atlas and Southern Morocco* (London: George Philip and Son, 1889), 350. The Jewish community of Casablanca surpassed that of Marrakesh as Morocco's largest in the 1930s.

9. Marrakesh was unusual in terms of its municipal administration. It had not one but two pashas. The first was the pasha or *qâʾid* of the *madîna* (sometimes referred to as the "governor" in European sources). The second, known simply as "the pasha,"

ruled over the *qasba* and the *mallâh*, and by extension the Jewish communities of the countryside around Marrakesh. His jurisdiction is confirmed by official *makhzan* documents, including the following: "Thus the Jews living in the countryside are under our authority as Jews of the *qasba*, and they will be ruled by the same law that rules over the Jews of Marrakesh." Direction des Archives Royales (hereafter DAR), Marrakesh 7, 18 Safar 1303/26 November 1885, Umalik. The Pasha also named the *shaykh al-yahûd* for the wider region. Archives of the *Alliance Israélite Universelle* (hereafter AAIU), Maroc.VII.B.1852, [n/a] 1914, Danon.

10. Marrakesh was the home of southern Morocco's only schools for advanced rabbinical training.

11. *Times of Morocco*, 15 December 1888.

12. Jewish merchants were the primary link between city and countryside throughout North Africa. Daniel Schroeter explains: "The very fact that the Jews were not rooted in rural society, with tribal or kinship ties, meant that they did not constitute a political threat and were therefore more trustworthy in economic matters. Paradoxically, this marginality was the guarantee of a neutrality which was in the interest of all parties to maintain under normal conditions." *Merchants of Essaouira: Urban Society and Imperialism in Southwestern Morocco, 1844–1886* (Cambridge: Cambridge University Press, 1988), 86. A similar point is made by Dale Eickelman, *Knowledge and Power in Morocco* (Princeton: Princeton University Press, 1985), 66.

13. Such activities were much lauded by the A.I.U.: "Many Jews roam the countryside...buying indigenous goods and selling European goods to the Arabs. The French find in the Jews active assistants, devoted to their beautiful cause." AAIU, Maroc II.B.9–13, 31 May 1928, Goldenberg.

14. Since much of the slave trade was conducted in private homes by Muslim brokers rather than in the public market, Jews did participate in these exchanges. Europeans were also forbidden to attend the slave auctions, yet many managed to observe the sales surreptitiously. See Public Record Office (hereafter PRO), FO 174: 85, 12 April 1876, Hay.

15. José Benéch, *Essai d'explication d'un mellah (ghetto marocain); un des aspects du judaïsme* (Paris: Larose, c.1940), 48.Gaston Deverdun, *Marrakech des origines à 1912*, 2 vols. (Rabat: Editions Techniques Nord-Africaines, 1959), 1:563. Benéch implies that the jewelers actually lived in their ateliers, making them the only Jews to reside outside the *mallâh* in Marrakesh during the pre-Protectorate period, though this cannot be corroborated by other sources. Benéch, 47.

16. With its application to the Jewish quarter of Marrakesh, the toponym "*mallâh*" passed into generic usage. Following a similar trajectory as the word "ghetto," that originally referred to the foundry in Venice where that city's Jews were transferred, "*mallâh*" originally referred to a specific geographic area in Fez (the salt marsh area) where the Jews of the northern Moroccan city were transferred in 1438. Several decades passed before the term "*mallâh*" entered into local, and eventually European, terminology with reference to Marrakesh, but eventually all Jewish neighborhoods in Morocco, walled or not, were referred to by that name.

17. In some Moroccan cities, such as Essaouira, individual Jews were able to circumvent the requirement of residing in the *mallâh*. See Schroeter, *Merchants of Essaouira*, 19. This was not the case in Marrakesh. Segregation was abolished by the Protectorate authorities after 1912.

18. Mohammed Naciri, "Regards sur l'évolution de la citadinité au Maroc," in *URBAMA*, Université de Tours (1985), 37–59.

19. See, for example, DAR, Marrakesh 12, 4 Dhu al-Qaʿda 1321/22 January 1904, Corcos; and DAR, Marrakesh 1, 4 Shaʿban 1265/25 June 1849, Ibn Mushâsh.

20. In the late nineteenth century, Jewish butchers in the *mallâh* were repeatedly chastised by the authorities for illegally slaughtering female cows. DAR, Marrakesh 4, 17 Muharram 1297/31 December 1879, ʿAbd al-Allah b. Ibrahim.

21. AAIU, Maroc XXIV.E.384–393, 22 January 1934, Bibasse.

22. PRO/FO 174: 95, 19 December 1878, Maclean. Cotton was carried by Jewish peddlers from Marrakesh to places as far away as Tindûf, deep in the Sahara. Y.D. Sémach, "Un rabbin voyageur marocain: Mordochée Aby Serour," *Hespéris* 8 (1928): 389.

23. The Jews recognized the value of their goods and services to the rest of the city, and did not hesitate to use it as leverage with the municipal authorities, as when they "talked of...ceasing to do business" in retaliation for the beating of a local Jewish woman by soldiers. PRO/FO 413: 18, 24 October 1892, Payton.

24. Paul Wheatley has observed for the first four centuries of Muslim expansion in particular, "the urban process in the Middle East and North Africa...was principally one of adaptation and accretion rather than creation." *The Places Where Men Pray Together* (Chicago: University of Chicago Press, 2001), 263.

25. Allen Fromherz, "Marrakech: City as Doctrine," unpublished paper presented at the annual meeting of the Middle East Studies Association, Washington, D.C.,November 2005.

26. Debate exists as to whether Marrakesh was founded in 1062 or 1070, and hence whether Abu Bakr or Ibn Tashfîn should be considered the city's true founder, with most scholars now agreeing on the later date. Ronald Messier, "Rereading Medieval Sources through Multidisciplinary Glasses," in Michel Le Gall and Kenneth Perkins, eds., *The Maghrib in Question: Essays in History and Historiography* (Austin: University of Texas Press, 1997), 177–178; Vincent Lagardère, *Les Almoravides jusqu'au règne de Yûsuf b. Tasfîn* (Paris: l'Harmattan, 1989), 74–76.

27. Paul Pascon, *Capitalism and Agriculture in the Haouz of Marrakesh*, transl. Edwin Vaughan and Veronique Ingman , ed. John Hall (London: Kegan Paul International, 1986), 38. The Rahamna maintained close relations with the Jews of Marrakesh for centuries.

28. According to the twelfth-century geographer Muhammad al-Idrîsî, the Almoravid Sultan 'Ali b. Yûsuf [r.1106–1142] forbade Jews to spend the night in Marrakesh, though they were permitted, and perhaps even encouraged, to enter the city by day to pursue "the business and services that are their particular specialty." Reinhart Dozy and Michael De Goeje, eds. and transl., *Description de l'Afrique et de l'Espagne, par Edrisi*, 2 vols. (Leiden: E. J. Brill, 1866), 2:79. Muslim sources do not make explicit mention of the persecution of Moroccan Jews by the Almohads, though the topic is treated at length in Jewish sources. See, for example, Maimonides' "Epistle to the Jews of Yemen," translated by S.D. Goitein and reprinted in Norman Stillman, *The Jews of Arab Lands* (Philadelphia: Jewish Publication Society, 1979), 233–248. Maimonides was living in Fez as a refugee from Spain at the time. In the Epistle, he recounts the forced conversions taking place under Almohad rule in North Africa in order to reassure his co-religionists in Yemen who were facing a similar threat. See also the famous elegy of the poet Abraham Ibn Ezra, which can be found in David Kohn, *Rabi Avraham Ibn Ézra: Kovets hokhmat ha-Raba', shirav u-melitsotav, hidotav u-mikhtamav ` im toladeto* (Warsaw: Hotsa'at Ahi 'asaf, 1894), 140–143.

29. Diego de Torres, *Relación del origen y suceso de los Xarifes y del estado de los reinos de Marruecos, Fez, y Tarudante que tienen usurpados* (Seville: Casa Francisco Perez, 1586), ed. Mercedes García-Arenal (Madrid: Siglo Veintiuno, 1980), 93. Aswâl is also the location of the first house built in Marrakesh, suggesting that the Jewish settlement in this part of the city was very old. Deverdun, *Marrakech* 1:339.

30. Jean Mocquet, "Voyage de Jean Mocquet au Maroc," in *Les sources inédites de l'histoire du Maroc*, deuxième série, *Archives et bibliothèques de France*, ed. Henry de Castries, Pierre de Cenival, and Philippe de Cossé Brissac, 6 vols. (Paris: E. Leroux, 1922–1960), 2:400.

31. On the founding of the Fez *mallâh*, see Chapter 3.

32. For a full discussion of the various causes of "mallâhization" in Marrakesh, see Emily R. Gottreich, "On the Origins of the *Mellah* of Marrakesh," *International Journal of Middle East Studies*, 35, 2 (May 2003): 287–305.

33. Torres, *Relación del origen*, 295. Henry Koehler, "La Kasbah Saadienne de Marrakech," *Hespéris* 27 (1940): 4, n.2.

34. Jacques Meunié and Henri Terasse, *Nouvelles recherches archéologiques à Marrakech* (Paris: Arts et métiers graphiques, 1957), 47–48. For a full treatment of the grid in the history of the city, see Spiro Kostof, *The City Shaped: Urban Patterns and Meanings through History* (Boston: Little, Brown, 1991), 95–157. David Elalouf, "Une architecture juive?" in André Goldenberg, ed., *Les juifs du Maroc* (Paris: Editions du Scribe, 1992), 303–307.

35. Adrien Matham, "Le Palais d'el Bedi et l'oeuvre de Matham," in *Les sources inédites de l'histoire du Maroc*, première série, *Archives et bibliothèques des Pays Bas*, ed. Henry de Castries, 6 vols. (Paris: E. Leroux, 1913), 4: 570–623. Deverdun, *Marrakech*, 1:365–366.

36. This stands in contrast to the European ghetto, which was generally locked from the outside by non-Jews, increasing the sense of imprisonment and isolation. Because the door to the Marrakesh *mallâh* was locked from the inside, Jews controlled the entry.

37. Mohammed Kenbib, *Juifs et musulmans au Maroc, 1859–1948* (Rabat: Faculté des Lettres et des Sciences Humaines, 1994), 394–400.

38. AAIU, Maroc II.B.9–13, 10 March 1929, Goldenberg. Isaachar Ben-Ami, *Saint Veneration among the Jews in Morocco* (Detroit: Wayne State University Press, 1998), 252. This behavior may be attributed not only to Ben Attar's relic, but also to the probable existence of a *mezuzah* on the upper right-hand side of the gate's entryway, which Jews customarily kiss when passing into or out of domestic space. A *mezuzah* in the gate suggests that the entire *mallâh* was considered domestic space.

39. *Times of Morocco*, 29 September 1888.

40. Colonial administrators were obsessed with issues of health and hygiene; here, this fear is coupled with the A.I.U.'s disdain for the popular religious practices. AAIU, Maroc II.B.9–13, 10 March 1929, Goldenberg.

41. According to Ben-Ami, ninety Jewish saints are said to be recognized by Muslims in Morocco, and thirty-six Muslim saints are recognized by Jews. See Ben-Ami, *Saint Veneration*, 131.

42. The pioneering work on this topic is Edward Westermarck, *Ritual and Belief in Morocco*, 2 vols. (New York: University Books, 1968). See also Ernest Gellner, *Saints of the Atlas* (Chicago: University of Chicago Press, 1969), and Vincent Cornell, *Realm of the Saint: Power and Authority in Moroccan Sufism* (Austin: University of Texas Press, 1998). Saint veneration among Moroccan Jews specifically is treated in Ben-Ami, *Saint Veneration*; Yoram Bilu, *Without Bounds: The Life and Death of Rabbi Ya'aqov Wazana* (Detroit: Wayne State University Press, 2000); and most recently Oren Kosansky, *All Dear Unto God: Saints, Pilgrimage, and Textual Practice in Jewish Morocco*, PhD diss., University of Michigan, 2003).

43. Issachar Ben-Ami, *Culte des saints et pèlerinages judéo-musulmans au Maroc* (Paris: Editions Maisonneuve & Larose, 1990), 179.

44. Ben-Ami, *Culte des saints*, 179.

45. Louis Voinot, *Pèlerinages judéo-musulmans du Maroc* (Paris, 1948), 52. Benéch, *Essai d'explication*, 181.

46. Ben-Ami, *Saint Veneration*, 277–279, 311–312, 260–263.

47. Thomas Willan, *Studies in Elizabethan Foreign Trade* (Manchester, UK.: Manchester University Press, 1959), 224.

48. Mocquet, "Voyages," 2: 400.

49. Albert Savine, *Dans les Fers du Moghreb* (Paris: Michaud, 1912), 12–13.

50. Hamid Triki and Bernard Rosenberger, "Famines et epidémies au Maroc aux XVIe et XVIIe siècles," *Hespéris-Tamuda* 14 (1974): 109–175; 15 (1974): 5–103. Deverdun, *Marrakech*, 1:365–366.

51. Thomas Hodgkin reported that the Marrakesh *mallâh* was "densely inhabited" and that the narrowness of the streets made it "extremely difficult to move through the crowd," even when blows were used to clear the way. Thomas Hodgkin, *Narrative of a Journey to Morocco in 1863 and 1864* (London: T.C. Newby, 1866), 85. The French military officer Jules Erckmann, who visited Marrakesh in the late 1870s, commented that the *mallâh* was remarkable for two things: "the dirtiness of its streets and the density of its population." *Le Maroc moderne* (Paris: Challamel Ainé, 1885), 190.

52. "Israélites du Maroc," *Bulletin de l'Alliance Israélite Universelle*, 25 (1900), 95. Erckmann, *Le Maroc moderne*, 191.

53. Using data from an 1890 census, the Jewish quarter's density is calculated at .0287 inhabitants per square meter. The census did not count young children. DAR, *al-Tartib al-'amm*, 6 Rabi' II 1308/19 November 1890. By the twentieth century, the population of the *mallâh* exceeded 1,000 inhabitants per hectare. Deverdun, *Marrakech*, 1:563.

54. José Benéch, *Essai d'explication*, 2.

55. Pascale Saisset, *Heures juives au Maroc* (Paris: Rieder, 1930), 145–146.

56. AAIU, Maroc XXV.E.394–397, 5 October 1917, Eskanazi.

57. See, for example, "Congratulatory address to the Emperor," from the Anglo-Jewish Association asking Mawlay Hassan I to continue good treatment of the Jews: PRO/FO 174: 291, 9 January 1874.

58. Bibliothèque Nationale and Archives, Rabat (hereafter B.N.R.), Rasâ'il muhtasib Murrâkush Mawlay `Abd Allah al-Bukîlî, D3410: 150, 17 Shawwâl 1309/15 May 1892.

59. DAR, al-Tartîb al-`âmm, 21 Safâr 1309/26 September 1891, Eliyahu b. Sussan and Yeshu'a Corcos.

60. DAR, Marrakesh 4, 11 Muharram 1297/25 December 1879, `Umanâ' al-Amrâs. DAR, al-tartîb al-`âmm, 21 Safar 1309/ 26 September 1891, Eliyahu b. Sussan and Yeshu'a Corcos.

61. PRO/FO 413: 21, 25 April 1894, Satow.

62. DAR, al-tartîb al-`âmm, Marrakesh 8, 22 Shawwâl 1307/11 June 1890, Umâlik.

63. PRO/ FO 413: 48, n/d, Nairn.

64. DAR, al-tartîb al-`âmm, 6 Râbi` II 1308/19 November 1890.

65. *Times of Morocco*, 25 October 1890.

66. Friedrich Schwerdtfeger, *Traditional Housing in African Cities: A Comparative Study of Houses in Zaria, Ibadan, and Marrakech* (New York: J. Wiley, 1982), 218.

67. With no drainage system, the disposal of waste was a major health concern in the *mallâh*. It was known for the huge mountain of garbage that stood more than 10 meters high at the end of the *rue du Cimitière*. Few visitors failed to comment on it. See, for example, Maurice de Périgny, *Au Maroc: Marrakech et les Portes du Sud* (Paris: Pierre Roger et Cie., 1918), 140–141; the garbage heap is also marked on the 1899 map of Marrakesh by N. Larras in Deverdun, *Marrakech*, 2: Plate 103.

68. S. L. Bensussan, "In Red Marrakesh," *The Fortnightly Review*, old series, 82 (1904): 434.

69. High on the list of concerns for the contemporary Jewish community of Marrakesh is to have the original street names and corresponding signage restored to the *mallâh*.

70. Jérome Tharaud and Jean Tharaud, *Marrakech, ou les seigneurs de l'Atlas* (Paris: Librairie Plon, 1920), 132.

71. AAIU, Maroc III.C.10, 20 December 1900, Levy.

72. DAR, Marrakesh 6, 18 Sha'ban 1301/14 June 1884, the two `amîn-s of Marrakesh, Buzîd and Bannânî. Corcos' right to these markets was revoked in 1893: BNR, Rasâ'il muhtasib Marrâkush Mawlay 'Abd Allah al-Bukîlî, D3410: 119, 23 Dhû al-Hijja 1310/8 July 1893.

73. The barley contract can be found in DAR, al-Yahûd 2, 15 Dhû al-Qa`da 1323/11 December 1905, `Abd al-Hafîz.

74. DAR, Marrakesh 9, 11 Ramadan 1310/29 March 1893, al-Mustafâ.

75. Hodgkin, *Narrative*, 86–87.

76. An additional synagogue existed in the lepers' quarter just outside the city walls at Bab Dukkala, where sufferers were segregated by religion. Paul Lambert, "Notice sur la Ville de Maroc," *Bulletin de la Société de Géographie de Paris* (1868), 445.

77. Haim Zafrani, *Pédagogie juive en terre d'Islam* (Paris: Maisonneuve, 1969), 42–43.

78. AAIU, France IX.A.67–73, 8 August 1876, Halévy.

79. A small number of newer synagogues in other parts of the city serve the remaining Jews of Marrakesh.

80. Schroeter, *Merchants of Essaouira*, esp. 85–116; 'Umar Afa, *al-Sahara' wa-Sûs min khilâl al-wathâ'iq wa-al-makhtûtât* (Rabat: Kulliyat al-Adâb wal-`ulûm al-Insanîya, 2001).

81. Paul Pascon, *Le Haouz de Marrakech* (Rabat: Centre Universitaire de la Recherche Scientifique, 1983); Deverdun, *Marrakech*, 1:117.

82. As noted by Dale Eickelman. *Knowledge and Power in Morocco*, 76.

83. Emily Gottreich, *The Mellah of Marrakesh: Jewish and Muslim Space in Morocco's Red City* (Bloomington: Indiana University Press, 2006), especially Chapter 5 for the connection between rural populations and Marrakesh Jewry in the 1907 insurrection known as the "Hafidhiyya."

SUSAN GILSON MILLER

5

THE BENI IDER QUARTER OF TANGIER IN 1900: HYBRIDITY AS A SOCIAL PRACTICE

A QUESTION OF HYBRIDITY

In 1888, the first foreign-language tourist guide to Morocco was published in Tangier, authored by the French journalist Kerdec Chény. The *Guide du Voyageur au Maroc* surveyed the whole country, but it was most informative about Tangier itself, the ancient port town poised at the meeting point of the Mediterranean and the Atlantic Ocean. After treating the usual topics of climate, geography, and local history, the *Guide* offered the following advice:

> The tourist new to Morocco could suffer from a false impression of the country if he should [only] visit Tangier. In this town, the population is mixed....The *mellah* —the ancient ghetto of the Jews—does not exist. People speak Arabic, Spanish, French and English. It is a mongrelized and nondescript place (*une ville bâtarde et neutre*) that is not longer entirely Moroccan, but not quite European. The pure forms of the Moorish houses are overwhelmed by new construction that expands day by day, marred by horrid green shutters and the awkward proportions of a hybrid architecture (*une architecture hybride*) whose only European feature is its rigidity and banality. For the artist, it is devastating; the old friend that was Tangier has lost its good looks and is about to die. (p. 95)

At the end of the nineteenth century Morocco was not yet colonized by Europe, yet its coastal towns were already much affected by Western influence.[1] For some, this was a deficit, for it meant that Morocco had begun to lose that primal quality of timelessness that traditionally attracted foreigners to the East. Indeed, discovering the sensation of "being out of time" was often the raison d'être of the Moroccan journey, seducing travelers from Eugène Delacroix to Pierre Loti. Kerdec Chény's use of the word "hybridity" reminds us that the notion is not a recent one, and that as early as 1888, foreigners arriving in Tangier were struck by the town's human and architectural diversity. The dolorous image of Tangier as a *ville bâtarde,* suffering irreparable losses because of its contact with modernity, leads us to think about how cities change, and how change is historically categorized and described. All cities are hybrid to some extent, but certain ones have made hybridity into an emblem of their uniqueness. Tangier is such a place.

For Kerdec Chény, eclecticism was a defect. Along with other intellectuals of his day, he regarded hybridity as an aberration, a biological misstep, and a movement away from the unadulterated forms that represented the highest level of human progress. In an era obsessed by matters of race, possessing qualities of hybridity was generally regarded as a sign of imperfection. Since then, notions of hybridity have radically evolved, not only in the realm of biology, but also in the realm of culture. Today, hybridity is widely viewed as a virtue, evoking a heterogeneity indicative of societal strength. In the writings of postcolonial scholars, it assumes even more powerful connotations, representing native resistance to colonial inroads. Yet it remains a slippery term, showing up in diverse settings and changing its meaning depending on its context. Recently, architectural historians have used it as a means of comparing urbanisms, especially those relating to cities of empire, for it neatly captures some of the ambiguities inherent in the stylistic mixing that empire imposed. In this context too, however, the notion of hybridity is never simple and rarely stands alone, but is often complicated by its relation to other equally elusive concepts, such as cosmopolitanism and identity.[2]

While remaining attentive to its analytical complexity, here I shall use the term in a rather straightforward way, as the frame for the dynamic spatial and social transformations that took place in late nineteenth century Tangier. If nothing else, Tangier

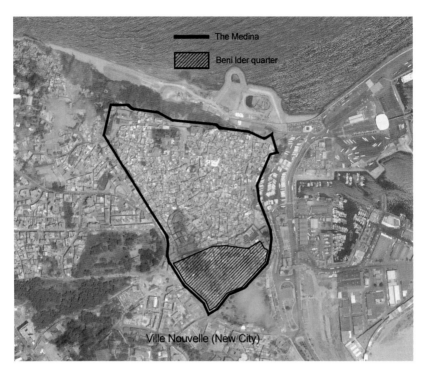

Map of the *madîna* of Tangier showing the location of the Beni Ider quarter

was a city of mixing and meeting. But it was also a city of rigorous order that grew out of a historical milieu in which various groups and communities maintained strict borders, in direct contrast to the idea of *metissage*. Competing tendencies—acculturation on the one hand and rigorous exclusion on the other—shaped the image of Tangier, perplexing foreign visitors by their contradictions and the variety of visual experiences they imposed. The setting for our inquiry is the old *madîna* of Tangier, where streets and buildings have retained their nineteenth-century aspect beneath a thin veneer of modernity. The Beni Ider quarter, historically the most diverse of Tangier's neighborhoods, is the site we have chosen to explore the historical processes that enabled minorities to occupy and transform a neighborhood, and in so doing, endow it with qualities of cultural hybridity that came to be representative of Tangier as a whole.

At this point one might reasonably ask: To what extent can one part of the city serve as a representation of the collectivity? How much is Greenwich Village a synecdoche for New York City, or the Marais for Paris? Isolating a section of a great city, and asserting that it stands for something greater, is problematic if one's insistence on likeness goes too far. But Tangier in 1900, with a population of about 30,000, was not New York or Paris. A mixed quarter in the heart of the city had an overwhelming influence on the rest. In the minds of many, the Beni Ider quarter *was* Tangier. Here we shall examine the history, morphology, and growth of this quarter, and ask how it came to have such an overwhelming influence on the character of the town. We have chosen

View of the *madîna* from the rooftops

the late nineteenth century as our moment, for it was then that people of differing mentalities and viewpoints interacted through the new media of mass-circulation newspapers, printed books, and memoirs that provide the textual component of our study. We begin by exploring the background to the many changes that took place at the turn of the last century.

TANGIER AND ITS PEOPLE

Located on the fringes of the ancient world, Tangier most likely began as a Phoenician trading post. Berber chieftains called the place Tingis and settled it well before the Romans invaded Morocco in 42 CE. The Romans stayed for about 500 years, and when they left, most of Tangier's inhabitants had become Christian. Archeologists have unearthed scattered vestiges of Roman rule: broken columns in the courtyard of the governor's palace, the remains of an aqueduct, a mosaic floor beneath the main street. The Romans were followed by Vandals, Goths, and Byzantines, each passing through without leaving a trace.[3]

During the Muslim invasion of the seventh century, Tangier's main role was as a jumping-off point to Spain, where the thrust of conquest was directed. References to Tangier are few and far between during this time. Despite its commercial and strategic importance, the town did not take a leading position in the struggles that perturbed the western Maghrib throughout the medieval period. In the fifteenth century, Tangier reemerged into Mediterranean history when Catholic Iberians wrested it away from the Moroccan Muslim sultanate; thereafter, the city remained in foreign hands for more than two centuries. First the Portuguese and the Spanish appended it to their growing African empires. Portuguese sources speak of a prosperous city with a cathedral located in the main square. A mixed population of Spanish, Portuguese, Arabs, Berbers, black Africans, and even some Jews filled a marketplace that offered goods "equal to what one would find in Europe."[4]

In 1661, Tangier passed to the English crown as part of the dowry of Catherine of Braganza, the "sad and barren" bride of Charles II.[5] Its new masters coveted it as a base to monitor the naval maneuvers of France and Spain, Britain's great rivals for Mediterranean supremacy. During a twenty-year English occupation, the town was populated mainly by soldiers and workmen engaged in building a breakwater to improve the port. In 1669, the Bohemian artist Wenceslaus Hollar made a series of superb engravings showing the main features of the colony, its walls and fortifications, its gates and main thoroughfares, its half-timbered houses with pitched roofs evoking a disciplined domesticity. The street pattern shown in these engravings conforms closely to the street pattern we know today. The Beni Ider quarter is clearly visible, with many open spaces and gardens.[6]

But the apparent orderliness of Hollar's renderings masked a project in deep trouble. The incessant attacks of Muslim *mujâhidîn* (holy warriors) sapped the strength of the garrison and Parliament's willingness to pay for it. In 1684 the English decided to

Hollar's map of Tangier, 1669. The Beni Ider quarter is at the apex of the triangle.

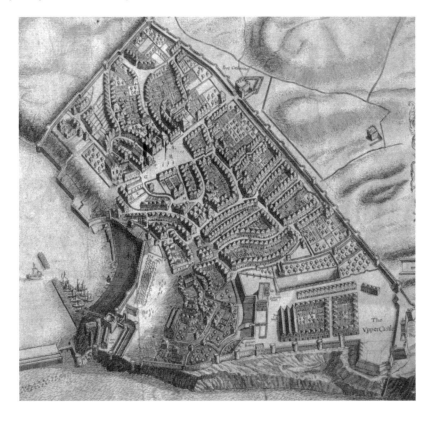

abandon the place, after blowing up the military installations, the ramparts, the houses, and the half-built breakwater. Of all the works constructed during 200 years of foreign rule, practically nothing remained. Tangier returned to Moroccan control under the powerful Mawlay Isma`îl, a sultan of the `Alawî dynasty that rules Morocco to this day. After Mawlay Isma`îl's death in 1727, northern Morocco became virtually independent under the rule of warlords from the nearby Riff Mountains who provided the troops that liberated the town and continued to govern it for the next two centuries. The city and its hinterland soon developed its own character based on its militant leadership, its proximity to Europe, and its resistance to centralized rule.

THE EUROPEANS

Because of its place on the threshold of Morocco, Tangier was the landfall for foreign visitors. In the late seventeenth and early eighteenth centuries, diplomatic relations between Morocco and Europe centered on the ransoming of captives seized by Moroccan corsairs cruising the Mediterranean coasts. Foreign embassies had to make the arduous journey to the interior, where the *makhzan* (government) resided, to conduct the lengthy negotiations that sometimes led to their release. After the suppression of piracy in the early nineteenth century, the main subject of diplomacy was trade and the opening of Moroccan ports to European business. Wishing to encourage these commercial ventures, but at the same time reluctant to receive foreigners in the cities of the interior, Sultan Muhammad b. `Abd Allâh (r. 1757–1790) decided to settle them in Tangier.[7]

This decision completely changed the character of the town, giving it an even more distinctively European flavor. The diplomatic presence, combined with the growth in overseas trade, transformed Tangier from a sleepy military outpost into an international crossroads. In 1800, the European population consisted of a handful of foreign diplomats living amid a sea of Muslims; by the mid-nineteenth century, the diplomatic contingent had become a significant factor in local politics. Nearly all the major powers had representatives in Tangier who handled commercial affairs, looked after their own nationals, and presided over the consular courts that provided an alternative to the local legal system. In addition to city residences furnished in a luxurious and comfortable style, the diplomats maintained large country houses embellished by extensive gardens and fruit orchards.[8]

Tangier's reputation as an open city soon attracted political refugees from all over Europe, making it a safe haven for colorful characters in search of a temporary home. It became Europe's doppelganger, a place where the residue from continental upheavals washed ashore. Aristocrats fleeing the fury of the French Revolution would stop briefly at Gibraltar and catch a fishing boat that would take them to the other side, where there was no limit on the duration of a stay. According to French historian J-L. Miège, some 200 political refugees arrived in Tangier during the revolutionary period.[9]

But the main source of exiles was Spain. At first, the Spanish emigrés were mainly intellectuals fleeing the failed uprisings of the 1840s, but later in the century, the agricultural crisis in Andalusia and the harsh repression of the anarchist movement brought a different social category. By the 1880s, the foreign population of Tangier was overwhelmingly working-class Spanish, influencing the language heard in the streets, the local foods, even the hours of work. Mixed among them were the occasional scoundrels and low-lifes, but the majority were "honest" workmen: the carpenters, masons, blacksmiths, and petty tradesmen who helped to build modern Tangier.[10] Most eventually moved on, but some stayed and became the nucleus of a permanent Spanish settlement that included shopkeepers, artists, and members of religious orders, as well as a handful of fiery radicals linked with the international workers' movement.[11]

After a series of free trade agreements were imposed on Morocco at mid-century by the European powers, the number of foreign businessmen multiplied rapidly; they opened shops, built hotels, and initiated a sustained building boom that was to last throughout the rest of the century. The flow of people and capital into Tangier produced a demand for Western amenities unknown in other Moroccan towns. By the closing years of the century, a telephone system, telegraph offices, reliable communications by sea, banking facilities, doctors and hospitals, frequent mail service, department stores and restaurants contributed to a manner of living that was palpably European. Moreover, the visual beauty of the place attracted artists of world repute. Sargent, Fortuny, Gérôme, Tiffany, Benjamin-Constant, and Matisse were some of the best known, but others of lesser fame came too, to sketch the natives, the marketplace, the walls bathed in a lambent light.[12] Writers, intellectuals, world travelers, pensioners, and adventurers of all types were drawn there for the climate, the *paysage*, and the easy living, imprinting the town with a decidedly cosmopolitan stamp.

JEWISH TANGIER

Jews were an important part of Tangier's population. Most were descended from Jews who fled Granada in 1492, when the Catholic monarchs dismantled the remnants of a 700-year-old Muslim civilization, with its rich Jewish component. Evicted from Spain, the *expulsados* scattered around the Mediterranean basin, avoiding Tangier, then under Portuguese rule. Having already sampled the Catholic brand of co-existence, they preferred the Muslim variety instead, and those who reached Morocco usually headed for Fez. Protected under Muslim law, Jews in Morocco for the most part lived a tranquil existence in a Berber- or Arabic-speaking context, dispersed in communities large and small as far as the remotest desert regions. The Iberian influx dramatically changed the make-up of many of these communities, introducing new social mores and ritual practices, and even a new language, the *haketiya,* or spoken Ladino, particular to the Jews of Northern Morocco.

In Tangier, a tiny Jewish settlement existed already in the late sixteenth century. We know this from the retelling of their delivery from the sword of the Portuguese King Sebastian, who invaded Morocco in 1578. During the English period (1662–1684) other

Jews arrived in Tangier, but their numbers were so small they were barely able to main-tain a single synagogue.[13] In the late eighteenth century, the Italian Jewish traveler Samuel Romanelli gave a mixed report on Tangier's Jews, steeped in overtones of European superiority:

> They are goodhearted folk, charitable and hospitable to strangers. They honor the Torah and study it. They hold the European Jews who come there in high esteem and call them "freemen"...The women are good-looking and have a robust build. However, they are rather like dumb beasts, having no part in science, understand-ing, or knowledge. They do not know how to speak, read or write Hebrew, Arabic or Standard Spanish. The women, like the men, speak a mixed language...[of] Spanish with a Portuguese accent. [14]

A steady trickle of Jews continued to migrate to Tangier throughout the nineteenth cen-tury, mainly from nearby northern towns such as Tetuan, Larache, Meknes, and Fez, but also from further south, from Essaouira (Mogador) and Marrakesh. Some found work in the foreign consulates or in the new houses of commerce, while others engaged in crafts or petty trade. The consular employees often received extraterritorial status from their employers, allowing them to elude the vicissitudes of local law. The newcomers settled throughout the *madîna*, and Tangier became famous among Moroccan towns because it had no separate Jewish quarter. In 1789, the English doctor William Lempriere visited Tangier and noted that, "contrary to the usual custom in Barbary, the Moors and the Jews live intermixed in Tangier, and maintain a more friendly intercourse than else-where in this quarter of the globe."[15] Tangier became known as the place where Jews walked freely in the streets, dressed like Europeans, displaying a newfound sense of self-worth different from Jews elsewhere in Morocco. Endowed with a feeling of *droit de cité*, and after 1864, enjoying the benefits of a modern education through the French-run schools of the Alliance Israélite Universelle, a handful of Jews rose to prominence and joined the urban elite.[16]

Haim Benchimol was a leader of Tangier Jewry at the end of the nineteenth centu-ry whose own story tells of this steady climb. Although his official position was that of humble "second dragoman" of the French Legation, in fact he was one of the richest men in Tangier, owner of extensive properties, an agent for European companies, cattle dealer, newspaper owner, and banker.[17] In his later years, he endowed a Jewish hospital, the first of its kind in Morocco, and gave generously to other charities. Under his cap-taincy, the Tangier Jewish community modeled itself after Western European Jewry in its pursuit of a bourgeois-inspired modernity.[18] No wonder that some Muslims reacted to the Jewish success with bitterness, finding themselves outdistanced by these par-venus. Writing around 1915, local historian Muhammad Skîrij may have been thinking of Haim Benchimol when he wrote:

> The commerce of the *madina* is entirely in the hands of the Jews who have ingrati-ated themselves with the foreigners....They are in need of the judgment of Allah

upon their deeds....The Jew is only interested in his own profit, and in lighting the spark of alienation between groups in order to extend his own advantage and to preserve his nearness to those in charge.[19]

Others must have shared Skîrij's chagrin at the profound shift that had taken place during the second half of the nineteenth century that reshuffled traditional hierarchies and gave a small but highly influential coterie of Jews a decisive role in the local economy.

MUSLIM TANGIER

Skîrij's anger was not that of a displaced member of the old guard, since he, too, was a newcomer to Tangier. When the Portuguese seized the town in the late fifteenth century, all of its native inhabitants fled. The repopulation of the city in the seventeenth century took place under the leadership of rustic chieftains from the nearby Riff Mountains. For generations to come, these rough-hewn Riffians maintained their position at the top of the social ladder, commanding all the important administrative posts.[20] But in the late nineteenth century, the rapid growth of commerce created a need for a cadre of "new men" capable of keeping accounts, organizing data, and corresponding correctly with the central government. Furthermore, Sultan Mawlay al-Hassan I (r. 1873–1895) decided to rebuild the fortifications around Tangier, launching a project that called for skilled engineers trained in European building arts. Newcomers from all parts of Morocco flocked to Tangier to take advantage of its thriving port economy. Among them was the Skîrij family, originally from Fez. They established a foothold in Tangier when young Zubayr Skîrij was assigned to the task of rebuilding the fortifications surrounding Tangier's port. Around 1900, Zubayr settled permanently in Tangier and not long after, he invited his young nephew Muhammad Skîrij of Fez to join him.[21]

Muhammad Skîrij was a highly literate and well-educated man.[22] Not long after his arrival in Tangier, he was employed as notary (`adl) in the customs house, and later as a teacher in the mosque school (madrasa). In his spare time, he wrote history, becoming the unofficial chronicler of the city with his multivolume work, Riyâdh al-Bahja fî Târîkh Tanja.[23] Coincidentally, he also owned a house in the Beni Ider quarter that is still inhabited by members of his family. The influx of "new men" like Skîrij introduced a dynamic element into the hitherto closed Muslim society of Tangier. However, it was not always a smooth integration. The newcomers were caught in a three-sided competition for influence; on the one hand were the upstart Jews and meddlesome Europeans, and on the other side, the Riffian old guard, who resented the cultivated manners of the Fâsî intellectuals such as Muhammad Skîrij. It is no wonder that Skîrij and others like him felt angered and alienated by the reorganization of political authority and financial power that foreign influence entailed.

Deposed rulers also gravitated to Tangier, as did their entourages. In the aftermath of the dynastic struggles that undermined the Moroccan monarchy at the turn of the last century, Tangier became the refuge for ex-sultans and their attendants: Sultan `Abd al-`Azîz, unseated in 1907 by his brother `Abd al-Hâfidh, settled in Tangier; his hapless brother was soon to follow, after he too was forced to abdicate by the French in 1912. ʿÀbd al-Hâfidh built not one, but two great palaces in Tangier, one in the Hasnûna quarter outside the walled town and the other on the nearby Mountain. After clear-cutting the ancient forest surrounding his mountain retreat to improve his view of the sea, he decided he did not like Tangier after all, and moved to Spain. Others of the deposed royal circle made Tangier their home, such as the exceedingly rich Mahdî al-Manabbhî, former Minister of War and devotee of all things British.

These displaced notables introduced a worldly element into Tangier, challenging the authority of the old Riffian families who for generations had maintained a grip on power. Well-traveled and familiar with modern ways, open to a dialogue with Europeans, they also placed their imprint on the town. They inserted themselves in the economic sphere, building alliances across communal boundaries, deploying their capital and linking up with non-Muslim investors to launch new building projects, putting aside ancient religious and tribal loyalties in search of new forms of wealth. They too were participants in the transformation of Tangier, although their role has been underplayed by historians who have ignored local entrepreneurs and concentrated instead on the more visible foreigners.[24]

THE BENI IDER QUARTER IN 1900

In 1900, the Beni Ider quarter was one of fourteen subdivisions of the city.[25] The source of its name is a matter of debate. Some quarters in Tangier were named for sites located within them—Dâr al-Barûd, for example, the site of an ancient powder magazine— while other quarters were named after the tribes who settled there after the Muslim retaking of the city. The Beni Ider is a tribe of the Jbala region to the south of Tangier. Because this tribe participated in the reconquest, it has been widely assumed that the quarter was named for them, although no sources actually corroborate this.

Another story circulating in Tangier is that the quarter was named for the Jewish Benider family of Tetuan. Abraham Benider was born in Tetuan in the early eighteenth century, lived in Tangier and Gibraltar, and went to London in 1734 as the interpreter for a Moroccan embassy. His son, Jacob, served the governor of Gibraltar in negotiations with Morocco over commercial matters in 1767. Later, Jacob was appointed Vice-Consul of Great Britain in Tangier, Tetuan, and Salé, where he collected customs duties on British ships entering Moroccan ports. In 1772, he was working for the Moroccan sultan, this time carrying letters to London announcing the expulsion of foreign merchants from Tetuan. The Beniders were typical of a small but influential group of Moroccan "court Jews" who had worked their way upward through their skills at diplomacy and capital accumulation.[26] Given the importance of the Benider family, it is conceivable that the quarter was named after them, although a firm connection is yet to be established. Names are important for many reasons, but mainly because they reflect attitudes. Whether it was the Jewish Benider family or the Muslim tribe that gave its name to the quarter is less important than the fact that ownership of the name is claimed by two different communities, each having, in its own eyes, a reasonable justification.[27]

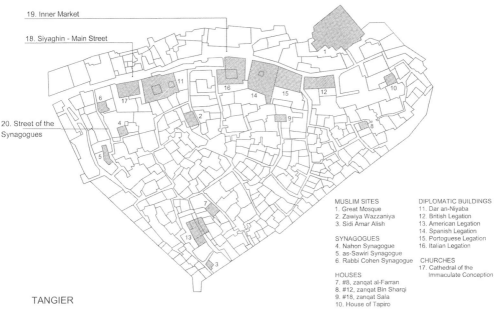

19. Inner Market

18. Siyaghin - Main Street

20. Street of the
Synagogues

11

16   14   15   12   10

6   17

4   2   9

5

7

13

3

TANGIER

MUSLIM SITES
1. Great Mosque
2. Zawiya Wazzaniya
3. Sidi Amar Alish

SYNAGOGUES
4. Nahon Synagogue
5. as-Sawiri Synagogue
6. Rabbi Cohen Synagogue

HOUSES
7. #8, zanqat al-Farran
8. #12, zanqat Bin Sharqi
9. #18, zanqat Sala
10. House of Tapiro

DIPLOMATIC BUILDINGS
11. Dar an-Niyaba
12. British Legation
13. American Legation
14. Spanish Legation
15. Portoguese Legation
16. Italian Legation

CHURCHES
17. Cathedral of the
    Immaculate Conception

Plan of the Beni Ider quarter

The Beni Ider was the largest and most important quarter of the *madîna,* encompassing some of Tangier's most prestigious sites, such as the Great Mosque, the diplomatic legations, two Muslim shrines, and almost all of its synagogues. The surface area within the walls is 26 hectares, and 6 of them belong to the Beni Ider, about 23 percent of the whole. Edouard Michaux-Bellaire, writing in 1921, said that the Beni Ider quarter was "the most important" of the *madîna,* covering the entire southern part of the old city from the main street of the Siyâghîn to the southern ramparts, and including the Inner Market (*sûq al-dâkhil*) and the Great Mosque.[28]

Five exits led outward from the quarter: two leading to the main street, one to the Inner Market, two others onto the street leading to the port, and the last leading to the street along the ramparts. All the principal streets of the quarter met at its center, forming a key intersection. The ample street network, coupled with the numerous exits, made it one of the most porous parts of the city. It was the preferred place to live because of its proximity to markets, the port, and the gate leading to the hinterland. Another important feature was an abundance of water in a city famous for its droughts. The principal underground water conduit of Tangier ran down the length of the main street that formed one edge of the quarter, while two fountains along the way served its inhabitants. Because of its steeply descending topography, the Beni Ider also enjoyed good drainage and freedom from the foul odors that plagued other parts of the town. An exception was the lowest part of the quarter, close to the port, marked on a seventeenth-century map as "the Common Sewer."[29]

Maps made during the English occupation of Tangier show the Beni Ider quarter divided into plots ("fruitlands") assigned to agricultural purposes; housing was less dense here than elsewhere in the town, and there was much open space. The quarter remained relatively empty throughout the eighteenth century. The toponym first appears in the records of the religious endowments or habûs [pl. ahbâs] in 1812. Thereafter it appears often, and by the mid-nineteenth century it was completely built up and had become one of the more populous quarters of the town.[30]

Although it was primarily a residential quarter, the Beni Ider contained important religious, commercial, and diplomatic sites. In 1889, Budgett Meakin, owner and editor of the English-language Times of Morocco, took an imaginary tour around the town that was published in the columns of his newspaper.[31] His "Stroll Around Tangier " mentions all parts of the madîna, but it was especially detailed about the neighborhood of the Beni Ider, where his newspaper's offices were located. Meakin points out legations, a theater, and bread ovens, showing that in addition to residences, the quarter had a strong commercial component with an ethnically mixed ownership that offered a wide range of services. (See Appendix: Meakin's List).

The large number of places of worship in the quarter reflected its religious diversity: the Great Mosque anchored its southern periphery, the Cathedral of the Immaculate Conception buttressed its eastern flank, the zâwiya (sanctuary) of sharîfs of Wazzân was located at its geographical center, and an entire street was lined with synagogues. The synagogues ranged in style from the exquisite Masaat Moshe, built by the wealthy Nahon banking family and modeled after the El Tránsito of Toledo, to the tiny hole-in-the wall prayer room of a humble rabbi. Despite this impressive inventory of religious sites, the quarter offered little to satisfy the orientalist imagination, since—from the outside, at least—its main attributes were its tortuous turnings and blind walls. But with Meakin's guide in hand, the fanciful tourist could walk its streets and conjure up life behind the blank façades.

The diversity of the Beni Ider quarter was also reflected in the street names that suggested a pastiche of ownership: zanqat (alley) Toledano, zanqat Mawlây al-Tayyib, zanqat Carambo. The polyglot nature of the street names was not by accident; over the years, Christians and Jews had acquired houses and empty lots in the Beni Ider adjacent to Muslim-owned property, thus planting their feet firmly in the quarter. The inspectors of the religious endowments had contributed to this tangling of ethnicities by permitting non-Muslims to acquire properties from the habûs, the most important property-owner in the town. All parts of the social spectrum were represented in the Beni Ider, from the rich to the very poor, and including Muslims, Christians, and Jews.[32]

While human diversity was one feature of the quarter, another was the juxtaposition of architectural styles, with Western forms competing and merging with local building types in a fusion of aesthetic elements that foreshadowed the hybrid colonial architecture later produced in Morocco's cities under the French Protectorate.[33] Balustrades, balconies, ornamental doors, archways, exterior windows, and shutters borrowed from the southern Mediterranean vocabulary made their appearance alongside the austere façades and simple shapes of the older courtyard houses. Cross-fertilization in the Beni Ider was aided by the fact that people lived cheek-by-jowl, with ideas passing quickly from one homeowner to another. Although no one aesthetic emerged, a constellation of similar ideas gained currency and reappeared in various settings. The following survey of some of the representative building types in the quarter around 1900 shows how building practices reflected the tastes of a rapidly Europeanizing and multi-ethnic society.

HOUSING THE DIPLOMATS

The most monumental structures in the Beni Ider quarter were the diplomatic offices-cum-residence. Most of the legations were clustered around the edge of the Inner Market, with the exception of the American Legation located deep inside the quarter. In their design and decor, the legations represent the intermingling of Moroccan and European styles at the most sumptuous level; in fact, they represented a new typology in the *madîna*: "urban palaces" as compared with the surrounding houses of more modest proportions. These properties passed into European hands through various quiet means, since most of them were acquired in an era when foreigners were not officially permitted to buy property in Morocco.

The American Legation is a case in point. In 1797, Sultan Sulaymân (r. 1792–1822), eager for the foreign diplomats to settle in Tangier, ordered the pasha of the town to "lend" the American representative a house "on the main street" so that he could live "like the other consuls."[34] Perhaps this was the "horrid house" that Consul James Simpson referred to in 1816, when he pleaded with his superiors in Washington for funds to purchase a "National House...fitted in a state of elegance" like the other diplomatic residences.[35] This request was apparently denied. However, in 1821 Sultan Sulaymân, perhaps having second thoughts, granted the American consul the right to live "rent-free" in a different house deep inside the Beni Ider quarter, and gave him permission to make improvements to the building at the consul's own expense. This building, now known as the Old American Legation, is located on the street that eventually came to be called *zanqat Amarika*—the Street of America.

While the consul had full use of the property, its was still officially owned by the Moroccan government.[36] Succeeding American diplomats added to the building at every opportunity, and eventually it became a sprawling warren of forty-plus rooms, anterooms, pavilions, and courtyards connected by an overhead passageway that spanned the street. Some additions were paid for out of the diplomatic operating budget, while others were made from the consul's own pocket, further confusing the question of ownership. Was the building U.S. government property, the private property of the resident foreign representative, the property of the Moroccan government, or a mixture of all three? Finally, in 1891, Consul-General Felix Mathews, born in Tangier and wise in local ways, succeeded in gaining full legal ownership of the property for the U.S. government by extracting a *mulkîya*, or title deed, from the Moroccan authorities based on his "intimate friendship" with the governor. He touted his victory in a letter to Washington, claiming "the site of this building is the best and healthiest in the town, situated in the most elevated place with a magnificent view of the bay, Straits, and back country."[37] A contemporary photograph shows a large and comfortable draw-

The courtyard of the Old American Legation

ing room furnished with a forest of chairs, tables, and commodes in the latest Victorian fashion. The American Legation was a looming presence in the heart of Beni Ider, a clear example of the centrality of the diplomatic function to the life of the town.[38]

On the exterior, the diplomatic buildings stood out from the rest of the urban fabric because of their distinctive size and regular fenestration, so different from the surrounding Moroccan houses; on the interior, however, their basic form was often simply a variant of the native courtyard house. They were embellished with elements that were both foreign and familiar, with many references to the local building culture. Covered galleries, overhanging balconies on the upper floors, the use of pointed and horseshoe arches and stone paving, brilliant mosaics (*zulaij*), and carved plaster bands (*jibs*) gave color and texture. The Spanish Legation, for example, greeted the visitor with an ornate stone entryway and an inner courtyard with neoclassical columns, much like an elegant Madrid apartment house. The British Consulate, also built according to a courtyard plan, had an interior English garden "in which the trees and shrubs had grown to such a size that flowers could no longer be cultivated."[39] The garden was used to house a menagerie that included, at various times, a leopard, gazelles, wild sheep, and a boar. The Portuguese Legation was a courtyard house of refined proportions. Access to the second floor was via a grand staircase located directly opposite the principal entryway. Lodged between the old English and Spanish consular buildings, it had served as the Portuguese Legation since 1780, making it the oldest diplomatic building in continual use.[40] The Italian Legation in the Inner Market represents a type that was a distinct departure from other buildings of the diplomatic genre. A side entrance led into a long lateral corridor, with the ground floor divided into individual shops, while the second floor housed diplomatic offices. Its long façade, with a double row of tall windows overlooking the busy street, gave the impression of an extroverted building standing in sharp contrast to the more usual introverted courtyard type.

The architecture of the diplomatic houses drew on different aspects of Mediterranean sensibility, and their semipublic nature meant that their novelties were on display. Indoor plumbing, the assignment of specific rooms for a specific use, closets and wardrobes, even the use of chairs and tables, were unfamiliar innovations, not to speak of the pianos, paintings, and other furnishings that were de rigueur in the diplomatic household. Over time, and especially as private wealth became more commonplace in Tangier, the culture of bourgeois comfort introduced and propagated by European diplomats became widely diffused throughout middle-class society as the standard to which upwardly mobile families of all ethnicities aspired.

Courtyard of the Portuguese Legation

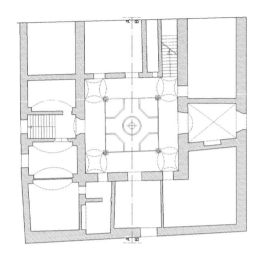

Top, right: Ground-floor plan, Portuguese Legation

Middle: Section of the Portuguese Legation

Below, right: Façade of the Italian Legation showing fenestration

Below: The façade of the Italian Legation facing the Little Market (*al-sûq al-saghîr*)

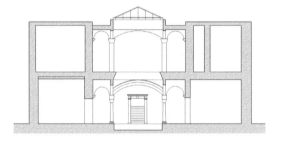

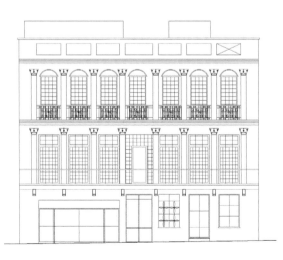

The building known as Dâr al-Niyâba exemplifies the processes whereby diplomatic architecture became a medium for expressing the heteroclite taste identified with premodern Tangier. This edifice is so old that its origins have been forgotten. It may have been built during the Portuguese occupation and somehow escaped destruction by the English in the seventeenth century.[41] In 1816, the building was given by the Moroccan government to the French to serve as their consulate. An 1830s inventory describes it as having a large open courtyard surrounded by four "arabesque " columns in brick; on the second floor, an apartment with an office, a commodious *salon de compagnie*, a dining room, and windows with "a view across the Strait." Despite these amenities, the French diplomats who lived there never considered the building sufficiently grand, and in 1850 it reverted to the Moroccan government to house the Moroccan Ministry of Foreign Affairs.[42] Today the structure is the location of the municipal administration of the *madîna* and is in a piteously dilapidated state, despite its historical distinction. It remains a prime example of the cross-fertilization typical of the quarter—a building that passed back and forth between foreign and local hands, absorbing stylistic elements from each.

Top, left: Ground-floor plan, Dâr al-Niyâba

Below, left: Section, Dâr al-Niyâba

Below, right: Courtyard of Dâr al-Niyâba

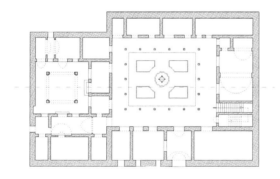

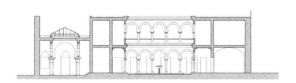

PRIVATE RESIDENCES

In the late eighteenth century, the Italian traveler Samuel Romanelli described a household that belonged to Jews and was typical of "middling" domestic architecture of that time:

> The plan of the house is a square built around a courtyard....There are no real windows, only two or three holes the size of a brick on the doorway of each room. Small mirrors hang on the walls, as well as glass lamps that are lit on the Sabbath eve. Their table looks like a stool, and there are no chairs, for they sit on the floor like the Arabs....Their roofs have parapets and are connected to one another in such a fashion that by way of the rooftops, one can go from house to house and courtyard to courtyard. The entranceway to the court[yard] is small and low so that even dwarfs would have to bow down....Near[by] are the privies stinking with excrement. Most of the houses have only one story, but a few have two or three.... Nearly all of the houses were of this plan. Only the homes of the Christian consuls were laid out in the manner of European houses.[43]

Fifty years later, the change was striking, and genuinely sumptuous houses were being built in the Beni Ider quarter. A visitor noted in 1863 that houses of the Jewish elite "were well supplied with European furniture and ornamental works."[44] In 1878, a Muslim named Muhammad al-Zuwwâq paid the truly princely sum of 1,159 *mithqâl*s to repair a house in the Beni Ider quarter.[45] Some of these luxurious houses are still in use, and a comparison between them and their earlier prototypes allows us to visualize

Plan and sections, house no. 8, rue du Four (*zanqat al-Farrân*)

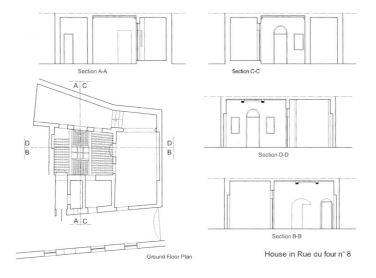

Section A-A

Section C-C

Section D-D

Section B-B

Ground Floor Plan

House in Rue du four n° 8

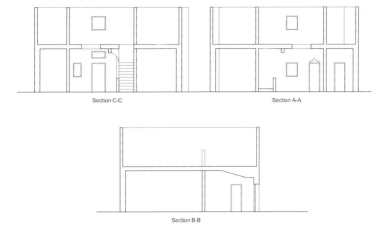

Section C-C   Section A-A

Section B-B

Sections, house no. 12, *zanqat* Bin Sharqî

how the simple, one-storied courtyard house evolved into its elaborate and multistoried variant.

The house at No. 8 Zanqat al-Farrân is probably closest to the "primitive" type that existed before 1860. The house consists of a single story with the rooms arranged around the courtyard in somewhat symmetrical manner, with a direct access to the outside. The courtyard itself is more or less rectangular, with the outer wall following the outline traced by the street. The house located at No. 12, Zanqat Bin Sharqî, is also of this type, but a second story has been added. A more fully developed example of the courtyard type is the house of Hamîd Bin `Abd al-Sadîq at No.18, Zanqat Salé. Located at the end of a cul-de-sac, this large mansion belongs to one of the oldest and most prestigious Muslim families of Tangier. A three-story edifice built around 1900, the house is notable because of its elegant proportions and rich interior decoration in the form of carved stonework on the columns and colored glass inserts around doors and windows. On the ground level, the staircase is off to one side, maximizing interior space. A balcony enclosed by wrought-iron railings surrounds the courtyard at each interior level.

An unusual feature of this house is the *minzah*, a separate windowed compartment set atop the flat roof and reached by a small staircase, where the family members would pass the evening during the hot summer months. The house also had a private *hammâm* (bathing room) and a glass roof over the courtyard to protect it from rain. The Bin `Abd al-Sadîq house, along with many other houses built in the Beni Ider quarter during the last third of the nineteenth century, is distinguished by the use of modern methods of construction. Iron structural beams in the ceilings, arches made of brick, and walls and floors made of reinforced concrete appear in this and other houses of the quarter, showing the influence of materials and techniques imported from Europe. Even the use of wrought-iron railings is an innovation; the same feature in a Fez house of the same period would have been made of wood. The *hammâm* was also unusual and

Section of the house of Bin `Abd al-Sadîq, *zanqat* Salé

Courtyard of the house of Bin `Abd al-Sadîq

required a sophisticated system for storing and delivering hot water. The *minzah* was a truly sumptuous appurtenance and a sign of considerable wealth. Used mainly by the men of the family, it was the setting for late-night conversations and poetry readings, the entertainments of a leisured class.

A final example of the evolution of the courtyard type is the house of the Spanish painter José Tapiró y Baró (1836–1913), a friend of the renowned Spanish painter Mariano Fortuny. Tapiró first visited Tangier with Fortuny in 1871 and returned often, eventually acquiring his own house in the Beni Ider quarter. Remodeled to suit the painter's needs, his house has survived in remarkably good condition and is a stunning example of a successful marriage of European and Moroccan styles. It is a courtyard house with a side stairway, but there the conformity ends. The many apertures that punctuate the façade and let in light, the Spanish tiles that add brilliant color to the dark interior surfaces, the ornate woodwork, all speak of a sense of refinement and love of color. This jewel box of a house represents a cultural syncretism inspired by the Spanish Baroque but tempered by the austerity of the Moorish courtyard house—a *madîna* dwelling adapted to suit the tastes of a European aesthete.[46]

`Abd Samâd Skîrij, son of the historian Muhammad Skîrij and long-time resident of the Beni Ider quarter, helped me to understand the critical relationship between space and self-identity that existed in the minds of the residents of the quarter.[47] He told me that until the late nineteenth century, the quarter was overwhelmingly Jewish and European. Then middle-class Muslims decided to settle there to "recuperate" this choice neighborhood, and in so doing, slowly and purposefully altered its composition. The Muslims built family houses over abandoned ruins, in places where storehouses (*funduqs*) once stood, or in empty plots close to the walls. Meanwhile, Spanish workers moved into *barracas* (shacks) in the lower part of the quarter nearer to the beach. Thus a kind of de facto economic and social separation evolved: Jews concentrated in the

Plan and section of the house of the artist José Tapiró y Baró

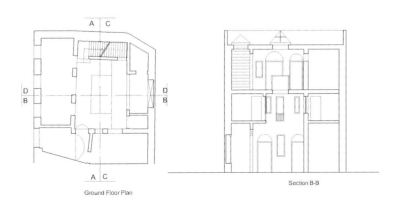

Ground Floor Plan

Section B-B

upper parts of the quarter, Muslims settled in the middle parts, diplomats along the edge, and poorer Europeans clustered in the lower parts. But Jews, Muslims, and Christians still shared the same pathways, used the same bread ovens, and patronized the same shops. While the home was a private space, a stroll down the street could mean a face-to-face encounter with a neighbor of a different religious persuasion. If there was one outstanding characteristic of the Beni Ider quarter, it was the sharing of public space among all three faiths.

The cosmopolitan atmosphere of the streets was the aspect that former residents mentioned most when recalling life in the quarter of their childhood.[48] The encounter with others in the public sphere gave no one group complete ownership over the whole. The human mix, the frequency of contact, and most of all, the overwhelming presence of densely packed religious sites important to each of the three faiths imposed a need for mutual acceptance. Rather than polarizing the inhabitants of the quarter into separate groups, the overlapping vectors of religious intensity demanded that they find a way to coexist. Over time, the residents of the quarter assented to an arrangement founded on the tacit understanding that they would not only "tolerate" but also yield actual physical space to one another. This reciprocity was an important factor that allowed a spirit of *convivencia* to take root and flourish in Tangier. The Beni Ider quarter was the principal site for observing how the disposition and use of space influenced the making of a unique social model—for that time and place—founded on a compact of mutual acceptance that the authorities did little to modify or resist.

SYNAGOGUES, MOSQUES, AND CHURCHES

What religious monuments symbolized this spatial reciprocity? The numerous syna-gogues of the quarter are barely identifiable as houses of worship from the exterior. They were "private" in the sense that their owner was usually a patron who regarded the synagogue as his personal property. Each synagogue had its own group of regulars, who, together with the patron and his family, formed a tight social network that could be activated beyond the walls of the synagogue, in business, in politics, and in mar-riage. In Tangier, the synagogue was a definer of social status and an extension of one's persona. The synagogue owned by the Sharîqî family from Essaouira (Mogador), who settled in Tangier in the late eighteenth century, exemplifies this constellation of val-ues. The family bought a house in the Beni Ider and then acquired the adjoining prop-erty. On the combined parcels they built the largest Jewish house of worship in the *madîna*. The building was dedicated in 1863 and named *Shaarit Yosef* ("The Remnant of Joseph") after the head of the family, but the Jews of Tangier called it the Synagogue as-Sawîrî, "the synagogue of the man from Mogador," underscoring the non-local origins of its founder.[49]

Shaarit Yosef, like most Moroccan synagogues, is a rectangular room measuring approximately 40 x 25 feet on which a certain code of order has been imposed. On the eastern-facing wall is the Holy Ark (*aron ha-kodesh*) containing the sacred scrolls of law. On the wall opposite is the *tevah*, the rostrum where the prayer-leader stands. The rest of the room is filled with freestanding benches, while a separate section for women occupies the mezzanine. The building was constructed of masonry and re-inforced concrete using modern techniques, and no expense was spared. This was the synagogue of a *parvenu*, an Arabic-speaking Jew from the south of Morocco, whose provincial origins were overlooked by the more "worldly" Spanish-speaking Jews of Tangier because of his generosity and civic mindedness.

Nearby and rivaling it was *Maasat Moshe*, a synagogue built in 1878 by the banker Moses Nahon, scion of an old Spanish-Jewish family. A simple barrel-vault structure, this synagogue is remarkable for the richness of its interior décor. The walls of ornamental stucco (*jibs*) are covered with intricate floral designs and Arabic script in the *mudéjar* style. The references to al-Andalus announced that the patron was a man of taste and refinement. The contrast between this synagogue and *Shaarit Yosef* is striking. One spoke of old wealth and Iberian roots, the other spoke of new money and innovation. Each had its own unique character, determined by its interior decoration, its member-ship, even the melodies that floated out into the street. And these were only two; there were half a dozen more synagogues in the Beni Ider quarter, each proposing a different social reference. The Jews of Tangier were not homogeneous, but varied according to class, place of origin, profession, and place of worship; the varieties of synagogue archi-tecture reflected their rich social complexity.

Below, left: Interior of the Sawiri synagogue

Below, right: Section of the Sawiri synagogue

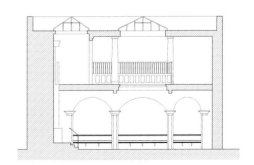

Muslim space in the Beni Ider is represented by two monuments that also demonstrate extremes: on the one hand, the elaborate *zâwiya* (lodge) and tomb of the Wazzânî *sharîf*s, a family known throughout Morocco; and on the other, the modest shrine of a popular local saint, Sîdî `Amr`Alîsh. Although their origins and size differ, both places are connected to the history of Tangier, and their stories indicate how events inside the Beni Ider quarter contributed to shaping the image of the greater city.

The Wazzânîyya brotherhood, or *tarîqa*, was the most powerful religious confederacy in the north of Morocco in the nineteenth century. Located in the small hill town of Wazzan amid a fertile agricultural region, the *sharîf*s of Wazzan garnered great power during the eighteenth century. With their reputation for saintliness and their negotiating skills, they became major allies of the ruling 'Alawî dynasty. They even extended

Above: Interior of the Nahon synagogue

Below: Section of the Nahon synagogue

Opposite: Doorway of the Wazzânîyya lodge

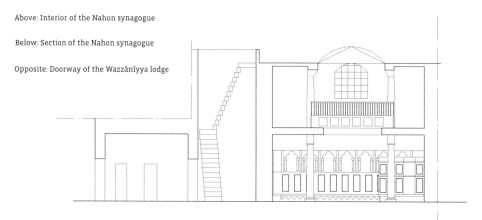

their authority into Algeria, where they commanded a lucrative network of lodges.[50] By the mid-nineteenth century, their interests had spread to Tangier, where they acquired extensive properties, including a large house in the *madîna* called Dâr al-Damâna (House of Refuge), and a mosque complex in the Beni Ider. In the 1850s the head of the family was Mawlay `Àbd al-Salâm, an eccentric character who prided himself on his friendly relations with foreigners. He preferred Tangier and its cosmopolitan environment to provincial Wazzan, and eventually settled there. Budgett Meakin considered him one of the more exotic sights on his "stroll" about Tangier:

> If the saint was at home, we would find him uncomfortably perched on a chair in some old French uniform, in a semi-European looking room; neither black nor comely, but nearly the former and by no means approaching the latter, very agreeable when he likes.[51]

Despite his benign appearance, Mawlay `Àbd al-Salâm was a wily operator. Reading the political winds after Morocco's disastrous defeat in its 1859–60 war with Spain, he acquired French protection in the belief that it would guarantee him access to his Algerian patrimony. Meanwhile, his attraction to things foreign became an obsession. In addition to French protection, money, and uniforms, he acquired an English wife, Miss Emily Keene, who wrote about their strange alliance in a remarkable memoir entitled *The Story of My Life*.[52] The *sharîf*'s marriage with a non-Muslim estranged him even further from his family, and rounded out the tragicomic aspects of his life. His political capital evaporated when his relations with the *makhzan* soured, hastening a decline caused by alcoholism and ill health. His shortcomings, however, were not evident to his many followers, who still considered him a great saint. They flocked to him while he was alive and created a tumult when he died. Emily describes his raucous funeral in Tangier in 1892:

> The crowd was so dense that I was told one could have walked from the *zowia* [the house where he died] to Mulay Taib's mosque [in the Beni Ider quarter] on the people's heads....Men sobbed aloud, women became hysterical and tore their hair...men rushed to re-cover them with the *haik* (cloak)....People fainted and were with difficulty rescued from being trodden underfoot.[53]

The sons of Mawlay `Àbd al-Salâm had wished for him to be buried in the holy city of Wazzân, but the *sharîf* preferred Tangier as his final resting place. His grave was dug in a chamber in the family mosque in the Beni Ider, and both the empty bier and the board used for washing the body were broken up as relics for the faithful. With the internment of Mawlay `Àbd al-Salâm, the Beni Ider mosque was transformed into a pilgrimage site. Now called the *zâwiya* of the Wazzânîyya, it became one of the principal monuments of the quarter, according to Muhammad Skîrij:

> Every Friday a group spends the night in the tomb of Sîdî `Abd al-Salâm reading the *Dalâ'il al-Khayrât* of the Imâm al-Jazuli who was his *shaykh*. Also, a big celebra-

tion is held in this *zâwiya* on the night of the birthday of the Prophet during which delegations come from every direction and all parts of the city, and the *ashrâf* [nobility; descendents of the Prophet] are there in all their splendor. [54]

The imposing *zâwiya* is located at the geographical center of the Beni Ider, where the major streets intersect. An ornate doorway announces its presence at the street level, while its large *qubba* (dome) is easily detected from the rooftops. It is the only *zâwiya* in the quarter. Its isolation is a kind of metaphor for Mawlay `Àbd al-Salam's own estrangement, and underscores his desire to remain close to the foreigners who had befriended him.

At the other end of the spectrum is the shrine of the local saint Sîdî `Amar 'Alîsh, located in a narrow alley behind the American Legation. His full name was `Àmar bin Abî al-`Abbâs al-Rîffî al-Tafarsîtî al-Tanjî.[55] His forefathers came from "noble rural stock" and were among the warriors who retook the city from the English in the seventeenth century. The shrine is on the left-hand side of the lane, covered by a dome about 3 meters wide. Sidi `Amar died in 1842 and was buried in the family house. He was popular because of his miracle working, and because of the mystical visions he experienced. One day, according to the *Riyâdh al-Bahja,* he was making an excursion to a place known as Ghandûrî, when suddenly he bent over and picked up a poisonous snake and experienced a "confusion of mind." Fearing for his sanity, his friends put him in chains and brought him to a saint to be cured. But the saint was furious at their actions, and ordered them to set him free, shouting: "We fill him with life, and you say he is crazy!"[56]

Doorway of the tomb of Sîdî `Amr `Alîsh

Sîdî `Amar was known for his defiant attitude toward authority. One day he went to the house of the military commander of Tangier, `Ali bin `Abd al-Sadîq, also located in the Beni Ider quarter, and knocked at the door, calling out: "Whoever has money may enter, but if he has none, he should go away." His arrogant disdain for both wealth and position endeared him to the common people, and his tomb became the scene of popular night vigils, earning him the title of "the *faqîh* (teacher) of Saturday night."[57]

The two Muslim sites in the Beni Ider represent distinct opposites: the richly endowed *zâwiya* of the Wazzânî nobility and the simple tomb of the eccentric holy man who scorned money and power. Sîdî `Amar came out of a cultural milieu that was urban and local, while the *sharif*s of Wazzân were interlopers whose power base was distant and tribal. So we are reminded that the forms of religious experience and the potential sites of worship available in the Beni Ider to the Muslim believer, as well as to his Jewish counterpart, covered a broad spectrum of possibilities.

Finally, our list of monumental buildings would not be complete without mentioning the Cathedral of the Immaculate Conception, maintained by the Franciscan Order of Friars, located in the Beni Ider and the only Christian house of worship within the *madîna*. In 1871, the Spanish government bought the property, the former Swedish consulate, and converted it into a church. Nestled between a Jewish synagogue and the Moroccan Ministry of Foreign Affairs, the church was inaugurated in October 1881. Its location on the main street celebrated the central place of the Catholic faith in Tangier's public life. It also reflected the increasing size of a European population that was overwhelmingly Spanish. The building was a simple basilica with an entry ornamented in the *mudéjar* style; a bell tower displaying a clock thrust itself into the skyline.[58]

Padre José Lerchundi, a Catholic missionary and scholar, headed the Franciscan mission at the time.[59] Under his direction, the Franciscans worked their way into the social fabric of the town through their patronage of schools, a hospital, a soup kitchen, and a printing press, putting aside blatant proselytizing in favor of good works. The church attracted worshippers from "all social classes," but they were mainly from the Spanish working class, and on one Sunday morning in 1888, three separate masses had to be held to accommodate all the worshippers.[60] The Spanish ambassador declared that "The Roman Catholic Church in Morocco is under the special patronage and protection of Spain," and other nations ceded to his claim without much argument.[61]

The peal of church bells announcing the hour of the mass was a regular feature of *madîna* life for years. Unlike other Moroccan towns where the ringing of church bells was forbidden, in Tangier the practice was protected by the consuls. The Cathedral was not simply neutral space; like other European institutions, it too emitted an aura of safety. In 1912, when France declared its Protectorate over Morocco, the sultan's troops in Tangier mutinied and refused to take an oath of loyalty to the new regime. Fearing for their lives, the soldiers sought refuge in the cathedral.[62] Complex attitudes toward the religion of the other did not inhibit boundary-crossing in times of trouble.

THEORIZING THE MULTIETHNIC QUARTER

Around the Muslim Mediterranean, in cities both ancient and new, the second half of the nineteenth century was a time of explosive change. In port cities such as Alexandria, Salonica, Beirut, Istanbul, Algiers, and Tunis, minority communities radically repositioned themselves vis-à-vis the majority. In the back streets of the city, where for generations Muslims, Jews, and Christians had worked out a modus vivendi, old contracts based on notions of hierarchy and subordination were being replaced by new social compacts premised on principles of class, wealth, and economic prowess. An implicit acceptance of hybridity—always part of the scene—suddenly moved into the foreground as the leitmotif of a new state of affairs. Cultural borrowings and the breaching of borders once considered fixed and now turned malleable became a topic of public discussion and debate.

In Tangier, a similar social revolution was taking place. New money emerged from rural, minority, and foreign origins and began to operate across ethnic and religious lines, accelerating the effects of an already perturbed social order. This revolution could be seen at many levels, but its most patent expression was in the streets and neighborhoods of the city, where alien "intrusions" were readily being absorbed into local use. Thus the "horrid green shutters" became part of the Moroccan vernacular, to the displeasure of those who worried about keeping things separate and pure. The rapid evolution in taste and values was true not only for Tangier; it was part of a larger and exceedingly complex social and historical process that was engulfing the Mediterranean region as a whole, and its Muslim parts in particular.

Postcolonial thinkers have theorized hybridity as a strategy for negating the effects of domination by adopting new vernaculars that separated the colonizer from the colonized and kept the former at bay.[63] But eclecticism and acceptance of the unfamiliar were not only defense mechanisms; they were also positive strategies adopted by the new native middle class that allowed it to profit from an era of opportunity. Through their willingness to host a spectrum of people, ideas, and physical forms, native Moroccans, both Muslim and Jewish, absorbed authoritative paradigms from the West and transformed them into localisms. They tried to overcome some of the worst effects of an incipient colonization by bridging the gap between themselves and the outside, and in the process, disrupted ancient hierarchies of order. Indeed, in Tangier it was often difficult to tell who or what was "native" and who or what was "foreign." Was the Beni Ider house, with its balconies and balustrades, any less Moroccan than the austere exterior of the *qasba* palace? Was the Spanish cigarette worker any less of a *tanjawi* than the Riffian muleteer? A mingling of tastes and genres blurred social categories, and the old fault lines that separated foreigner from native, Jew from Muslim, city-dweller from countryman became less salient.

Behind this tolerance were important structural factors, including the near-absence of the state in regulating local affairs. Tangier stood in sharp contrast with cities of the interior, where, under the watchful eye of the state and the religious establishment, a strict separation was enforced. Tangier was considered liminal space, too distant and foreign, rarely visited by sultans, and widely perceived to be different from the rest of Morocco. Freedom from centralized control allowed minority-majority relations to be far more relaxed and locally determined. As we have seen, local officials not only removed barriers to mixing, they sometimes inadvertently encouraged it by facilitating the means that allowed Christians, Muslims, and Jews to live side-by-side. The attitude of those in charge of the religious endowments (habûs) was central to this process; driven more by the thirst for profit than by scruples, officials of the habûs at the end of the nineteenth century began to concede properties for all sorts of commercial and non-commercial endeavors to the highest bidder, regardless of his religious affiliation.[64]

The human makeup of the town was another factor promoting hybridity. The resident diplomats, the swarms of tourists and travelers, the prevalence of gens de passage associated with a port environment created an open attitude toward outsiders. In a sense, they were the lifeblood of the town, driving its commercial success. Paradoxically, the constant stream of new faces not only undermined feelings of exclusivity, but also forged a sense of local identity. The cafés with their incessant talk in many languages, the newspapers in correspondence with the exterior, the many sites of sociability where people could meet at all hours of the day, contributed to the cosmopolitan mood. As Simon Levy has written, Tangier was a place where the grocery store owner could easily speak four languages.[65] Local people took pride in their sophistication and knowledge of the outside world. Architecture reflected this heterogeneity, with its repertoire of styles, its references to other times and places, its abandonment of strict codes and usages. Ironically, the diffusion of taste produced a strong feeling of the local; to be of Tangier was to be at home in the world.

This is not to say that the mix of elements that made up this diverse social world coexisted in perfect tranquility—far from it. All this rubbing of the elbows came at a cost. We cannot ignore the conflicts and injuries that emerged from so much close living. The weekly press documented the fistfights and stabbings, the petty snatches and daring robberies, the demonstrations and protests that resulted from the intense mixing of peoples, religions, and social classes. A Jew insulted on the way to a wedding, a Christian assaulted by thugs on the main street, and a Muslim mistakenly shot at in the dark as a suspected thief made front-page news.[66] Beneath the apparent tranquility there was a simmering tension arising from disparities in wealth, belief, and social power. Tolerance may have been the rule, but only up to a certain point; after that, older loyalties came into play. The saints' tombs, the church, the synagogues, and the Jewish cemetery were all visual reminders that certain fundamental differences could never be bridged.

When we speak about hybridity, we must recognize that it takes on various forms and functions, depending on time and place. One of those functions is the promotion of social cohesion. Deplored by outsiders such as Kerdec Chény, who felt it undermined the social order, hybridity was embraced by locals for precisely the same reason, for it carved out a territory where native and non-native could meet on more or less equal terms. The Muslims of Tangier reluctantly acceded to their loss of dominance (and not without bitterness), but in the end, they were not excluded. Mixing was the inevitable result of the coming of modernity; rather than being divisive, it formed the basis for a new framework of understanding among ethnic groups. In other words, hybridity allowed for a positive redefinition of this small universe, thus opening the field of action and circumventing the stultifying culture of exclusivity that was the *raison d'être* of both the encroaching colonial order and the archaic system known as the *makhzan*. For all its drawbacks, hybridity was liberating. For that reason, above all others, it was seized upon by the people of the Tangier and made the emblem of the city of their affections.

APPENDIX: MEAKIN'S LIST OF IMPORTANT SITES IN THE BENI IDER QUARTER (1881)

Place name	Type	Community
Garat Mawlay al-Tayyib	shrine	Muslim
Bank Nahon	bank	Jewish
Franciscan church	church	European
Italian Legation	diplomatic	European
Spanish Legation	diplomatic	European
American Consulate	diplomatic	European
Portuguese Legation	diplomatic	European
British Legation	diplomatic	European
Fonda de Nicholas	fountain	European
Hotel Central	hotel	European
British Consul	house	European
Sr. Tapiró	house/studio	European
Dar al-Niyaba	office	Muslim
Times of Morocco	newspaper	European
El Eco Mauritano	newspaper	European
Gibraltar boats	office	European
Ferran Gamoori	oven	Muslim
French restaurant	restaurant	European
Franciscan school, boys	school	European
Franciscan school, girls	school	European
Jewish girls' school	school	Jewish
Zanqat Carambo	street	European
Z. Dar Portugez	street	European
D. Aflalo	street	Jewish
Z. Nahon	street	Jewish
Tawahin	street	Jewish
Z. El Mellah	street	Jewish
Z. Toledano	street	Jewish

Z. Mawlay al-Tayyib	street	Muslim
Z. Hayani	street	Muslim
Z. al-Sami'a	street	Muslim
Z. Balga	street	Muslim
Z. Darqawi	street	Muslim
Z. Furran al-Hamrani	street/oven	Muslim
Z. Furran Johnnie	street/oven	Muslim
Zawiya Mawlay al-Tayyib al-Wazzani	shrine	Muslim
Sidi `Amr `Alish	shrine	Muslim
Franciscan church	church	European
Synagogue Etz-Hayyim	synagogue	Jewish
Synagogue Nahon	synagogue	Jewish
Synagogue Shriqi	synagogue	Jewish
Synagogue Laredo	synagogue	Jewish
Theater	theater	Jewish/European

Source: *Times of Morocco*, No. 169, 2 February 1889: No.170, 9 February 1889; No. 171, 16 February 1889.

Notes

1. There are numerous studies of the impact of modernity on port cities of the Muslim Mediterranean. A good overview is Michael J. Reimer, "Ottoman-Arab Seaports in the Nineteenth Century: Social Change in Alexandria, Beirut, and Tunis," in R. Kasaba, ed. *Cities in the World System* (Westport, CT; Greenwood Press, 1991), 135–156. See also the following case studies: Zeynep Çelik, *The Remaking of Istanbul: Portrait of an Ottoman City in the Nineteenth Century* (Seattle: University of Washington Press, 1986), and by the same author, *Urban Forms and Colonial Confrontations: Algiers under French Rule* (Berkeley, CA: University of California Press, 1997); Michael J. Reimer, *Colonial Bridgehead: Government and Society in Alexandria, 1807–1882* (Boulder, CO: Westview Press, 1997); Mia Fuller, "Preservation and Self-Absorption: Italian Colonisation and the Walled City of Tripoli, Libya," in S. Slyomovics, *The Walled City in Literature, Architecture and History: the Living Medina in the Maghrib* (London: Frank Cass, 2001), 121–154; Mark Mazower, *Salonica, City of Ghosts: Christians, Muslims and Jews, 1430–1950* (London: Harper Collins, 2004). A study from a typological perspective is Attilio Petruccioli, ed., *Rethinking [the] XIXth Century City* (Cambridge, MA: Aga Khan Program for Islamic Architecture, 1998).

2. *International Encyclopedia of the Behavioral and Social Sciences*, s.v. "Hybridity."

Electronic resource: doi: 10.1016/B0-08-043076-7/00890-1. Homi K. Bhabha, "Signs Taken for Wonders: Questions of Ambivalence and Authority under a Tree Outside Delhi, May 1817," *Critical Inquiry* 12 (1985): 144–165; Nezar AlSayyad, *Hybrid Urbanism: On the Identity Discourse and the Built Environment* (Westport, CT; London: Praeger, 2001).

3. E. Michaux-Bellaire, *Tanger et sa zone*, vol. 7, *Villes et tribus du Maroc* (Paris: Ernest Leroux, 1921), 35. B. Rosenberger, "Les premières villes islamiques du Maroc: géographie et functions," in *Genèse de la ville islamique en al-Andalus et au Maghreb occidental*, Patrice Cressier et Mercedes García-Arenal, eds. (Madrid: Casa de Velasquez, 1998), 229–255, and especially pp. 230–232.

4. Michaux-Bellaire, *Tanger et sa zone*, 69.

5. Linda Colley, *Captives: Britain, Empire and the World, 1600–1850* (London: Pimlico, 2003), 24.

6. Collection of the Tangier American Legation Museum (TALM), Tangier, Morocco.

7. Ramon Lourido-Diaz, "Le Sultan Sidi Muhammad b. 'Abd Allah et l'institution de la représentation consulaire à Tanger," in *Tanger, 1800–1956: Contribution à l'histoire récente du Maroc* (Rabat: Faculté des Lettres et des Sciences humaines, 1991), 9–28.

8. British Consul John H. Drummond Hay is a prime example of a diplomat whose life became entwined with the history of Tangier. Sportsman, schemer, and shrewd observer of events, during his forty-year period of service in Morocco, he shaped an

entire era thorough his close relationships with the court, his credibility at the Home Office, and his bold interventions in local affairs. See Khalid Ben Srhir, *Britain and Morocco during the Embassy of John Drummond Hay, 1845–1886* (London and New York: Routledge Curzon, 2005).

9. J-L. Miège, "Les Réfugiés politiques à Tanger; 1796–1875," *Revue Africaine* LI, 1–2, (1957): 133.

10. *Times of Morocco*, 10 and 24 March 1888. According to the newspaper, in 1885 there were 500 Spaniards in Tangier; by 1888, the Spanish population had reached 3,000 out of a total population of 20,000–25,000. Budgett Meakin, the English editor of the *Times of Morocco*, disliked the Spanish settlers and blamed them for having introduced vice in the form of wine-shops, gambling houses, and the use of tobacco. See his *The Land of the Moors* (London: Swann Sonnenschein, 1901), 101.

11. J-L. Miège , *Le Maroc et L'Europe*, 4 vols. (Rabat: Editions La Porte, 1989) 4: 292–293. On the first of May, 1891 Tangier saw its first street demonstration led by a small group of Spanish "socialists." *Times of Morocco*, 2 May 1891.

12. Andrew Clandermond and Terence MacCarthy, *A Dictionary of Painters in Tangier* (Tangier: Black Eagle Press for the Lawrence-Arnott Gallery, 2003), passim.

13. The "rescue" of the Jews from the Portuguese in the sixteenth century was recorded in a special Purim text. See Abraham I. Laredo,"Les Pûrîm de Tanger," *Hespéris* XXXV (1948): 193–203, and by the same author and J.M. Millás, "Las lápidas sepulcrales antropomorfas de los cementarios israelitas de Alcazarquivir y Tánger, *Sefarad*, 9,2 (1949): 421–432. On the Portuguese invasion of Morocco in 1578 and its implantation in Moroccan memory, see Lucette Valensi, *Fables de la mémoire: la glorieuse bataille des trois rois* (Paris: Seuil, 1992).

14. Samuel Romanelli was born in Mantua in 1757 and educated in Italy before beginning the life of an itinerant scholar. He arrived in Morocco quite by accident in 1786 in the company of a merchant whom he had met in Gibraltar. He had a penchant for disaster. He lost his passport and was left stranded in the Maghrib for four years, eking out his living by working as a teacher, preacher, scribe, and accountant. His travel account written in Hebrew was first published in Berlin in 1792. References here are to the excellent English translation by Norman and Yedida Stillman, *Travail in an Arab Land* (Tuscaloosa: University of Alabama Press, 1989), 1–3, 28–31.

15. William Lempriere, *A Tour from Gibraltar to Tangier, Sallee, Mogodore, Santa Cruz, and Tarudant; and Thence over Mount Atlas to Morocco: Including a Particular Account of the Royal Harem*, 3rd ed. (Richmond, VA: William Pritchard, 1800), 5.

16. Tangier's Jews were multilingual. At home they spoke a dialect of Spanish called *haketiya* that was a mixture of Spanish, Hebrew, and Arabic; in the street, they spoke modern Spanish and dialectical Arabic; in addition, some had an ability in French and English. They also knew Biblical Hebrew, Italian, and Portuguese. The first school of the A.I.U. opened its doors in Tangier in 1864. See Michael Laskier, *The Alliance Israélite Universelle and the Jewish Communities of Morocco* (Albany: SUNY Press, 1983), Chapter 2.

17. Mohamed Kenbib, "Tanger 1767–1957," *Tribune juive*, 11, 5 (March 1994): 67.

18. Susan Gilson Miller, "Dhimma Reconsidered; Jews, Taxes, and Royal Authority in Nineteenth-Century Tangier," in *In the Shadow of the Sultan; Culture, Power and Politics in Morocco*, Rahma Bourqia and S. G. Miller, eds. (Cambridge, MA: Harvard University Press, 1999), 103–128; Joseph Bengio, and J-L. Miège "La communauté juive de Tanger dans les années 1860, 'Les Actas'," *Maroc-Europe 6* (1994):151–165; J. Bengio, "La Junta selecta: Le comité de la communauté juive de Tanger," *Maroc-Europe 6* (1994):167–214.

19. Muhammad b. Muhammad Skîrij, *Riyâdh al-bahja fî akhbâr Tanja*, Bibliothèque Nationale et archives, Rabat, MS No. 1452. Unpublished. The copy used here is from the Sbihi Library, Salé.

20. Michaux-Bellaire, *Tanger et sa zone*, 195.

21. Muhammad al-Manûnî, *Mazâhir Yaqzat al-Maghrib al-Hadîth*. 2 vols. (Casablanca: al-Mudâris, 1985): I, 102; Ben Srhir, *Britain and Morocco*, 231. In 1877, Zubayr was sent abroad to England to study civil engineering at Chatham and Woolwich. On his return, he was commended by British Consul John H. Drummond Hay as a man of "superior character" and the product of "good English training." Public Record Office (PRO), London, FO 174/144 Hay to Minister Bargash, 12 July 1880.

22. Muhammed Skîrij attended the Qayrawîyîn, the venerable mosque university of Fez, reputedly the oldest university in the Islamic world, founded in the ninth century.

23. See note 19 for bibliographical details.

24. Pierre Guillen, "Les milieux d'affaires français et le Maroc à l'aube du xxe siècle," *Revue historique* 229 (1963): 397–422. European actors are understandably more visible in the Western archives that form the main source for the rare scholarly studies of this period.

25. The evolution of the Beni Ider quarter can be traced through various documents. Municipal archives for the precolonial period are nonexistent, except for the records of the religious endowments, or *habûs* (pl. *ahbâs*). The name Beni Ider occurs with some frequency in the *habûs* records of Tangier. Newspaper reports, travelers' impressions, foreign archives, and personal memoirs are also useful. The chronicle of Muhammad Skîrij, *Riyadh al-bahja*, is invaluable. Colonial scholars offer credible insights. Georges Salmon, a member of the French-sponsored *Mission scientifique*, wrote several key articles on Tangier published in *Archives marocaines*, vols. 1 and 2, noted in the bibliography at the end of this volume.

26. Jacob Benider's story is told in Nicole S. Serfaty, *Les courtisans juifs des sultans marocains:*

hommes politiques et hauts dignitaires, XIIIe-XVIIIe siècles (Saint-Denis: Bouchène, 1999), 197–202; see also Cecil Roth, "Jacob Benider: Moroccan Envoy, 1772," *The Jewish Historical Society of England Miscellanies*, part II (1935), 84–91.Other portraits of pre-modern Moroccan "court Jews" are Daniel J. Schroeter, *The Sultan's Jew: Morocco and the Sephardi World* (Stanford: Stanford University Press, 2002), and Mercedes García-Arenal and Gerard Albert Wiegers, *A Man of Three Worlds: Samuel Pallache, a Moroccan Jew in Catholic and Protestant Europe* (Baltimore: Johns Hopkins University Press, 2003).

27. Abraham I. Laredo, *Les Noms des juifs du Maroc; Essai d'onomastique judéo-marocaine* (Madrid: Instituto B. Arias Montano, 1978), 628.

28. Michaux-Bellaire, *Tanger et sa zone*,185. On the surface area of the quarter, see *S.D.A.U. Tanger: Schéma Directeur d'aménagement urbaine* (Ministère de l'habitat et de l'aménagement du territoire, Secretariat général, Direction de l'urbanisme et de l'architecture, Division de la planification urbaine, Délégation regionale de Tanger, 1983), 529.

29. Serious water problems affected town politics. See Susan Gilson Miller, "Watering the Garden of Tangier: Colonial Contestations in a Moroccan City," in *The Walled Arab City in Architecture, Literature, and History: The Living Medina*, ed. Susan Slyomovics (London: Frank Cass, 2001): 25–50.

30. Map collection, Tangier American Legation Museum (hereafter, TALM). The originals are in the Public Record Office, London, M.P.H. 1/4,7,21,25,29,30,32,43,45,54. The *habûs* records show that the *nâdhir*, the overseer of the endowment, bought an empty lot in the Beni Ider quarter from a certain Mas`ûd al-Wariarghli for 6 *ûqîya*s in 1153/1740. Mas`ûd is a distinctly Jewish name. E. Michaux-Bellaire, *Les Habous de Tanger: Registre officiel d'actes et de documents, part 2, Analyses et extraits* (Paris: Ernest Leroux, 1914), 132. For more on the *habûs* of Tangier, see Susan Gilson Miller, "Finding Order in the City: The *Hubûs* of the Great Mosque of Tangier as an Agent of Urban Change," *Muqarnas* 22 (2005):262–280.

31. *Times of Morocco*, no. 169, 2 February 1889; no.170, 9 February 1889; no. 171, 16 February 1889.

32. Miller, "Finding Order in the City," 272–273.

33. Documented in François Béguin, *Arabisances: décor architectural et tracé urbain en Afrique du Nord 1830–1950* ([Paris]: Dunod, 1983).

34. Michaux-Bellaire, *Habous de Tanger*, part 2, 44; according to an 1808 map, this house was located behind the Swedish consulate on the Siyaghîn. See Jacques Caillé, *La Mission du Capitaine Burel au Maroc en 1808: documents en partie inédits* (Paris: Arts et Métiers Graphiques, 1953), map found between pages 86 and 87.

35. Archives of the TALM relating to the Consular Property, Simpson to the Secretary of the Treasury, July 1816.

36. The U.S. government held what was known as a *tanfîdha*, or right of occupancy; it did not constitute legal ownership. Nor was the property "a gift to the US government in 1821," as has been widely proclaimed. Rather, the U.S. government had the right to use the property at the pleasure of the *makhzan*. *Makhzan* properties were routinely handed out in this manner, as favors and rewards. See Salmon, "L'administration marocaine a Tanger," 33–34.

37. TALM, Property file, Mathews to State, 27 May 1891. The building, still owned by the U.S. Government, is now a National Historical Landmark—the only such landmark outside the United States. It is the home to a first-rate museum and research library. See http://www.legation.org.

38. The photograph was on display in the TALM Museum as of May, 2006.

39. The building was designed by an English architect and built in 1791, when James Mario Matra was consul. Hans Christian Andersen, the Danish folklorist, visited it in 1862 and wrote that "in this house there was every English convenience, even to a fireplace." L. A. E. Drummond-Hay Brooks and A. E. Drummond-Hay, *A Memoir of Sir John Drummond Hay, P.C., K.C.B., G.C.M.G., Sometime Minister at The Court of Morocco Based on His Journals and Correspondence* (London: J. Murray, 1896), 221–225.

40. Ramon Lourido-Diaz, "Le Sultan Sidi Muhammad," 21.

41. Dâr an-Niyâba means literally "The House of Representation," and refers to the house as seat of the sultan's representative in Tangier vis-à-vis the foreign powers; hence, "Ministry of Foreign Affairs" in contemporary parlance. It served that function from the mid-nineteenth century until the coming of the Protectorates in 1912. Dr. Nadia Erzini, architectural historian, makes valuable observations about its provenance in her unpublished manuscript, *Tangier as 'Diplomatic Capital' of Morocco from 1773 to 1912: A Study of the City and Its Architecture*, n.d., 44.

42. See note 40. Drawings of the site were made by the well-known French architect Pascal Xavier Coste in 1847. Coste worked in Egypt and Persia before coming to Morocco. He also contributed to the architecture of his home town Marseilles. For a discussion of Dâr an-Niyâba and Coste's mission, see Patrick Boulanger, "Le Projet de Pascal Coste pour Tanger (1847–1850), *Revue Maroc-Europe* 6 (1994), 245–254. See also *Times of Morocco*, 22 September 1900. For a study of Coste's design work in Egypt, see André Raymond, "Muhammad Alî et Pascal Coste," in *Pascal Coste ou l'architecture cosmopolite*, Daniel Armogathe et Sylviane Leprun, eds. (Paris: L'Harmattan, 1990): 24–33.

43. Romanelli, *Travail in an Arab land*, 25–26.

44. H. Guedalla, *Refutation of an anonymous article in the "Jewish World" entitled Secret History of Sir M. Montefiore's Mission to Morocco in 1863–64* (London: Darling and Son, 1880), 15. Guedalla, the former British Lord Mayor's nephew, accompanied him on his famous trip to Morocco in 1863–64.

45. Michaux-Bellaire, *Habous de Tanger*, part 2, 196.

46. Today the house is owned by Abdellah El-Gourd, jazz musician and collaborator of the African-American jazz artist Randy Weston. For information on Tapiró, see Clandermond and MacCarthy, *A Dictionary of Painters*, 281. See also *The Times of Morocco*, 15 May 1897, "A Visit to Sr. Tapiró's Studio."

47. Interview with A. Skîrij in his home, 27 June 2002.

48. I. J. Assayag wrote in his sentimental memoir of early twentieth century Tangier that in the Beni Ider quarter, *"tous les habitant, chrétiens, musulmans et juifs vivaient en étroite amitié...."* (all the inhabitants, Christian, Muslim and Jew, lived in close harmony). *Tanger...Regards sur le passé... Ce qu'il faut* (Casablanca: Najah El Jadida, 2001), 129.

49. For more background on the construction of this synagogue, see Susan Gilson Miller, "Apportioning Sacred Space in a Moroccan City: The Case of Tangier, 1860–1912," *City & Society* 13 (2001): 68–71.

50. E. Michaux-Bellaire, "La Maison d'Ouezzane," *Revue du monde musulman* 5 (1908): 23–89; George Joffé, "The Zawiya of Wazzan: Relations of Shurafa and Tribe up to 1860," in *Tribe and State: Essays in Honor of David Montgomery Hart*, G. Joffé and C. R. Pennell, eds. (Cambridgeshire: MENAS, 1991), 84–118.

51. *The Times of Morocco*, "A Stroll around Tangier," 16 February 1889.

52. Emily Keene, Shareefa of Wazan, with S. L. Bensusan, *My Life Story* (London: E. Arnold, 1911). Many accounts circulate as to how the Sharif and the English lady met. Michaux-Bellaire says that Emily was a *demoiselle de compagnie* (nanny) to a rich American family that the Sharif often visited. Another version is that they encountered each other while out riding, and yet another fancifully claimed that the Sharif spotted Emily as she sat in the window brushing her luxuriant red hair. The marriage was not a happy one, despite Emily's claims to the contrary, and it ended in bitterness and recrimination.

53. Ibid., 252.

54. Skîrij, *Riyadh al-Bahja*, unpaged.

55. There are different spellings and pronunciations of the name by which he was popularly known. Skîrij calls him Amr al-'Alîsh, while Michaux-Bellaire refers to him as Alilech (*Tanger et sa zone*, 331).

56. Skîrij, *Riyadh al-Bahja*, unpaged.

57. Ibid. Skîrij reports that the *qubba* of Sîdî Amr was ordered built by the *qâ'id* Bû Silhâm, who was an admirer of his miracle-working.

58. The Franciscans arrived in Marrakesh in the thirteenth century and established a mission in Tangier after the Portuguese conquest in 1471. They were expelled by the English in 1662, who purged the town of all "Romish" influences. They returned in the middle of the eighteenth century and established a hospice in the Beni Ider quarter between the Wazzânî *zâwiya* and the Jewish "*mellah*" (street of the synagogues), according to Michaux-Bellaire. (*Tanger et sa zone*, 351). Along with other Christian missionaries,

they were again expelled in the time of Sultan Yazid (reigned 1790–92) but returned in 1794 and have been there ever since. Not all Spanish residents were "good" Catholics; some were decidedly anti-clerical and refused to either register births or allow priests to officiate at their burials. The bells of the Cathedral have been silent for years. A recent renovation removed them altogether and replaced the bell tower with a plain copper-clad dome.

59. Lerchundi arrived in Morocco in 1862 as a young priest and was sent to Tetuan, where he studied Arabic. In 1870 he published the first grammar book of dialectal Moroccan Arabic entitled *Rudimentos del árabe vulgar, que se habla en el Imperio de Marruecos, con numerosos ejercicios y temas aplicados a la teoría*. A great admirer of Moroccan culture, he possessed a liberal mentality that endeared him to *tangerinos* of all persuasions. Isaac Laredo, *Memorias de un viejo Tangerino* (Madrid: C. Bermejo, 1935), 155–158; See also A. Peteiro Frieire, "El Padre Lerchundi, hombre de iglesia y renovador de la misión franciscana de Marruecos," in G. C. Moralejo and R. Lourido Diaz, *Marruecos y el padre Lerchundi* (Madrid: MAPFRE, 1996), 35–52; R. Lourido-Diaz, "Jose Lerchundi y las relaciones culturales Hispano-marroquies de finales del XIX," *Hespéris-Tamuda*, XXX,1 (1992): 39–66.

60. *Times of Morocco*, 11 February 1888.

61. *Times of Morocco*, 12 October 1889.

62. *Times of Morocco*, 24 June 1912.

63. Bhabha, "Signs Taken for Wonders," 154–157, 160.

64. Miller, "Finding Order in the City," 273–274.

65. Anonymous, "Le judaisme tangérois et son essor au xixe siècle," unpublished manuscript, private collection, n.d.

66. Articles frequently appeared in the local press documenting acts of violence across communal bounds. See, for example, *Times of Morocco*, 12 October 1889, "Brutal Assault"; 31 May 1890, "Murder at Tangier"; 4 October 1890, "Attempted Murder"; 16 May 1891, "A Fracas in the Sok"; 21 October 1891, "Another Moor Murdered"; 20 May 1899, "An Arbitrary Act"; 5 September 1903, "Hooliganism"; 2 April 1904, "Jew Baiting in Effigy"; 11 March 1905, "Outrage"; 24 November 1906, in the "Weekly Notes" column, an article describing "a scuffle between a Sharif and a Spaniard." On the other hand, popular attitudes disfavored conflict and opinion veered toward finding "an identity of interest" between Muslims and Europeans. An editorial entitled "The Moors of Tangier" that appeared shortly after the establishment of the French and Spanish Protectorates, when the status of Tangier was as yet undetermined, lauded the concept of peaceful coexistence. (3 April 1913).

KAREN A. LEAL

6

THE BALAT DISTRICT OF ISTANBUL: MULTIETHNICITY ON THE GOLDEN HORN

Halfway up the Golden Horn, the estuary that bisects the European side of Istanbul, the district of Balat is situated between Fener, from the Greek *phanar*, meaning lighthouse, and Ayvansaray, whose name reflects the Turkish pronunciation of Blachernae Palace, built by the Byzantine emperors. The name Balat is itself a reflection of the area's Byzantine heritage; it is a corruption of the Greek term *palation*, meaning "palace."[1] Just as the Ottoman Turkish names evoke the Byzantine past that bound these areas to one another, they also remind us of the many intertwining layers of identity of those who lived there. Today the area is inhabited primarily by Muslim Turkish migrants from the Black Sea region of Turkey, but for centuries Balat was home to Jewish, Greek Orthodox, Muslim, and Armenian subjects of the Ottoman Empire. They spoke Greek, Ladino, Armenian, Turkish, and perhaps French, as they interacted daily in marketplaces, synagogues, churches, and taverns, and on the streets, reenacting the ties that established their place as inhabitants of this vividly diverse district.

THE COURT RECORDS: A MIRROR OF OVERLAPPING IDENTITIES

The boundaries separating Balat from Fener and Ayvansaray were never clearly delineated. Likewise, the daily life of the nineteenth-century residents of Balat reflects the many ways in which they were interrelated religiously, linguistically, socially, and economically. According to the Ottoman court records, in 1816 a Jewish tobacconist by the name of Karakasoğlu Hananya veled-i Yako appeared before the *kadi* (chief judge) of Istanbul to document the transfer of equipment he used in practicing his trade from a shop near Arslan Wharf in the Dibek Quarter, located outside of Balat Gate, to a shop in the el-Hac İsa Quarter of Balat, located within the city walls. When the owner of the shop in Dibek, a Jew named Hayım, decided to annex the shop to his own house, Hananya was forced to move to another shop owned by a grocer named Haleblioğlu Yaşuva v. Avram. Though their confessional identities are clear from their names, the court record denotes each of them as a Jew through the use of the term *Yehudi,* in conformity with Ottoman scribal practice. In the decree, Yaşuva vows not to force out his new tenant by increasing the rent, the new location is officially noted, and a copy of the document is delivered into Hananya's possession. Witnessing this transaction were a group of Muslim officials: the steward of the tobacconists' guild, Ömer Agha, as well as the guild elders, es-Seyyid Mustafa Agha of Bebek, es-Seyyid Mustafa Agha of Bandırma, the prefect Mustafa Efendi, and the regulations officer, es-Seyyid Abdullah Çelebi.[2]

Map of Istanbul showing the location of Balat

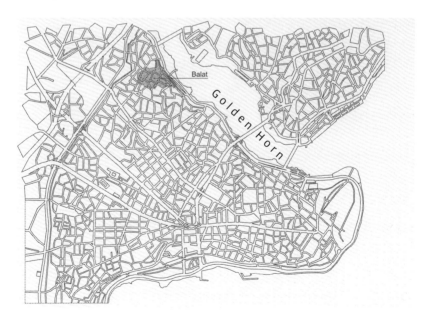

This routine transfer of property draws attention to the various ties that bound the parties to one another and to the quarters (*mahalle*s) of Balat, the district (*nahiye* or *semt*) of Istanbul where they lived and conducted business.[3] The three main actors were marked in the court record as members of the Jewish community, who most likely lived in this area before Mehmed II's conquest of Istanbul in 1453.[4] The business transaction also highlights the level of commercial activity in which Jewish merchants were engaged: leasing and renting properties, and, in this case, selling tobacco, fruits, and vegetables in stores located on the shores of the Golden Horn as well as inside the quarters of Balat within the city walls.

We must also be aware of other connections tying these men to their physical and sociocultural environment. A Jewish court operated in Balat, and non-Muslims were required to consult the Ottoman judicial system only in criminal cases. Nevertheless, there were still occasions when Jewish subjects of the empire, along with their Muslim, Greek Orthodox, and Armenian counterparts, resorted to the authority of Ottoman institutions such as the judicial system. They did this to have property transfers, matters of inheritance, and financial disputes—even ones in which only co-religionists were involved—noted in official state registers.[5]

A group of Muslim officials were present at the court proceedings: the steward, elders, and an officer of the guild to which the Jewish plaintiff belonged. Their tacit approval further imbues the transaction with a sense of legitimacy. The *kadi* court record thus points to an aspect of Karakasoğlu Hananya v. Yako's identity that was not contingent upon his religious background: namely, his membership in a guild that tied him to other tobacconists of varying confessional identities, Muslims in this case, but perhaps also Greek Orthodox Christians and Armenians as well. The legal and moral authority provided by the guild legitimizes a commercial deal he makes with a fellow Jew who is a member of yet another guild. In this small moment, multiple identities come into play, outlining the various ways that individuals could present themselves in the public sphere.

Another court case from the same year tells us something about the residential patterns of the Jewish population of Balat, though all the litigants in the matter were either Greek Orthodox or Muslim. In this instance, Yoan v. Paraşkeva, Yoan v. Hürmüz, and Andriya v. Lefter, members of the sesame oil makers' guild, filed a lawsuit against es-Seyyid Mehmed Arif Agha ibn Ismail, a proxy appearing on behalf of a Muslim woman named Şerife Fatıma Hanım ibnet el-Hac Ahmed. The lawsuit concerned an oil mill Fatıma Hanım owned in Balat. The Greek Orthodox plaintiffs had for some time rented this oil mill, located next to the Tokmak Bakery within Balat Gate, from the Muslim defendant for 15 *guruş* per month. When the mill was destroyed in a fire, the landlady wished to repossess the property and build in its place a *yehudihane*, a multistoried tenement specifically intended for Jewish families.[6] The plaintiffs argued that because this was an ancient oil mill and included in the regulations of their guild, Fatıma Hanım was legally obligated to restore the structure to its original state and rent it to them at the former price.

Muslim elders residing in Hacı İsa, Hızır Çavuş, Hammamcı Muhyiddin, and Hace Kasım Gonani, all quarters of Balat, confirmed that the oil mill had been there for nine-ty years and argued that it should be rebuilt. The court ruled accordingly and ordered the defendant Fatıma Hanım to restore the mill.[7] This decree confirms that Muslim and Greek Orthodox subjects continued to reside in Balat alongside Jews in the early nine-teenth century. It also tells us that one savvy and enterprising Muslim property owner, herself a resident of the suburb of Bebek, believed there would be more profit in con-structing a building for Jewish families than in letting her Orthodox Christian tenants keep up an oil mill.

GARDEN OR GHETTO?

These cases point to the long-time presence of Jews in Balat, and serve to remind us that Greek Orthodox, Muslims, (and Armenians, though they do not appear here) also resided and conducted business in the district, exerting an influence over its physical and social makeup. The dynamic portrayal of Balat found in the Istanbul *kadi* court records stands in sharp contrast to the scene of abject poverty and misery described by the Italian traveler Edmundo de Amicis decades later, in his travel account, *Constantinople*:

> The vast ghetta [*sic*] of Balata...winds like a disgusting serpent along the shore of the Golden Horn. I pushed on even into the most wretched alleys, in the midst of houses "encrusted with mould," like the banks in the Dantesque circle, through cross ways, where I wished for stilts and stopped my nose.[8]

De Amicis draws a sharply negative comparison between the Jewish residents of Balat and those he encountered while touring the Jewish quarter of Tangier: while the coun-tenances of the Balat Jews are drawn and "pinched," drained of all "vitality," those of Tangier are "well-rounded," with "brilliant coloring" and "piercing eyes."[9]

Another voyager who toured the area in the early twentieth century, Bertrand Bareilles, echoing de Amicis, remarked that Balat, together with Hasköy, Ortaköy, and Kuzguncuk (also districts with large Jewish populations located outside the city walls), were [some of] "the most pitiful suburbs that can be seen in Constantinople."[10] This image of filthy, poverty-stricken neighborhoods was also perpetuated by Jews. Writing in 1875, Nissim Béhar, a teacher of the French Alliance Israélite Universelle (A.I.U.), described the Jews of Balat as "seedy [in their] appearance...quick-tempered, loud, selfish, unscrupulous in their means of making money, opposed to all work, and accus-tomed to living from hand to mouth."[11] Later, a director of one of the A.I.U. schools char-acterized the area by the shore as the "true Balat," a slum looked down upon by more affluent Jews, whose air was "poisoned by an unidentifiable stench of frying, rotten eggs and herring."[12]

No ramparts had ever partitioned Jewish or any other non-Muslim subjects from the rest of Istanbul, though a section of the ancient Byzantine walls encompassing the

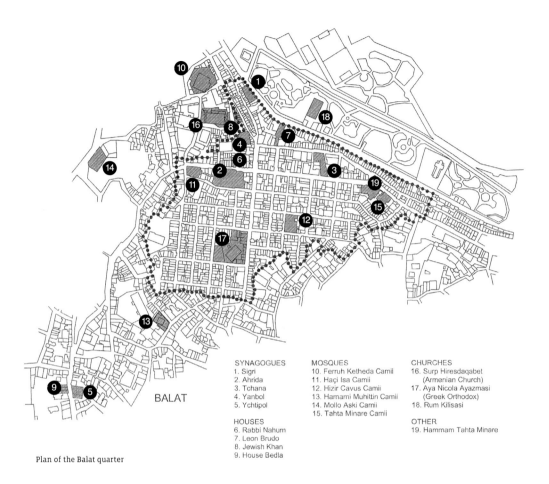

SYNAGOGUES
1. Sigri
2. Ahrida
3. Tchana
4. Yanbol
5. Ychtipol

HOUSES
6. Rabbi Nahum
7. Leon Brudo
8. Jewish Khan
9. House Bedla

MOSQUES
10. Ferruh Ketheda Camii
11. Haçi Isa Camii
12. Hizir Cavus Camii
13. Hamami Muhittin Camii
14. Mollo Aski Camii
15. Tahta Minare Camii

CHURCHES
16. Surp Hiresdaqabet
    (Armenian Church)
17. Aya Nicola Ayazmasi
    (Greek Orthodox)
18. Rum Kilisasi

OTHER
19. Hammam Tahta Minare

BALAT

Plan of the Balat quarter

city divided the district itself into two areas, Outer Balat and Inner Balat.[13] Despite the
absence of any physical dividers, by the beginning of the twentieth century Balat—
where Greek Orthodox, Armenian, and Bulgarian Orthodox churches shared space with
mosques and synagogues—came to be regarded as a poor Jewish ghetto, decrepit and
dank, its open sewers spilling their contents into the Golden Horn, with decaying fruit
scattered across the marketplace.

Why this impression? Foreign tourists to Balat frequently passed through only one
section located outside the city walls, and thus may have acquired a one-sided view of
the area. They may not have been aware of the lower population density and abundant
green spaces in the Kasturiya Quarter, or of the many refreshing gardens found in
Ichtipol, both also part of Balat.[14] Thus, although the perception of Balat as a Jewish
slum may have accurately reflected the situation in one part of it by the turn of the century, it may not have been representative of Balat as a whole. Ottoman registers and
European travelogues provide vastly opposing images of Balat in the nineteenth century.
The network of intercommunal interactions and interdependence revealed in the
state decrees is confronted with the depiction of a truncated piece of the district por-

trayed as representative of the "true Balat." Whereas tobacconists, grocers, sesame oil makers, and property owners such as Ömer Agha, Hananya, Yaşuva, Andriya, Yoan, and Şerife Fatıma Hanım create the image of a vibrant district pulsating with energy and life, Europeans portrayed a decaying and stagnant Jewish ghetto.

These starkly contrasting images demand a consideration of how an earlier flexibility in boundaries and spatial identities eventually gave way to the rigid definition of what it meant to be from Balat by the turn of the twentieth century. It is important to note that the *Tanzimat*, the period of Ottoman reform lasting from 1839 until 1876, separated these two portrayals; therefore we must consider temporal boundaries as well. Between the time when three Jewish men registered their property transfer with the Ottoman authorities early in the nineteenth century, and European observers began depicting the district as economically depressed at century's end, Balat experienced political, socioeconomic, and cultural changes that affected the city and the empire as a whole, and especially its non-Muslim populations. Internal and intercommunal divisions, conflicts and rivalries fueled in part by actions initiated by the Ottoman state, set the Jewish community off on a different trajectory from that of the Greek Orthodox, Armenian, and even Muslim communities. These differences affected the cultural outlook of Jewish *Balatlıs*, the physical state of the district, and self-perceptions of one's place as a *Balatlı* in Istanbul.

It is my contention that the tendency to project the image of Balat after the *Tanzimat* back on previous centuries has deeply influenced perceptions of the ethnoreligious composition of this district. To portray the evolution of the district with greater accuracy, we must reexamine the documentation about Balat and its people from the historiographic, demographic, and architectural points of view.

REVISITING THE HISTORIOGRAPHY OF OTTOMAN JEWRY

According to sixteenth-century Hebrew sources, the new Ottoman rulers appointed Moses Kapsali as Chief Rabbi of the entire Jewish community, an office parallel with that of the Greek Orthodox Patriarch. However, there is "no evidence that such a post existed...no evidence that [Kapsali] was the sole vehicle for Ottoman dealings with Jews or *vice versa*," and no evidence that his authority extended beyond the city.[15] To some, the appointment may have symbolized the integrity and unity of the community. However, after the death of Kapsali's successor, Elijah Mizrahi, in the sixteenth century, no single authority emerged to lead until the nineteenth century. In 1835, Abraham Levy was elected and confirmed by the government as the Chief Rabbi, the definitive head of the Jewish *millet* (*yehudi milleti*).[16]

The persistence of this foundation myth, despite evidence to the contrary, is related to the concept of the Ottoman institution of the "*millet* system" as it has been defined in the historiography of the Ottoman Empire since the nineteenth century by Turkish and non-Turkish historians alike. Until recently, it was commonly accepted that the Ottoman state contained a system of *millets*, or legally sanctioned religious communities under the authority of the central government. This system was instituted by

Sultan Mehmed II after the conquest of the city to regulate the lives of the empire's Greek Orthodox, Armenian, and Jewish subjects, known as *dhimmî*s, in reference to the Islamic concept of the *ahl al-dhimma*, or "the people of the covenant."[17] More recent research suggests that the institutional character of the *millet* system may have been overemphasized; rather, it would perhaps better be seen as "a set of arrangements" negotiated over the centuries between the Ottoman authorities and their non-Muslim peoples, granting *dhimmî*s varying amounts of sovereignty over their respective communities.[18]

The use of the term *millet* to describe the Ottoman-*dhimmî* relationship was in fact a nineteenth-century European anachronism appropriated by the Ottoman authorities themselves during the *Tanzimat*.[19] The reforms instituted in this period by the Ottoman state were in part a response to the Greek insurrection of the 1820s that resulted in the establishment in 1831 of the first nation-state to be carved out of the Ottoman Empire. The Ottoman state reacted to the dismemberment of the empire by initiating a reorganization that critically altered its relations with its non-Muslim subjects. The special status of the *dhimmî* was eliminated and, in its place, the principle of equality between Muslim and non-Muslim "citizens" was instituted. Specific leaders were appointed to head the various non-Muslim *millet*s that were now transformed into defined entities under the authority of the central government. The special poll tax (*cizye*) imposed on non-Muslims was rescinded, and Jews and Christians became Ottoman citizens required to fulfill their military obligations to the state.[20] These changes transformed the state's attitude toward its non-Muslim subjects; they also may have influenced how the residents of Balat envisioned themselves and the place of their *mahalle* vis-à-vis Greater Istanbul.

As the institution of the *millet* system crystallized in the course of the nineteenth century, the word *millet* that for centuries had symbolized a religious community converged with the Western concept of the "nation," the connotation it retains in Turkish today. The various *millet*s were perceived as distinct "nations" subsumed under Ottoman rule. To demonstrate the age-old existence of these redefined "*millet*s/ nations," and to substantiate a claim to nationhood based on those imagined pasts, various nationalist historiographies adopted the notion that the *millet* system, as it functioned in the nineteenth century, had existed since the reign of Mehmed II. It was this fifteenth-century sultan who purportedly appointed specific *milletbaşı*s (communal leaders) for each of the three non-Muslim communities of the empire: Moses Kapsali for the Jews, Gennadios Scholarios for the Greek Orthodox, and Hovakim of Bursa for the Armenians. This interpretation of the "*millet* system" promoted an insular approach to the histories of the non-Muslim communities that paid little attention to the connections between these groups and the larger Ottoman society. Thus, for example, Greek historian Constantine Paparrigopoulos (1815–1891) stressed the modern Greek state's Hellenic patrimony and its ties with its classical Greek and Byzantine past, regarding the period of Ottoman rule as little more than a period of occupation.

No such claims to separate statehood existed with respect to the Ottoman Jewish community in the nineteenth century. Nevertheless, a similar insular approach left its mark on the study of Ottoman Jewish history, so that, until recently, it has been framed in terms of its role in the development of a general Jewish history, and not in terms of its place within the Ottoman past. The Jews of the Ottoman Empire were often portrayed as a distinct group living in a sociocultural vacuum, set within, yet apart from, the larger Ottoman Muslim-Orthodox Christian-Armenian milieu.[21] Moreover, the "lachrymose tradition" that pervades Jewish historiography, according to which the Jewish diaspora is perceived as having lived an insurmountable tragedy, also contributed to the tendency to regard the Ottoman Jewish community as an entity unto itself.[22] Some scholars of Jewish studies continue to interpret the history of Ottoman Jewry in this way[23] despite innovative approaches adopted by historians such as Benjamin Braude, Joseph Hacker,[24] and Avigdor Levy, who notes that: "the net result [of the traditional insular interpretation]...has been that the achievements of Ottoman Jewry have rarely been examined as a unique expression of Jewish life as it was shaped by the sociopolitical realities prevailing in the Ottoman Empire."[25]

In the case of the history of a district such as Balat, there has been a similar inclination to project back on previous centuries the image the district had acquired by the early 1900s of being distinctively Jewish. One encounters titles such as *Balat, faubourg juif d'Istanbul* ["Balat, the Jewish District of Istanbul"] that foster the image of Balat as a strictly Jewish section of the city.[26] Turkish scholars, too, have fallen prey to this tendency. For example, according to the entry on "Balat" in the *İstanbul Ansiklopedisi*, "in Istanbul when the word 'Balat' is mentioned the word 'Jew' comes to mind, when 'Jew' is mentioned, 'Balat' comes to mind."[27] This statement ignores the fact that other elements of Ottoman culture also exerted an influence on the social, economic, cultural, demographic, and architectural significance of the district. The essentializing concept of the "Islamic city" as a monolithic entity made up of distinct quarters providing city residents with little chance of either horizontal or vertical mobility may also have played a role in perpetuating the image of Balat as the "Jewish" district located next to Fener, the prototypical "Greek Orthodox" district.[28]

It is true that Jews were a presence in Balat by the end of the fifteenth century, and exerted an especially strong influence in the district at the turn of the twentieth century. Nevertheless, the role played by other individuals and groups residing in the district (not always to be defined ethno-religiously) in the centuries prior to the *Tanzimat*, and also during and after it, must also be taken into consideration to achieve a clearer understanding of how Balat functioned, how it was tied to the districts that surrounded it, and how the inhabitants of Balat perceived their place in this milieu. Here we shall argue that it was precisely the ambiguity of the various demographic and geographic boundaries surrounding Balat—both from the perspective of the Ottoman administration and from that of the inhabitants themselves—that was the source of the dynamism of Balat.

THE GEOGRAPHY OF IDENTITY

In his examination of the Kasap Ilyas Quarter of the district of Davud Paşa, Cem Behar highlights the localized nature of Istanbulites' sense of loyalty to the urban spaces they inhabited. The walled city of Istanbul comprised a number of *mahalle*s, or neighborhoods, whose boundaries often varied over the centuries, each composed of not more than fifteen streets organized around a main road (*tarik-i am*) and most often a house of worship such as a mosque, church, synagogue, or perhaps a dervish lodge that often indicated the ethno-religious identity of its residents.[29] According to Behar, "these urban neighborhood units...fostered a durable sense of local identity and cohesion."[30]

Several *mahalle*s constituted a *semt*, or district, whose name was often related to a noteworthy landmark, individual or, sometimes, the city gates, such as Fener (Lighthouse), Ayvansaray (Blachernae Palace), Beyazıt (in honor of the Sultan), and Edirnekapı (Edirne Gate). These larger spaces engendered less of a sense of loyalty among residents, though their names were probably more familiar to Istanbulites living in other parts of the city than those of the individual *mahalle*s (just as Brooklyn might be more familiar than Greenpoint or Red Hook to Manhattanites and Bronxites). Thus despite the emphasis on Balat as a whole in the secondary sources, the residents of the district may actually have felt more of a sense of attachment to one particular *mahalle*, for example, el-Hac İsa or Dibek, rather than Balat, though of course when they ventured beyond their "turf" that loyalty may have extended more readily to include the entire district.[31] Ottoman sources such as court records and *divan* registers often refer to the particular *mahalle* litigants resided in rather than to the larger district such as Balat. In such instances the individual in question is identified by his or her religion (e.g., Kevork nām Ermenī, "an Armenian named Kevork"), as well as by the quarter or neighborhood in which he or she resided: "the petitioner, the described individual Christian woman Maryora, daughter of Panayot, one of the [female] residents of Mirahur Quarter, and her natural born adult son, non-Muslim Manol, son of Dimitri."[32]

Minna Rozen has suggested that the Ottomans regarded the members of each religious community residing in a particular neighborhood as a distinct entity: "Thus, people of different religions who lived next door to each other belonged to different *mahalle*s, while people of the same religion who did not live in relative proximity could belong to the same *mahalle*."[33] She further argues that this understanding of *mahalle* was in conformance with the Jewish community's use of the term *qahal*, a Hebrew word meaning a group of Jews from the same region who belonged to the same synagogue in Istanbul.[34] While Rozen's interpretation of *qahal* makes sense in terms of the composition of Jewish congregations, the wording of Ottoman court and *divan* records suggests that from the Ottoman administrative perspective, the *mahalle* was a specific locale to which subjects of various confessional identities belonged. Thus if Muslim and non-Muslim residents from the same neighborhood were submitting a petition together, they would all be named as coming from the same *mahalle*. Moreover, beginning in the late seventeenth century, distinct words meaning "resident" were applied to Muslims, as opposed to Christians and Jews.[35] In this respect, the Ottoman discourse recognized members of various communities as belonging to the same quarter or district, even as it was developing a specialized terminology to distinguish Muslim from non-Muslim residents.[36] Nevertheless, some quarters would have higher concentrations of one particular confessional group over another, and thus come to be regarded in the popular mind as a "Jewish quarter" or a "Muslim quarter." Such was the case with the lower part of Balat along the Golden Horn, which was more closely associated with Jews than were other sections of the district located within the city walls.

OUTER BALAT/ INNER BALAT

The area of Balat located outside the city walls, now in an advanced state of decay, was long identified with the Jewish community. One of the main parts of Afuera Balat ("Outer Balat") was the Karabaş Quarter, mockingly referred to as *Balat-sur-mer* [Balat-by-the-sea] by Jews who had left there and moved on to other parts of the city.[37] Here were located the main wharves where boats known as *kayık*s ferried passengers from Balat to Eyüp, and on the other side of the Golden Horn, to Galata and especially Hasköy.[38] Timber, coal, and wine were unloaded at these wharves daily. Nearby, open sewers spilled their contents into the Golden Horn, contributing to Balat's reputation as polluted, unhygienic, and odoriferous.[39] Opposite the Poli Yashan Synagogue (now destroyed, but dating back to the late fifteenth century) is the Dibek Quarter, where Hananya v. Yako had his tobacco shop in 1817. A school established by the Alliance Israélite Universelle in 1875 was also located in Dibek. Farther along on the shore approaching Ayvansaray is the Or ha-Hayyim Hospital, founded in 1858 and still in operation today. The ruins of more than 140 *yehudihane*s, the tenement structures meant to house multiple Jewish families, are found in the Lonca Quarter. On the other side of Karabaş Quarter, in the direction of Fener, where many wealthier Jews preferred to live, is Sığrı, the site of the former Selaniki synagogue close by Balat Gate. This synagogue, now a ruin, is a reminder of the Jews deported to Istanbul from Salonika in the latter half of the fifteenth century by Mehmed II. Yet even in this predominantly Jewish milieu, significant landmarks pointed to the other residents of the district: Greek Orthodox churches such as Aya Yani and, following the split from the Greek Orthodox Patriarchate in 1870, the imposing church of St. Stephen of the Bulgars, fabricated of iron cast in Vienna and floated by barge in sections down the Danube.[40]

While Outer Balat was crowded with coffeehouses and *yehudihane*s catering to the working class, Inner Balat, or "Ariento Balat," was the home of the wealthier merchants. The *kavafhane* (the "shoemakers' building") is located within what is left of Balat Gate; it was destroyed by an earthquake in 1894. Here Jewish, Greek Orthodox, Muslim, and Armenian shopkeepers and vendors interacted with one another regularly. Other quarters located within Inner Balat, such as Haci İsa, Hızır Çavuş, Hammamcı Muhyiddin, and Hace Kasım Gonani, contain landmarks that are a testimony to Balat's multiconfessional population.[41] The Ferrukh Kethüda Mosque located in Inner Balat was built by Sultan Süleyman's chief architect, Sinan, in 1562.[42] Considered one of the finest examples of a small mosque built in the classical style, its courtyard was the site of the Balat Kadi Court.[43] The Armenian church, Surp Hıraşdagebet, is nearby and still functioning, surrounded by Armenian residences.

The entry to the Saloniki synagogue, now a ruin

A stone's throw from the church was the Yanbol synagogue, perhaps the oldest in the quarter, with its rustic hand-painted ceiling in an Italian style. One hundred meters further on is the Ahrida synagogue, the main house of Jewish worship in the district, where the Messianic prophet Sabbetai Sevi is believed to have preached in the seventeenth century. This synagogue, founded by Romaniot Jews from Ohrid in Macedonia, was also the location of the Jewish court, or *Beit Din*. The building has been completely restored, with some attention paid to its original décor. The most notable feature is its prow-like *tevah*, or podium for the reading of the Torah, which stands in the middle of the meeting space. The synagogue was the largest in Balat, able to accommodate the entire male Jewish population.[44] Victorya Acu, a former resident of Balat, recalls:

> A vivid memory of Ahrida synagogue is surely my wedding. We had our wedding at Ahrida since Ahrida offered the ceremonies for free. Furthermore, it was larger than the other synagogues and thus the whole Jewish neighborhood could attend the ceremony. [45]

Just a few streets away and down a narrow alleyway is the Chana synagogue. Its plan, consisting of a series of consecutive rooms over a central courtyard connected by an exterior gallery, made it suitable for use as a *yeshiva*, or religious school, where Jewish boys and men came to study.

The Armenian church, Surp Hıreşdagabet

The Armenian school with the minaret of the Ferrukh Kethüda Mosque in the background

Painted ceiling of the Yanbol synagogue

Interior of the Yanbol synagogue

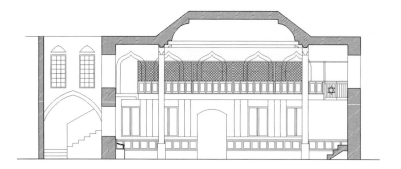

Section of the Yanbol synagogue

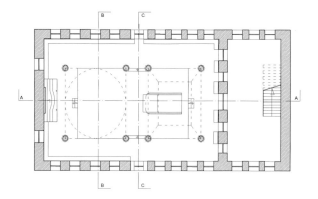

Ground-floor plan, the Ahrida synagogue

Sections, the Ahrida synagogue

The Ahrida synagogue entryway

Korin Suryano remembers:

> We attended the Chana and Yanbol synagogues: two very popular and crowded synagogues where people went to pray nearly everyday. I remember going to pray with my grandfather on Saturday mornings. In those times, people paid a lot of attention to wearing their best clothes and looking impeccable on Saturday mornings since Shabat was the most important day of the week. On major holidays, we had big festivities called *fiestas* in the synagogue. We sang religious songs and danced and had huge banquets.[46]

Not far away, in Fener, the Greek Orthodox community convened around the seat of the Patriarchate, located there since 1602. Although predominantly Greek, Fener was not off-bounds to Jews, at least not on its periphery. A neighborhood bathhouse (*hammâm*) was located in the Tahta Minare (Wooden Minaret) neighborhood on the border between Balat and Fener. It contained a *mikveh* (as did all the bathhouses of Balat) used by Jewish women to perform their ritual ablutions before the Sabbath, when it was closed to non-Jews. Victorya Acu recalls:

> I remember going to the *hammâm* once a week on Fridays before Sabbath dinner and the entry was one *para*. On the days of *mikveh* before marriage, women had big fiestas in the *hammam*. Everybody brought some food: dolmas, meatballs, pastries, etc. We also called for the gypsy musicians and a Jewish female drummer. We danced for hours and sang and shared news and gossip.[47]

This *hammâm* still functions today. It is said to be the oldest in Istanbul and may be regarded as the dividing point separating Balat from Fener, though in practice neither

Interior of the *hammam* of Tahta Minare

Entry to the Chana synagogue

Right: Entry to the Ichtipol synagogue

Below, right: House of the *shammash* (sexton) of the Ichtipol synagogue

Below, left: Storage closet in the courtyard of Ichtipol synagogue, perhaps the *genizah*

Plan and sections of the Ichtipol synagogue

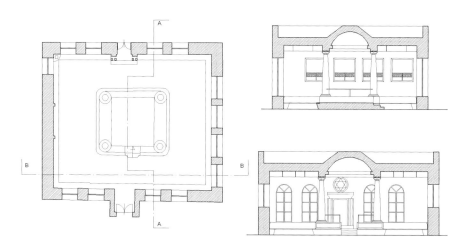

the residents themselves nor the Ottoman authorities seem to have been very concerned with making such distinctions.[48] As might be expected, Greek Orthodox Christians were more concentrated in the part of Balat that merged into Fener.

Further up the hill, and separated from the rest of Inner Balat, was Kasturiya Quarter, whose focal point was the Kasturiya Synagogue (now destroyed, with only the main portal remaining). It was founded after 1453 by a group of Jews originally from Castoria, Macedonia. Noted for its broad streets, this spacious quarter was home to the famous Palti family, one of whose forebears was the physician to the Sultan in the sixteenth century, when Jewish influence among the Ottomans was at its peak. Next to Kasturiya is the quarter of Ichtipol, containing a large and beautiful wooden synagogue of the same name. It was founded in the fifteenth century by Jews from Stip, in Macedonia. Although the Ichtipol quarter was predominantly Jewish, many Greek Orthodox families settled around the nearby Kariye Cami, the former Byzantine Church of the Chora. Ichtipol was one of the quarters most adversely affected by the destructive fires that Istanbul experienced over the centuries.[49] Remarkably, the synagogue and the large wooden house of the *shammash* (beadle), opposite the synagogue, have survived in good condition. They are among the largest wooden structures still intact in Balat—fragile monuments of unique historical significance.

"BALAT SAKİNLERİNDEN": THE POPULATING OF BALAT

The profile of the district comes to life when one considers the activities and lives of the inhabitants who made this area overlooking the Golden Horn their own. Even prior to the conquest of the city by Sultan Mehmed II in 1453, it appears that Romaniot Greek-speaking Jews highly acculturated to the larger Byzantine society resided in the area of Constantinople that would come to be known as Balat.[50] While it is not clear whether the synagogues Poli Hadash and Poli Yashan ("New City" and "Old City," respectively), whose remains can still be seen near Dibek today, date from the Byzantine era, their Greek names point to the influence exerted by the Romaniot Jews, who were eventually settled along both sides of the Golden Horn.[51] Historian Abraham Galanté, citing a *firman* (decree) of 1694 authorizing the restoration of these synagogues, has suggested that the synagogues in the Haci Isa Quarter of Balat, whose residents came originally from the Balkan cities of Ohrid, Karaferya, and Yanbol, may have been established even before the conquest.[52] Though Varol questions the reliability of this supposition due to the late date of the *firman*, she does acknowledge the likelihood of a Jewish presence in Balat before 1453, given the Jewish settlement across the Golden Horn in Pikridion (Ottoman Hasköy) as well as the proximity of Balat to the cemetery near Eğrikapı (the Byzantine Kaligarya Gate), where Moses Kapsali was buried.[53]

However, Balat does not figure prominently among those areas to which Jews who fled Istanbul prior to the conquest returned when ordered to do so by Sultan Mehmed II. Instead, they were settled primarily in another area bounded by Eminönü, Sirkeci, Tahtakale, and Mahmut Paşa, along with Romaniot Greek and Turkish-speaking Jews deported from Anatolia and the Balkans to Istanbul.[54] Not long after, in the 1470s,

Ashkenazi Jews fleeing persecution in Bavaria sought refuge in Istanbul; they chose to reside further up the Golden Horn in Hasköy. These Jews, as well as Karaites, for whom the district of Karaköy is said to have been named, were among those listed in a register from 1540 that identified the congregations whose taxes were used to support the *vakı* (endowment) of Mehmed II. Some Jews do appear to have taken up residence in Balat in the late fifteenth and sixteenth centuries. An endowment deed (*vakfiye*) from the late fifteenth century mentions Balat among the districts populated by Jews.[55]

Following the expulsions from Spain and Portugal in 1492, waves of Sephardic immigrants entered the empire, settling first in the Balkans and eventually in the capital city. Istanbul thus became the city with the second-largest Jewish population, superseded only by Salonika. Welcomed by the Ottomans, who recognized their professional skills, these Jews were classified in state registers as *kendi gelen* ("one who came on his own accord") as opposed to those who were *sürgünlüler*, or forcibly transferred. The Sephardic Jews settled in numbers in the area around Eminönü, given its proximity to the customs house and wharves that were crucial to their commercial endeavors, though others also chose areas along the Golden Horn, including Hasköy and Balat.

The Greek-speaking Romaniot and the Spanish-speaking Sephardic Jews, each with their own customs, culture, and language, vied for predominance throughout the sixteenth century and early seventeenth centuries. The conflagration of 1660 that consumed a great part of the city led to a demographic shift that increased the concentration of Sephardic Jews in Balat, which became a more heavily Jewish area on the whole. Meanwhile, members of the Greek Orthodox elite known as Phanariots, in reference to the residences they had established in Fener/Phanar, began their rise to prominence in the Ottoman bureaucracy in the latter half of the seventeenth century. The Phanariots replaced members of the Jewish elite who had enjoyed high status in the sixteenth century, such as Moses Hamon, physician to Sultan Süleyman, and Don Joseph Nasi, the wealthy banker who became the Duke of Naxos.

Turhan Valide Sultan, the mother of Mehmet IV, used the fire of 1660 as an opportunity to resume work on the mosque in Eminönü. Jews who lived in the vicinity of the partially completed mosque were forced to move to other areas of the city. "This is how it came about that, between 1597 and the 1660s, the greater part of Istanbul Jews settled in Balat," Rozen tells us.[56] While 10-20 percent of the Jewish population of Istanbul resided in Balat in the 1590s, a century later almost a third of the community lived there, while 11 percent lived in Hasköy, with other smaller groups influencing the makeup of the nearby areas of Cebe Ali and Tekfur Sarayı.[57]

Expelled from their former homes in Eminönü, Sephardic Jews began to assert their presence in Balat, absorbing the Romaniot Jews living there into their Iberian culture. Ladino replaced Greek as the main spoken language of Jewish *Balatlı*s, though some Greek-speaking Jews still maintained ties to their influential Orthodox Christian neighbors in Fener, where more affluent Jews settled. A vestige of the withering Balkan roots were the synagogues with names such as Ahrida, Yanbol, Salonika, Veria (Turkish Karaferya), Kasturiya, and Ichtipol, that evoked their Romaniot origins. However, congregations founded on the basis of an exclusive cultural and linguistic heritage, whether it was Balkan or Iberian, eventually lost their defining element. A blurring of borders took place among the various sections of the Jewish community of Balat during the seventeenth and eighteenth centuries. Symbolic of this transformation is the sale of the Romaniot synagogue of Chana in Balat to the Sephardic community in 1663.[58] As the Jewish population became integrated, so did their communities of worship.

Eremya Çelebi (1637-1695), writing in the seventeenth century, commented that the Jewish population of Balat was larger than that of Hasköy, Beşiktaş, Ortaköy, Kuruçeşme, Kuzguncuk, Üsküdar, and Cengelköy. "They live on the outer part of Balat... here is a grand wharf at which dock ships bearing all sorts of goods," since, according to Çelebi, Jews never "stray far from the sea and always live on the shore."[59] In discussing a section of the shoreline in Ayvansaray, a little further down the Golden Horn from Balat, Çelebi notes that Jews lived there, reasoning that "since the rich live by the shore, the Jews are there."[60] Though it was poverty-stricken by the nineteenth century, in the 1600s, areas such as Karabaş appear to have been prime real estate.

While mostly Jews lived in Outer Balat, the area within the city walls was home to people of varying confessional identities. Çelebi describes the Armenian church of Surp Hıreşdagabet (Church of the Holy Archangels) that was originally a Greek Orthodox church called Taxiarchi ("Archangels," in reference to the Archangels Michael and Gabriel) dating from the thirteenth or fourteenth centuries.[61] Murad IV granted the decrepit Orthodox church to the Armenian community in 1627 when their own church (Surp Nikos in Edirnekapı) was confiscated to be converted into a mosque.[62] In 1628, permission was granted to the Armenians to repair their new house of worship.[63] Surp Hıreşdagabet was consecrated by the Armenian Patriarch Stephen of Bursa on 8 September 1631.[64] This church became a focal center for the Armenian community.[65] It contained a sacred spring visited by the faithful throughout the year, and in the eighteenth century, a school was established next to it.[66] Later, in 1779, Matteos Tıbır founded a press there, and scholars such as Kevork Tıbır, who was proficient in Persian, Arabic, and Hebrew, lived nearby. The deal brokered between the Sultan and the Armenians is noteworthy, for it was clearly within the sovereign's prerogative to confiscate the church in Edirnekapı without offering any compensation. Yet he did make amends, suggesting that he felt responsible for his Armenian subjects, who were crucial to the commercial success of the state.

The fact that the structure given to the Armenians was a dilapidated Greek church is also significant, for it indicates a long-standing Greek Orthodox presence in Balat. In 1591, Sultan Murad III had the Church of the Pammakaristos, the seat of the Greek Orthodox Patriarchate in Fatih, seized and converted into the Fethiye (Victory) Mosque, in celebration of his recent victory over the Safavids in Azerbaijan.[67] The Patriarchate was then temporarily moved to Panagaia Paramythias and the Church of St. Demetrius Kanavi in Balat.[68] Then, in 1602, Patriarch Jeremias II transferred the Patriarchate to the Church of St. George in Fener, where it remains to this day. Thus after several migrations, including a brief stay in Balat, the patriarchal authority found its final home in Fener. In the wake of this move, wealthy Greek families transplanted themselves to surround the seat of Greek Orthodox authority, constructing the stone houses for which Fener is renowned.[69]

The Greek Orthodox church Aya Nikola

The decline in influence of the Greek Orthodox with the Ottomans in the sixteenth and early seventeenth centuries (when Jewish dignitaries were the confidants of sultans) may in part account for the closing of other Greek Orthodox churches in Balat. According to a decree issued on 8 Rebiülevvel 973 (3 October 1565) a church located outside Balat Gate was shuttered on the order of the sultan.[70] When Christians tried to construct a new place of worship on the foundations of the old church, a complaint was registered that the new church was taller than the surrounding houses. A decree was issued ordering the building to be razed and stating that the Christians should no longer perform their "vain rites" there. The Muslim neighbors were exhorted to report any future infractions. In the early 1660s, the Greek Orthodox also lost ownership of church property near Balat Gate and Fener Gate that had been destroyed in a fire in 1633.[71]

Despite these setbacks, the Greek Orthodox maintained a foothold in Balat and were allowed to repair the Aya Nikola church after the fire of 1692.[72] Another fire ravaged Balat in 1729; following this disaster, a decree again granted permission to Greek Orthodox authorities to repair several of their churches in various parts of Balat, among them the Aya Yani in Karabaş Quarter, Küçük Meryem Ana in Haci İsa Quarter, Aya Nikola in Hammamcı Muhyiddin Quarter, and, near Tekfur Sarayı in Çakır Agha Quarter, Meryem Ana.[73] The transfer of synagogues from Romaniot to Sephardic Jews, the reincarnation of Greek Orthodox and Armenian churches as mosques, the transformation of Greek Orthodox into Armenian churches, and the renovation of all types of houses of worship evoke the fluidity of the social makeup of the district and the continual and ongoing transformations among the various communities that characterized life in Balat prior to the nineteenth century.

BALAT OR FENER?

The Ottoman state's view of the boundaries between Fener and Balat varied over the centuries. One of the buildings authorized for repair in the decree mentioned above was Hızır İlyas, "situated in Tahta Minare quarter within Fener Gate," while a decree from 1905 grants the Greek Orthodox Damyanos v. İstrati permission to open a tavern in the "Tahtaminare [sic] quarter of Balat."[74] Similarly, in a court decree issued in 1662, Hammamcı Muhyiddin quarter was named as part of Fener rather than Balat, as it was in the decree concerning the oil mill issued in 1817.[75] Some areas regarded as part of Fener in earlier centuries seem to have assimilated to Balat, at least from an administrative point of view, by the nineteenth and twentieth centuries.

The ambiguity regarding the borders may have also depended on the way a person identified himself. People living on the edge between the two areas may have felt more an affinity to one or the other. A Greek Orthodox resident might publicly express his attachment to the Patriarchate located in Fener, while actually having a greater sense of loyalty to his local church, such as Aya Nikola, located in Balat. In the court case that placed the Hammamcı Muhyiddin Quarter in Fener, the petitioners, an *imam* and the *muezzin*s of the neighborhood, claimed that the Jewish innkeeper was renting spaces to his co-religionists even though Muslims had always lived there. They "received a decree [from the representative of the grand vizier] ordering the expulsion of Jews from the quarter...[and] displayed it to the judge, who warned the owner of the

The main shopping street of Balat

inn to expel the Jewish tenants."[76] If the Muslim leaders identified themselves as being from Fener, they clearly did not associate that area exclusively with Greek Orthodox Christians. In the seventeenth century, the area appears to have been home to all three confessions.

In recording Fener or Balat as the name of the quarter, the perspective of the scribe may also have been a factor, though the scribe's decision only begs the question of the Ottoman state's perspective on where one area ended and the next began. Distinctions between Balat and Fener may not in fact have been a matter of great significance to the government, so long as the quarter in question was properly identified. In the seventeenth century, when litigants in court cases gave their identities, the district (*semt*) where they lived was often omitted altogether, as in "Mahmiyye-i Kostantiniyyeˊde el-Hāc ʿİsā Mahallesinde sākin Yahūdi tāifesinden Ohri cemāʾatine cemāʾat başı olan Salini veled-i Papule" ("Salini, son of Papule, a member of the Jewish community, the head of the Ohri Congregation, who resides in el-Hac İsa Quarter in the City of Constantinople").[77]

At the turn of the eighteenth century, some parts of the districts of Fener and Balat were so highly regarded that they were considered suitable addresses for statesmen and princes. Indeed, in the early 1700s, the former Grand Dragoman Alexander Mavrokordatos (1641-1709), father of Nicholas Mavrokordatos (1668–1730), who succeeded him as Grand Dragoman and later ruled the principalities of Wallachia and Moldavia, occupied a mansion near Fenerkapı.[78] The Transylvanian prince Tököli Imre (1657–1705), who was recognized by the Ottomans in the 1680s as the King of Upper Hungary, was also associated with the Fener/Balat area of Istanbul. An ally of the Ottomans in the war against the Habsburgs, he settled in Istanbul after being denied amnesty in the Treaty of Karlowitz signed in 1699. When his wife Zrini Ilona (Helen Zrinski) submitted a petition in 1700 explaining that her former residence was in ruins and uninhabitable, a decree was issued ordering that a new mansion (*konak*) be procured for her in either Fener or Balat.[79] From the Ottomans' point of view, either locale would have been appropriate for the wife of an esteemed ally. In the sixteenth and seventeenth centuries, Jewish notables such as the Nasi and Palti families occupied parts of Balat and Fener; by the 1700s, they were being supplanted by Orthodox luminaries and Christian anti-Habsburg nobility.

In the nineteenth century, another series of destructive fires between 1860 and 1890 completely changed the appearance of many parts of Istanbul. Burned-out neighborhoods constituted a "blank slate" and became places of experimentation for new concepts in urban planning imported from Europe.[80] In a large part of Balat, streets were reorganized into a grid, plot sizes were regularized, and attached houses built of stone and brick (*kargir*) replaced freestanding wooden structures. These changes, while architecturally significant, did not have a great impact on the social makeup of the neighborhoods. Confessional communities still owned much of the land, the task of rebuilding was mostly in private hands, and the multi-ethnic character of Balat remained intact.

Bow windows on the street leading to Fener

However, the new construction took on a distinct style of its own that became emblematic of the district as a whole. Many homes were rebuilt as row houses, with the bow-window (*oriel*) façade forming a rhythmic pattern running along the length of the street.[81] Houses were three stories in height, with each floor occupied by a different family, so that every house constituted its own unique social environment. Memories of communal living recur frequently in the recollections of former inhabitants:

> I was born in a three-floor wooden house in the Hizir Cavus Mahallesi [neighborhood of Balat] where my parents moved after a fire in Kuzguncuk where they had been living since they were newly married. Each family had its own floor yet there was always a very strong feeling of a family house. We were very close with our neighbors Mrs. Galikos and a Jewish family with three daughters who later moved to Israel. Our flat consisted of two bedrooms, a living room, a kitchen and a large hall. The apartment was of a decent size since we were a small family of four. Unlike other Jewish families, we did not live with our grandparents.[82]

The residence of Nahum Efendi, located across the street from the Ahrida Synagogue, is a "typical" Balat house consisting of three stories with a side entrance. Despite its modest appearance, the house was an important landmark for *Balatlı* Jews, for it was the home of the Chief Rabbi (*hahambaşı*) Haim Nahum, official head of the community, who filled the post in the waning days of the Empire.[83] The house has separate entryways to

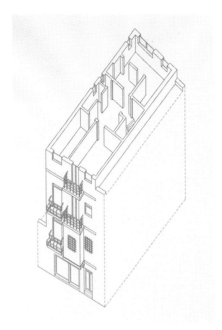
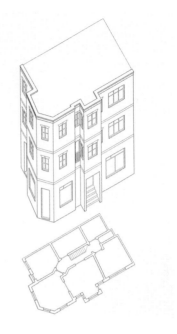

Left: The house of Leon Brudo, showing the interior plan

Right: The house of Rabbi Nahum facing the Ahrida synagogue, with ground plan

each of the apartments, and an *oriel* window facing the street. Beneath layers of more recent wall covering, the delicate hand-painted floral designs of an earlier era are still faintly visible on the interior walls, while a small balcony on the second floor has a wooden ceiling decorated with the Star of David, easily seen from the street below.

MOUNTING INTERCOMMUNAL STRIFE

In 1821, only a few years after the Greek Orthodox sesame oil makers had asserted their rights to a Muslim-owned oil mill in Balat, the place was the scene of a gruesome punishment meted out by Sultan Mahmud II to a Greek Orthodox subject. The Patriarch Gregorios V ordered the excommunication of the instigators of the Greek insurrection begun earlier that year in the principality of Moldavia. But the Sultan still suspected that his sympathies lay with the revolutionaries and the Philiki Etairia, the "Friendly Society," founded in 1814 to "liberate" the Greek Orthodox from Ottoman rule. The Sultan ordered the Patriarch to be hanged on April 22, the day before Easter, outside the Fener Gate. After the Patriarch's body lay unattended for three days, some Jewish criminals were commanded to throw the corpse in the Golden Horn.[84] Hostile feelings toward Jews often surfaced at Easter since they were believed to be responsible for Jesus' death. The forced involvement of two or three Jews in the undignified disposal of the Patriarch's remains further inflamed such sentiments. Robert Walsh describes how the unsettling news of the insurrection was received in Istanbul, even before the execution took place: "The Turks were walking slowly about, holding one hand on the hilt of their *yataghans* (a heavy curved knife)...while the Greeks and Jews, whenever they met them, got out of their way, into some store or coffeehouse that happened to be open."[85] Walsh was speaking about Pera specifically, but tensions must also have run high in the neighborhoods near the Patriarchate.

Not long thereafter, several Jewish bankers were caught up in the reaction to the destruction of the Janissary corps in 1826. After the defeat of the Greek forces at Missolonghi, Mahmud II, seeking to resume the reforms begun under Sultan Selim, announced in a *Hatt-i-Şerif* (imperial decree) the formation of a new military organization. When the Janissaries tried to stage a revolt in protest, they were immediately cut down, but not before they had pressured several Jewish bankers and tax farmers, including the wealthy Isaac Behor Carmona, to provide them with financing. These Jews were put to death after being denounced by another banker, the Armenian Aziz Artin. After this incident, the position of Jewish bankers vis-à-vis the Ottoman state was greatly compromised, much to the benefit of their Armenian counterparts.[86]

Though there are no reports of actions against the Jews of Fener and Balat following these incidents, they highlight a marked change in the sociocultural milieu beginning in the mid-nineteenth century. From the state's perspective, the boundaries between Fener and Balat were nebulous, and many documents continue to identify the same neighborhood as belonging to Fener at one point and to Balat at another.[87] Despite this ambiguity, there appears to have been a hardening of the lines among the different confessional groups of Balat, manifested in the ever more violent nature of intercommunal confrontations. Armenians, Muslims, and Greek Orthodox Christians still lived cheek by jowl in Balat with their Jewish counterparts, yet the dynamics of the relationships and sense of interconnectedness seem to have been altered completely over the course of the century.

Although the Ottoman regime was the cause of the strife that occurred after the Patriarch's death, it alone cannot account for the large number of blood libel cases that pitted Orthodox Christians and Armenians of Balat against Jews beginning at midcentury. These cases are evidence of a new and unprecedented level of hostility. In 1874, the body of a Greek child named Antoine was found in Balat along the banks of the Golden Horn, near the home of a Jewish jeweler named Ishak Mizrahi. According to the Greek newspaper *Typos*, the boy, whose tongue had been cut out, seemed to have been a "sacrificial victim" worthy of "Polynesian cannibals."[88] An inquiry was opened and Greek doctors determined that the child had drowned; medical reports were widely disseminated to refute the Greek newspaper's claim. In spite of this, acts of vengeance were committed against Jews for weeks, and the authorities had to post guards around the Jewish neighborhoods to ensure the safety of their residents. The Chief Rabbi had to appeal to the Grand Vizier, the Greek Orthodox Patriarch, and the Minister of Religion before the violence subsided. News stories such as "L'Atroce Assassinat de Balata," ("A Vile Murder in Balat") must have engendered a sense of fear and isolation among Jewish *Balatlıs*.

In 1870, Greek Orthodox and Armenians filed a petition and tried to convince their Muslim neighbors to sign it. According to the complaint, the Jews harassed them and their children and interfered with their funeral processions.[89] A few years earlier, insulted by a scarecrow in the shape of a crucifix erected in the garden of a Jewish home, Greek Orthodox rioted in the streets, only stopping when the Patriarch and the Chief Rabbi intervened.[90] None of these events appears to have been incited or encouraged by the leaders of the Christian communities, who generally opposed the attacks on the Jewish community.[91] Muslims also registered complaints that the Jews of Balat were a threat to their children; in 1859, Emine Hatun accused a Jewish tinsmith and his sons of beating her crippled daughter Hadice.[92] It would be a mistake to assume that intercommunal friction colored all interactions among neighbors, children, merchants, customers, *imam*s, priests, and rabbis. Nevertheless, the violence that erupted appears to be a departure from the more peaceful nature of intercommunal relations in previous centuries.

The kinds of complaints that the Greek Orthodox, Muslims, and Armenians voiced against their Jewish neighbors also changed markedly. In the seventeenth century, Muslims of Hammamcı Muhyiddin Quarter expressed their discontent over a Jewish innkeeper who had rented rooms to Jews in what the Muslims argued had always been a Muslim neighborhood. The plaintiffs took their case to the court and the matter was adjudicated there. There is no mention of any violent acts, and the plaintiffs received a judgment in their favor. The basis of the complaint seems to have been "tradition"; namely, for years there had been no Jews in the neighborhood. Thus it was contrary to tradition to allow them to move in.

In this seventeenth-century case, both petitioners and defendant were operating within the framework of a society that implicitly acknowledged the superiority of Islam in myriad ways. The validity of the complaint was predicated on this tacit acknowledgment. Sumptuary laws and other rules that pointed to the lesser status of non-Muslims were well known, even if they were more often than not honored in the breach. Indeed, the Ottoman system of state was in general reactive, in the sense that it did not enforce law codes concerning the place of *dhimmî*s in Ottoman society until subjects registered a complaint concerning the actions of a non-Muslim and brought the matter to the attention of the Imperial Divan or the pertinent court. Thus in the case of the Jewish innkeeper, most likely the renting of rooms to Jews in Hammamcı Muhyiddin Quarter would have proceeded unimpeded had not the *imam* and his cohorts filed a petition exhorting the court to pay attention to "tradition" and a return to the status quo.

The "blood libel" cases filed in the mid-nineteenth century, however, were of an entirely different sort, not in any way predicated on the traditional system that guaranteed the non-Muslim's place in Ottoman society. What was behind this change? It is worth noting that in 1856, only a few years before the accusations of Jewish harassment of Greek Orthodox, Armenian, and Muslim children were made in Balat, another imperial rescript (*Hatt-i Humayun*) was issued at the urging of the French, Austrians, and British, asserting the equality of non-Muslims.[93] The rescript, in many ways a reaffirmation of the *Hatt-i Şerif* of Gülhane issued in 1839, signified the transformation of the non-Muslim subject from *dhimmî* to Ottoman citizen. Although it may not be possible to find a direct causal relationship between the issuance of the rescript and the intercommunal strife in Balat, nevertheless the writ represented the utter dismantling of the traditional system that defined the place of the Greek Orthodox, Armenians, and Jews in Ottoman society. The rescript and the social dislocations it caused may be considered at least in part a factor in the upheavals occurring in Balat in the 1860s-70s. It is not surprising that in this era Jewish families with means departed Balat for other, "safer," areas of Istanbul such as Galata, Ortaköy, and Kuzguncuk. Greek Orthodox families who could afford it also departed for other parts of the city or even the Kingdom of Greece, and rich Armenians too seem to have chosen to leave Balat at this time.

OTHER SOURCES OF INSTABILITY

Besides intercommunal strife, beginning in the 1840s Balat also witnessed changes in the maritime commerce of the once busy wharves and the satellite businesses dependent on them that negatively affected the factories and workshops along the shore.[94] The debilitating fires that occurred between the 1860s and 1890s destroyed homes, businesses, churches, and synagogues, not all of which were rebuilt. Fifteen hundred Jewish *Balatlıs* were left homeless as a result of one fire in 1865.[95] In this period of turmoil, many licenses to open taverns were granted. The economic decline and freer access to alcohol may have been two factors accounting for the rise in criminal activity that beset Balat in the later nineteenth and early twentieth centuries.

Balat was also the scene of much criminal activity related to the general economic malaise and urban blight witnessed by de Amicis. The 1860s saw a spate of burglaries that crossed confessional lines: in April 1862, Panayot, Mihael, Yani, and the rest of their Greek gang were equal-opportunity thieves who had no compunction against breaking and entering the shops of Greek barbers Hristo and İsak and the shop of Jewish tailor Salamon, while Muslim Ali of Tekfurdağ stripped his co-religionist Hatice Hanım's place bare.[96] Murders were not a rare occurrence either.[97] Thus, in addition to some particularly vicious displays of intercommunal hatred, the district experienced a crime wave whose victims were not only Jews but also Greek Orthodox, Muslim, and Armenian *Balatlıs* who could not move to safer areas.

MODERNITY AND ITS DISCONTENTS

As a result of the reforms called for in the *Hatt-i Şerif* of 1856, the authority of the Greek Orthodox and Armenian *millet*s' religious hierarchies, already weakened by internal division, now declined even further. Meanwhile, powerful secularizing and modernizing forces emerged to fill the void.[98] Wealthy Armenians, believing it their duty to raise the education level of the masses, opened a secondary school, Jemaran, in 1836.[99] The Greek Philological Society of Istanbul (*Ellinikos Filologıkos Sillogos Konstantinupoleos*), founded in 1861, promoted secular education among the Greeks.[100] In 1881, a large red-brick Greek Boys' School of Fener (*Fener Rum Erkek Lisesi*) was constructed on a hill overlooking the shore. The Jewish community was also in transition. While in the Greek Orthodox and Armenian communities, advocates of secularization were successful in implementing their goals, it was the traditional element that remained dominant among the Jews. The conflict between "reactionaries" and "modernizers" in the Jewish community had a particular result regarding the Jews of Balat.[101]

Over the centuries, powerful members of the Jewish laity acted as intermediaries with the government on behalf of their co-religionists. Their declining role resulted in increased power for the Chief Rabbi (*hahambaşı*) by the end of the nineteenth century. At the same time, a growing secular opposition to the power and control of the *hahambaşı* divided the Jewish community, with an especially sharp debate over the sort of educational system that would best serve them. Balat and Hasköy each had Talmud Torah schools, institutions that provided basic religious education but omitted modern subjects.[102] Religious leaders maintained that the instruction these schools offered provided a defense against the moral corruption they saw around them. Many rabbis also perceived secular education as a threat to their own professional positions.[103] Meanwhile, secular interests, including the French-sponsored Alliance Israélite Universelle (A.I.U.), argued against the traditional educational system, maintaining that the emphasis on religious instruction and Hebrew put the local community at a disadvantage vis-à-vis the Christian communities. There was also a fear that Jewish students would be drawn to the schools established by Protestant and Catholic missionaries in various areas of Istanbul. "The London Society for Promoting Christianity amongst the Jews" opened schools in Balat and Ortaköy in 1855 and one in Hasköy in 1864.[105] Indigent students were attracted to these schools, which often dispensed practical items such as clothing and food as well as knowledge. Though they do not appear to have been very successful in their proselytizing mission, the existence of these schools was a major preoccupation of the leaders of the community.

The situation changed dramatically when the A.I.U. began to introduce modern secular education in the district in the last decades of the nineteenth century. A primary school for boys was founded in Balat in 1875, and a girls' school was opened in 1882.[106] Subjects such as mathematics, history, and physics were taught. French, regarded as the language of "civilization" as well as of commerce, was introduced as a way to help Jews who knew only Ladino and perhaps Turkish to compete in the economic sector. Eventually, French became the language of choice for educated Jews. Thus a linguistic boundary that hindered Jewish economic and social advancement for decades was breached.

There was a strong moralizing aspect to the Alliance's agenda. Students were regarded as "Orientals" who had to be rehabilitated and elevated to the level of Jews in Europe. Alliance teachers in Balat often commented on the filth, stench, and overpopulation of the district, blaming it on the excessively high birth rate.[107] In 1875, teacher Nissim Béhar provided a harsh assessment of the Jewish areas of Balat.[108] According to Béhar, most Jews of the area were peddlers and dealers in second-hand goods, while the Christians (and some Muslims) engaged in the "skilled trades." There were also many Jewish beggars. Béhar explains:

[The Jews of Balat] have many natural gifts, but their vices dull or deaden their intelligence, give a sharp edge to their character, and leave them only with ruse or cleverness. They have more superstition than religion and although they pray in the temple almost every day, they do not truly think about God until poverty or illness keeps them from thinking about their own interests or pleasures. It can be said that the Jewish people are the least well considered here and the most despised; the Jews are the dregs of society. The Jews are made to suffer injustice only from the Greeks (the blood libel); but everyone despises them. A people may be persecuted unjustly, but when they are looked upon with general disdain, it must be that to some extent they are deserving of it.[109]

This image of pitiable uneducated Jewish *Balatlis* and the abysmal state of Balat's Jewish community may have been advanced to demonstrate how crucial was the presence of the A.I.U. But in the process, a particular mentality about Balat's Jews was formed that became increasingly difficult to change. Béhar's portrayal was soon corroborated by other visitors such as Edmondo de Amicis and, in the early twentieth century, Louis Bertrand and Bertrand Bareilles; as we have noted, these visitors may have seen only "Outer Balat," located outside the city walls, thereby giving them a biased impression.[110] However, this negative image was later reinforced by respected local scholars such as Abraham Galanté, himself a product of a French education, who, "on those rare occasions" when he referred to the population of Balat, "makes them appear as a rabble manipulated by obscurantists."[111]

By the early twentieth century, the changes wrought by the reforms of the *millet* system, economic decline, and natural disasters conspired to turn the once lively district where Ottoman Jewish, Muslim, Greek Orthodox, and Armenian subjects lived, worshipped, and conducted business together for centuries into a poor area. While scores of better-off Greek Orthodox, Armenian, Muslim, and Jewish families fled, Christians and Muslims continued to live there peaceably alongside Jews of a similar modest economic standing. Former Jewish residents have a fond recollection of growing up in the district during these years, remembering its multiethnic environment with a warm nostalgia:

Balat was a peaceful quarter where we were able to get along with people of different religions and backgrounds. It was a small neighborhood where people had close friendships and neighbors of intimacy.[112]

We had very good relations with Muslims and Greeks. As a Jewish family, we lived in a quarter of Balat that was predominantly Greek.[113]

Although most of the inhabitants were Jewish and lived according to Jewish customs, the Muslim presence...was very much felt. We had big festivities in the neighborhood during the Muslim holidays like Ramadan....People of all social classes and mixed backgrounds lived next to each other. In a way, Balat was a very cosmopolitan place where people learned to live harmoniously, disregarding any differences among themselves.[114]

THE PASSING OF "OLD BALAT"

The Balat of a vibrant multiethnicity was entering into its final stages. In the 1930s, the pro-nationalist policies of the Kemalist regime ushered in the final act, bringing to an end the laissez-faire pluralism that Balat's residents had enjoyed for centuries. Former residents recall the imposition of these policies by a state bent on secularizing and unifying the Turkish nation as a moment of crisis, when their own particularisms—shaped by school and home—were called into question by the new wave of reforms.

> All types of people were my friends until the Turkification attempts in 1930s, where people were forced to abandon their first languages and were forced to speak in Turkish. When the state's stand on Turkifying turned to lack of tolerance for multiculturalism, we started isolating ourselves from the outer society and found ourselves in a particularly Jewish social life.[115]

The house of Ben Porat next to Balat gate. Mixed religious references embellish the façade. The name of the original owner—Yosef Ben Porat—appears in Hebrew letters above the entryway.

I remember that we had very good relations with Greeks and Armenians but later on, when the Turkification of populations took place in 1940s, we started feeling insecure and isolating ourselves from Muslim Turks.[116]

Each piece in the mosaic that made up "old Balat" now retreated into self-absorption and finally, decomposition. The trend toward emigration accelerated, so that by the end of the twentieth century, few non-Muslims remained. In the past few decades, Turkish Muslims from the Black Sea region have settled into Balat and again transformed the place, just as the arrival of the Sephardic Jews did in the seventeenth century.

Some may regret the passing of "Old Balat." But it has not really been lost, merely reshaped as new patterns of existence emerge out of old ones and each new wave of inhabitants imparts its own character to the district, appropriating the houses, streets, and economic and cultural institutions, while altering them to suit their own purposes. The houses, churches, mosques, and synagogues of Balat provide material proof of a multiethnic conviviality that shaped the story of this district and made it the exemplar of a generous cosmopolitanism.

Notes

1. Jak Deleon, *Ancient Districts on the Golden Horn: Balat, Hasköy, Fener, Ayvansaray* (Istanbul: Gözlem Gazetecilik Basın ve Yayın, 1991), 21.

2. Şevki Nezihi Aykut and Nejdet Ertuğ, eds. *Şer'iyye Sicilleri'ne Göre İstanbul Tarihi: İstanbul Mahkemesi 121 Numaralı Şer'iyye Sicili 1231–1232/1816–1817 (Halil İnalcık Araştırma Projesi)* ["The History of Istanbul According to the Law Registers: Istanbul Law Court Register No. 121, 1816–1817 (The Halil İnalcık Research Project)"]. Under the supervision of Prof. Cemal Kafadar, Director of the Ottoman Court Records Project. (Istanbul: Sabancı University Press/Packard Humanities Institute, 2006).

3. The term *nahiye* appears in some Ottoman sources in connection with Balat and Fener; *semt* was encountered only rarely. Balat and Fener as a whole are also sometimes referred to as *mahalle*s in the primary sources. On other occasions, no specific term meaning "district" was employed in connection with place names such as Fener and Balat.

4. Romaniot (Greek-speaking) Jews were long-time residents of Constantinople. There is some evidence indicating that Jews inhabited this area of the city in the Byzantine era. Marie-Christine Varol, *Balat, faubourg juif d'Istanbul* (Istanbul: Éditions Isis, 1989), 1, 9.

5. Rodrigue has noted that the "decision of rabbinical courts in the Ottoman Empire very often remained inoperative if not approved by the Muslim courts, and that in many cases, the ensuing ambiguity led many Jews to go directly to Muslim courts to make sure that they received definite redress for their grievances." Aron Rodrigue, *French Jews, Turkish Jews: The Alliance Israélite Universelle and the Politics of Jewish Schooling in Turkey, 1860–1925* (Bloomington: Indiana University Press, 1990), 29.

6. I have not encountered in the Ottoman texts any examples of (hypothetical) "*rumhanes*" or "*ermenihanes*," i.e., residential buildings specifically designated for Greek Orthodox or Armenian families. The *yehudihane* appears to have been a unique form of housing intended specifically for Jews.

7. *Şer'iyye Sicilleri'ne Göre İstanbul Tarihi: İstanbul Mahkemesi 121 Numaralf Şer'iyye Sicili 1231–1232/1816–181*, decree #26a–2.

8. Edmondo de Amicis, *Constantinople*, transl. Caroline Tilton (New York: G.P. Putnam's Sons, 1878), 158. For a more recent Italian edition, see Edmondo de Amicis, *Constantinopoli* (Milan: Touring Club Italiano, 1997), 119–120.

9. René-Leclerc also commented upon the "upright, clear-eyed" and "jovial" manner of the Jews of Tangier, particularly in comparison with the "shocking and servile behavior of their co-religionists elsewhere." As quoted in Susan Gilson Miller, "Apportioning Sacred Space in a Moroccan City: The Case of Tangier, 1860–1912," *City &Society* 13, 1 (2001): 59

10. As quoted in Marie-Christine Bornes-Varol, "The Balat Quarter and Its Image: A Study of a Jewish Neighborhood in Istanbul," transl. Eric Fassin and Avigdor Levy, in *The Jews of the Ottoman Empire*, ed. Avigdor Levy (Princeton: The Darwin Press, 1994), 634.

11. Archives of the *Alliance Israélite Universelle*, Turquie XXV.E, transl. Aron Rodrigue, in Aron Rodrigue, *Jews and Muslims: Images of Sephardi and Eastern Jewries in Modern Times* (Seattle: University of Washington Press, 2003), 138. Nissim Béhar was the product of a Jewish school in Istanbul that taught French. When it became clear that the A.I.U. would not have enough French teachers to fill all its schools, it was decided that Turkish students such as Béhar would be trained as teachers, giving them an unprecedented opportunity. Rodrigue, *Jews and Muslims*, 34.

12. As quoted in Varol, "The Balat Quarter and Its Image," 634.

13. *Afuera Balat* and *Ariento Balat* were the Judeo-Spanish (Ladino) phrases the Jewish residents themselves employed.

14. Nur Akın, "Balat," *Dünden Bugüne İstanbul Ansiklopedisi* (Istanbul: Kültür Bakanlığı ve Tarih Vakfı, 1993–) vol. 2, 11. Varol, "The Balat Quarter and Its Image," 637–639. Similarly, in more recent decades, images disseminated by the media of burned-out and abandoned buildings in the South Bronx have become synonymous with the borough as a whole, even though the Bronx contains two of the largest parks in New York City.

15. Benjamin Braude, "Foundation Myths of the Millet System," in *Christians and Jews in the Ottoman Empire: The Functioning of a Plural Society*, eds. Benjamin Braude and Bernard Lewis, 2 vols. (New York: Holmes and Meier Publishers, 1982), I, 80; Joseph R. Hacker, "Ottoman Policy Toward the Jews and Jewish Attitudes toward the Ottomans during the Fifteenth Century," in *Christians and Jews in the Ottoman Empire: The Functioning of a Plural Society*, I, 119ff.

16. Ilan Karmi, *The Jewish Community of Istanbul in the Nineteenth Century: Social, Legal, and Administrative Transformations* (Istanbul: The Isis Press, 1996), 31.

17. According to Muslim law, like Greek Orthodox and Armenians, Jews were *dhimmī*s who were expected to fulfill their obligations (mainly financial) to the state in exchange for which they were guaranteed a special, though lesser, position in Ottoman society that implicitly acknowledged the supremacy of Muslims and Islam. Greek Orthodox subjects were generally referred to as *dhimmī*s (or later, as *rum*) in Ottoman bureaucratic sources such as the divan and court registers dating from the sixteenth century. Jews, on the other hand, were specifically called *yehudi*, while Armenians were called *ermeni* (and occasionally *dhimmî* as well). Karen A. Leal, "The Ottoman State and the Greek Orthodox of Istanbul: Sovereignty and Identity at the Turn of the Eighteenth Century" (PhD diss., Harvard University, 2003), 20 and 199–213.

18. Braude, "Foundation Myths of the Millet System," 74; Leal, "The Ottoman State," 20–21.

19. Braude, "Foundation Myths of the Millet System," 72–73.

20. In actuality, most non-Muslims were not eager to enter the Ottoman military. The government then made allowance for a special fee (*bedel-i askeriye*) that could be paid in lieu of service. Bernard Lewis, *The Emergence of Modern Turkey* (New York: Oxford University Press, 1968), 337. This fee was eliminated in 1909, after the Young Turk revolution, when conscription became compulsory for all. Rodrigue, *French Jews, Turkish Jews*, 32.

21. Jewish historiography is not concerned with refuting the influence of Ottoman culture, as is, for example, much of nineteenth- and twentieth-century Greek historiography. On the contrary, Jewish historiography has tended to emphasize Ottoman tolerance and "the thesis of continual peace and harmony among Ottomans/Turks and Jews." Marc David Baer, "Honored by the Glory of Islam: The Ottoman State, Non-Muslims, and Conversion to Islam in Late Seventeenth Century Istanbul and Rumelia" (PhD diss., University of Chicago, 2001), 41–42. See also Joseph R. Hacker, "Ottoman Policy toward the Jews and Jewish Attitudes toward the Ottomans during the Fifteenth Century," 117.

22. Sara Nur Yıldız, Review of *A History of the Jewish Community in Istanbul: The Formative Years, 1453–1566* by Minna Rozen (Boston: Brill, 2002), *H-Mideast-Medieval*, March, 2003. (July 1, 2005 <http://www.h-net.org/reviews/showrev.cgi?path=321061053042842.)

23. See comments by Avigdor Levy, *The Sephardim in the Ottoman Empire* (Princeton: The Darwin Press, 1992), 14. See also, Benjamin Braude, "The Nexus of Diaspora, Enlightenment, and Nation: Thoughts on Comparative History," in *Enlightenment and Diaspora: The Armenian and Jewish Cases*, eds. Richard G. Hovannisian and David N. Myers (Atlanta: Scholars Press, 1999), 10–12.

24. Yıldız has commented on the extent to which Hacker has "dispelled the prevailing stereotype of Jewish peaceful co-existence with Ottoman rule by exploring Mehmed II's *sürgün* (exile and re-settlement) policies toward the Romaniot and Karaite Jewish communities." Yıldız, Review of *History of the Jewish Community in Istanbul*. See J.R. Hacker, "The Sürgün System and Jewish Society in the Ottoman Empire during the Fifteenth to the Seventeenth Centuries," in *Ottoman and Turkish Jewry: Community and Leadership*, ed. Aron Rodrigue (Bloomington: Indiana University Press, 1992), 1–65.

25. Levy, *The Sephardim in the Ottoman Empire*, 14.

26. Varol, *Balat, faubourg juif d'Istanbul*.

27. Reşad Ekrem Koçu, "Balat," *İstanbul Ansiklopedisi*, ed. Reşad Ekrem Koçu (Istanbul: İstanbul Ansiklopedisi ve Neşriyat Kollektif Şirketi, 1960), 4, 1961.

28. Cem Behar, *A Neighborhood in Ottoman Istanbul: Fruit Vendors and Civil Servants in the Kasap İlyas Mahalle* (Albany: State University of New York

Press, 2003), 7. For a critique of the Orientalist paradigm, see among others, Janet L. Abu-Lughod, "The Islamic City – Historic Myth, Islamic Essence, and Contemporary Relevance," *International Journal of Middle East Studies* 19.2 (May 1987): 155–176.

29. Béhar, *A Neighborhood in Ottoman Istanbul*, 4. Still, archival evidence reveals many instances in which Greek Orthodox subjects had gradually encroached upon the areas surrounding a mosque, either renting or purchasing homes in the vicinity. (Leal, "The Ottoman State," 264–282).

30. Behar, *A Neighborhood in Ottoman Istanbul*, 4.

31. Reşad Ekrem Koçu, "Balat," *İstanbul Ansiklopedisi*, 4, 1961.

32. *İstanbul Mahkemesi 121 Numaralı Şer'iyye Sicili*, decree #44a–1: Mīrāḫūr mahallesi mütemekkinelerinden ʿarżıḥāl eden şaḫṣı muʿarrefe Māryora bint Panāyot nām naṣrāniyye ile ṣadrı kebīr oğlu Mānol veled-i Dımitrı nām ẓimmī ..."

33. Minna Rozen, "Public Space and Private Space Among the Jews of Istanbul in the Sixteenth and Seventeenth Centuries," *Turcica* 30 (1998): 337.

34. Rozen's concept of a "Jewish neighborhood" may be seen as another example of the tendency among scholars specializing in Jewish studies to see Jews as a distinct and separate entity within the larger society.

35. This terminology evolved over the centuries. Whereas in divan and court registers, one term, *sākin*, was generally applied to all Ottoman subjects in the sixteenth and part of the seventeenth centuries, by the late 1600s, the term *mütemmekin* was being used for Greek Orthodox, Armenians and Jews, with *sākin* reserved for Muslims specifically. Leal, "The Ottoman State," 224–229.

36. For an example of another way in which Ottoman texts distinguished Muslim from non-Muslim subjects see *İstanbul Mahkemesi 121 Numaralı Şer'iyye Sicili*, decree #30b-1 from the year 1817: "the [following residents] of Minor Çekmece District - Chief Farmer Halil Agha, Meckooğlu Süleyman Agha, the Royal Sergeant at Arms Usta-zade Ahmed Agha, Selim Agha, Haci Ahmed, and Benefşeli Mehmed Said, together with, from among the non-Muslims, Cicozçiftlikli Yorgi, Hazinedarçiftlikli Yanko, Terekanyalı Yani, Anbarlılı Yanako, Safralı Gülşenoğlu Kostandi and others - ..." The term *ahali* is inclusive of all the inhabitants of the district. However, when the non-Muslims are mentioned, they are referred to as part of the *re'aya*, a term that in earlier centuries had been applied to all tax-paying subjects of the Empire, but by the 1800s was used exclusively for non-Muslims. The Muslim residents are not marked as Muslim in the text; they are simply referred to as *kimesneler*, literally, "somebodies."

37. Varol, *Balat, faubourg juif d'Istanbul*, 6.

38. Many Jews resided in Hasköy as well, and an age-old rivalry existed between the two districts. A Ladino saying went as follows: "The lads of Balat are real strong youths, those of Hasköy are just dried raisins." Peter Mansel, *Constantinople: City of the World's Desire, 1453–1924* (New York: St. Martin's Press, 1998), 16.

39. Reşad Ekrem Koçu, "Balat Lağımları," *İstanbul Ansiklopedisi*, 4, 1972–73.

40. Edith Oyhon and Bente Etingü, *Churches in Istanbul* (Istanbul: Yapı Kredi Yayınları, 1999), 113–114.

41. These are some of the quarters named in Ottoman sources from the seventeenth and eighteenth centuries. Other quarters, such as that of Molla Aşık, appeared in nineteenth-century sources. The timing of the appearance of toponyms is somewhat of a mystery. Either certain areas such as this one did not have enough of a distinct identity to be considered a separate *mahalle* before the 1800s, or they simply did not figure in incidents mentioned in the sources from the earlier centuries.

42. Evliya Çelebi, *Evliya Çelebi Seyahātnāmesi, I. Kitap, Topkapı Serrayı Bağdat Yazmasının Transkripsiyonu-Dizini*, ed. Orhan Şaik Gökyay (Istanbul: Yapı Kredi Yayınları, 1996), 89a/5.

43. Reşad Ekrem Koçu, "Balat Mahkemesinin Kapatılması Vak'ası," *İstanbul Ansiklopedisi*, 4, 1973. The court of Balat was attached to the Office of the *Kadi* of Istanbul, though that judge did not adjudicate cases from that court himself; rather the duty was delegated to a substitute judge (*naib*).

44. Abraham Galanté, "Les Synagogues d'Istanbul," *HaMenora*, (August 1937): 106. Varol, "The Balat Quarter and Its Image," 637.

45. Victorya Acu, interview with Serra Levi, Hasköy, Summer 2003.

46. Interview with Serra Levi, Balat, Summer 2003.

47. Victorya Acu, interview with Serra Levi, Hasköy, Summer 2003; Varol, "The Balat Quarter and Its Image," 637.

48. Akın, "Balat," *Dünden Bugüne İstanbul Ansiklopedisi*, 2, 11. Even today, residents are vague about exactly where the dividing line between the two quarters is located.

49. Fires occurred in Balat in 1639, 1692, 1721, 1729, 1746, 1782, 1812, 1828, 1866, 1867, 1874, 1877, 1890, 1892, 1896, 1911, and 1912. Jak Deleon, "Balat Yangınları," *Dünden Bugüne İstanbul Ansiklopedisi*, 2, 12.

50. Varol, *Balat, faubourg juif d'Istanbul*, 1; Rozen, "Public Space and Private Space," 332.

51. Varol, *Balat, faubourg juif d'Istanbul*, 10.

52. Abraham (Avram) Galanté, *Histoire des Juifs de Turquie*, 9 vols. (Istanbul: Editions Isis, 1985), I: 99–100, 285–286.

53. Varol, *Balat, faubourg juif d'Istanbul*, 1, 9; Galanté, *Histoire des Juifs de Turquie*, I, 103, 173.

54. The deportations (*sürgün*) were carried out over two decades and led to the disappearance of the Jewish population of Anatolia and a drastic reduction of the Jewish communities in areas such as Macedonia and Bulgaria. Although those designated *sürgünlü* were forbidden to leave Istanbul, some Jews did manage to receive permission to return to their homes in the Balkans.

Rozen, *A History of the Jewish Community in Istanbul*, 45–47. See also J.R. Hacker, "The Sürgün System and Jewish Society in the Ottoman Empire during the Fifteenth to the Seventeenth Centuries," 1–65.

55. Abraham Galanté, *Histoire des Juifs de Turquie*, 2: 177, 183–184; Levy, *The Sephardim in the Ottoman Empire*, 7. Mantran does not accept Galanté's assertion, based on the eighteenth-century Armenian author P.G. Inciciyan, that Karaköy was named for the Karaites. Robert Mantran, *17. Yüzyılın İkinci Yarısında İstanbul: Kurumsal, İktisadi, Toplumsal Tarih Denemesi*, transl. Mehmet Ali Kılıçbay and Enver Özcan, 2 vols. (Ankara: Türk Tarih Kurumu, 1990), 1: 58. See also Rozen, *A History of the Jewish Community*, 59–60.

56. Rozen, "Public Space and Private Space Among the Jews of Istanbul in the Sixteenth and Seventeenth Centuries," 336.

57. Ibid., 337; Stéphane Yerasimos, "La communauté juive à Istanbul à la fin du XVIe siècle," *Turcica* 27 (1995): 121.

58. Galanté, *Histoire des Juifs de Turquie*, 2, 183; Naim Güleryüz, *İstanbul Sinagogları* (Istanbul: Naim Güleryüz, 1992), 14, 25. The court of the *hahambaşı* convened here every Monday and Thursday. A prison where those convicted could serve their sentences was located on the ground floor.

59. Eremya Çelebi Kömürcıyan, *İstanbul Tarihi*, transl. and eds., Hrand D. Andreasyan and Kevork Pamukcıyan (Istanbul: Eren Yayıncılık, 1988), 19.

60. Ibid.

61. Oyhon and Etingü, *Churches*, 103.

62. Kevork Pamukciyan, ed., Eremya Çelebi, *İstanbul Tarihi*, 170. Surp Nikos was originally an Orthodox Church established in the ninth century. The church, which later came under the charge of the Dominicans in Galata, was given to the Genoese and Armenians who were deported to this area of Istanbul from the town of Kaffa in the Crimea in the 1470s. It was named St. Nicholas des Latins (or Surp Nikos in Armenian). After it was converted to a mosque in 1630, it became known as the "Kefeli Camii," recalling the Crimean origins of many of the area's residents. Oyhon and Etingü, *Churches*, 52–53.

63. According to Oyhon and Etingü, the Armenians actually took possession of the church in 1629. *Churches*, 103.

64. Deleon, *Ancient Districts on the Golden Horn*, 34.

65. Perhaps in connection with the date of consecration, the second Friday in September is believed by many Istanbulites (of all faiths) to be a day of miracles when the infirmed who come to this church may be healed. Oyhon and Etingü, *Churches*, 103.

66. The school was rebuilt and named the Khorenyan School in 1816.

67. Rossitsa Gradeva, "Ottoman Policy Towards Christian Church Buildings," *Etudes Balkaniques* 4 (1994): 29; Steven Runciman, *The Great Church in Captivity: A Study of the Patriarchate of Constantinople From the Eve of the Turkish Conquest to the Greek War of Independence* (Cambridge: Cambridge University Press, 1968), 190. Runciman gives the year 1586.

68. Alexis Alexandris, *The Greek Minority of Istanbul and Greek –Turkish Relations 1918–1974* (Athens: Center for Asia Minor Studies, 1983), 24.

69. Haluk Sezgin, "Les maisons en pierre de Fener," *Observatoire urbain de l'Istanbul: Lettre de l'information* 5 (1993): 6–9.

70. Ahmed Refik [Altınay], *Onuncu Asr-ı Hicrî'de İstanbul Hayatı (1495–1591)* (Istanbul: Enderun Kitabevi, 1988).

71. Baer, "Honored by the Glory of Islam," 133; Galanté, *Histoire des Juifs de Turquie*, II, 182.

72. *Mühimme Defteri* 104, #654. After the fire of 1692, the Armenians and Jews were allowed to repair, respectively, the Surp Hıreşdagabet Church and the Ahrida Synagogue. The Ahrida was restored in the Baroque style characteristic of the period. Deleon, *Ancient Districts on the Golden Horn*, 27–29, 34; Naim Güleryüz, *The History of the Turkish Jews* (Istanbul: Gözlem Gazetecilik Basın ve Yayın, 2000), 21.

73. Ahmed Refik [Altınay], *Onikinci Asr-ı Hicrî'de İstanbul Hayatı (1689–1785)* (Istanbul: Enderun Kitabevi, 1988), 118.

74. ZB. *Dosya 372/Gömlek 116/Belge 1*.

75. Baer, "Honored by the Glory of Islam", 130–131.

76. Ibid.

77. *Şer'iye Sicilleri: Seçme Hükümler*, vol. II, ed. Türk Dünyası Araştırmaları Vakfı İlim Hey'eti, *Türk Dünyası Araştırmaları Vakfı Yayınları* 63 (Istanbul: Türk Dünyası Araştırmaları Vakfı, 1989), 266. See also 245–246; *Şer'iye Sicilleri: Mahiyeti, Toplu Kataloğu ve Seçme Hükümler*, vol. I, eds. Ahmet Akgündüz and Türk Dünyası Araştırmaları Vakfı İlim Hey'eti, *Türk Dünyası Araştırmaları Vakfı Yayınları* 52 (Istanbul: Türk Dünyası Araştırmaları Vakfı, 1989), 247, 270.

78. Refik [Altınay], *Onikinci Asr-ı Hicrî'de İstanbul Hayatı (1689–1785)*, 21.

79. Ibid., 31.

80. Zeynep Çelik, *The Remaking of Istanbul: Portrait of an Ottoman City in the Nineteenth Century* (Berkeley: University of California Press, 1993), ch. 3.

81. Rémi Stoquart, *Réhabilitation des quartiers de Balat et de Fener (péninsule historique d'Istanbul: diagnostic et propositions d'aménagement février 1998* ([Turkey?]: UNESCO, 1998), 32.

82. Leon Brudo, interview with Serra Levi, August 2003.

83. Esther Benbassa, ed., *Haim Nahum: A Sephardic Chief Rabbi in Politics, 1892–1923* (Tuscaloosa: University of Alabama Press, 1995).

84. Richard Clogg, *A Concise History of Greece* (New York: Cambridge University Press, 1992), 36–37.

85. Robert Walsh as quoted in Mansel, *Constantinople*, 241.

86. Karmi, *The Jewish Community of Istanbul in the Nineteenth Century*, 34; Lewis, *Modern Turkey*, 78; Rodrigue, *French Jews, Turkish Jews*, 27.

87. For example, Karabaş Quarter was sometimes identified as part of Balat, at other times part of Fener (cf. DH.EUM.3.Şb 9/43/1; ZB. 55/10/1). Several new *mahalle*s were identified in nineteenth- and early twentieth-century Ottoman sources, such as *Kiremit* and *Yazıcı*, names not seen in earlier sources.

88. Moise Franco, *Essai sur l'histoire des Israélites de l'empire ottoman depuis les origines jusqu'à nos jours* (Paris: Centre d'Etudes Don Isaac Abravanel, 1981), 229–230.

89. Y.PRK.ZB 1/81/1. See also Y. PRK. ZB 1/84 /1 in which Jewish boys were accused of harassing Armenian women in June 1881.

90. Varol, *Balat, faubourg juif d'Istanbul*, 24.

91. The Armenian Patriarch in 1889 stated that he did not condone the acts committed by ignorant people who should be arrested for their misdeeds (Y.PRK.ZB 8/6). On the other hand, in the "Balat Incident" the Greek Orthodox Patriarch did not intervene until requested to do so by the Chief Rabbi.

92. A.MKT.NZD 286/63/1.

93. Lewis, *Modern Turkey*, 115 ff.

94. Akın, "Balat," *Dünden Bugüne İstanbul Ansiklopedisi*, vol. 2, 11.

95. Walter F. Weiker, *Ottomans, Turks, and the Jewish Polity: A History of the Jews of Turkey* (Lanham: University Press of America, 1992), 129; Deleon, "Balat Yangınları," 12; Halil İnalcık, "Istanbul," *Encyclopedia of Islam*, vol. 4, 237.

96. A.MKT.MVL 143/85/2; 143/79/3; 145/12/1.

97. A.MKT.MVL 97/24/4; A.MKT.NZD 296/19/2; A.MKT.UM 496/69/1.

98. Kemal H. Karpat, "*Millet*s and Nationality: The Roots of the Incongruity of Nation and State in the Post-Ottoman Era," in *Christians and Jews in the Ottoman Empire: The Functioning of a Plural Society*, I, 164.

99. Hagop Barsoumian, "The Dual Role of the Armenian *Amira* Class within the Ottoman Government and the Armenian *Millet* (1750–1850)," in *Christians and Jews in the Ottoman Empire: The Functioning of a Plural Society*, I, 177.

100. Athanasia Anagnostopulu, "Tanzimat ve Rum Milletinin Kurumsal Çercevesi," in *19. Yüzyıl İstanbul'unda Gayrimüslimler*, ed. Pinelopi Stathis, trans. Foti and Stefo Benlisoy,*Tarih Vakfı Yurt Yayınları* 87 (Istanbul: Türkiye Ekonomik ve Toplumsal Tarih Vakfı, 1999), 22.

101. Karmi, *The Jewish Community of Istanbul in the Nineteenth Century*, 39. Karmi cautions against the perception that there were rigid lines between "conservative religious reactionaries" as opposed to "secular progressives." Chief Rabbi Ya'akov, who opened a school in 1849, considered himself a "progressive."

102. Rodrigue, *French Jews, Turkish Jews*, 36–37.

103. Ibid., 42.

104. Karmi, *The Jewish Community of Istanbul in the Nineteenth Century*, 63.

105. Rodrigue, *French Jews, Turkish Jews*, 37.

106. Rodrigue, *Jews and Muslims: Images of Sephardi and Eastern Jewries in Modern Times*, 20. Other schools were established in Hasköy, Galata, and Kuzguncuk in the 1870s.

107. Dumont has pointed out that emigration from the Balkans and Russia also contributed to the population increase. Paul Dumont,"Jewish Communities in Turkey during the Last Decades of the Nineteenth Century in the Light of the Archives of the *Alliance Israélite Universelle*," in *Christians and Jews in the Ottoman Empire: The Functioning of a Plural Society*, I, 212.

108. Rodrigue, *French Jews, Turkish Jews*, 72–73.

109. Archives of the *Alliance Israélite Universelle*, Turquie XXV.E, trans. Aron Rodrigue in Rodrigue, *Jews and Muslims: Images of Sephardi and Eastern Jewries in Modern Times*, 138–139.

110. Louis Bertrand, *Le mirage oriental* (Paris; Perrin et Cie., 1910); Bertrand Bareilles, *Constantinople - Ses cités franques et levantines* (Paris. Editions Bossard, 1918).

111. Varol, "The Balat Quarter and Its Image," 634.

112. Izak Negri, interview with Serra Levi, Hasköy, Summer 2003.

113. Avraham Asayas, interview with Serra Levi, Hasköy, Summer 2003.

114. Korin Suryano, interview with Serra Levi, Balat, Summer, 2003.

115. Avraham Asayas, interview with Serra Levi, Hasköy, Summer 2003.

116. Victorya Acu, interview with Serra Levi, Hasköy, Summer 2003.

BIBLIOGRAPHY

Abulafia, David *Frederick II: A Medieval Emperor.* London: Pimlico, 1988.

—. "The Jews in Sicily Under the Norman and Hohenstaufen Rulers." In *Ebrei e Sicilia.* Edited by N. Bucaria, M. Luzzati and A. Tarantino, 69–92. Palermo: Flaccovio, 2002.

Abu-Lughod, Janet. "The Islamic City: Historic Myth, Islamic Essence, and Contemporary Relevance." *International Journal of Middle Eastern Studies* 19 (1987): 155–176.

Afâ, `Umar. *al-Sahrâ wa-Sûs min khilâl al-wathâ'iq wa-al-makhtûtât: al-tawâsul wa-al-âfâq.* Silsilât nadawât wa-munâzarât, 96. Rabat: Kulliyât al-âdâb wa-al-'ulûm al-insânîya, 2001.

Africanus, Leo. *The History and Description of Africa,* translated by John Pory. 3 vols. New York: Burt Franklin, 1967.

Alexandris, Alexis P. *The Greek Minority of Istanbul and Greek-Turkish Relations, 1918–1974.* Athens: Centre of Asia Minor Studies, 1983.

Amahan, Ali, and Catherine Cambazard-Amahan. *Arrêts sur sites: le patrimoine culturel marocain.* Casablanca: Le Fennec, 1999.

Archivio di Stato di Bari, La Presenza ebraica in Puglia: Fonti Documentarie e bibliografiche. Bari: De Pascale, n.d.

Arnaldi, Girolamo. *Italy and Its Invaders.* Cambridge, MA: Harvard University Press, 2005.

Ashtor, Eliyahu. "Palermitan Jewry in the Fifteenth Century." In *The Jews and the Mediterranean Economy,* 219–241. London: Variorum, 1983.

Astarita, Tommaso. *Between Salt Water and Holy Water: A History of Southern Italy.* New York: Norton, 2005.

Aubin, Eugene. *Morocco of Today.* London: J. M. Dent & Co., 1906.

Backman, Clifford. *The Decline and Fall of Medieval Sicily: Politics, Religion, and Economy in The Reign of Frederick III, 1296–1337.* Cambridge: Cambridge University Press, 1995.

Baer, Marc David. "Honored by the Glory of Islam: The Ottoman State, Non-Muslims, and Conversion to Islam in Late Seventeenth Century Istanbul and Rumelia." Ph.D. diss. University of Chicago, 2001.

Bareilles, Bertrand. *Constantinople: Ses cités franques et levantines.* Paris: Bossard, 1918.

Behar, Cem. *A Neighborhood in Ottoman Istanbul: Fruit Vendors and Civil Servants in the Kasap Ilyas Mahalle.* Albany, NY: State University of New York Press, 2003.

Bellafiore, Giuseppe. "Architettura e forme urbane nella storia edilizia di Palermo." *Quaderno dell'Instituto di elementi di architettura dell'universita di Palermo,* 2–3 (1964): 51–74.

Ben-Ami, Issachar. *Culte des saints et pèlerinages judéo-musulmans au Maroc.* Paris: Maisonneuve Larose, 1990.

—. *Saint veneration among the Jews in Morocco.* Detroit: Wayne State University Press, 1998.

Benayahu, Meir, ed. *Divre ha-yamim shel Fes: gezerot u-me `ora`ot Yehude Fes ke-fi she-reshamum bene mishpahat Ibn Danan le-dorotehem ; ve-nilvah elehem tela`ot u-metsukot Yehude Fes me-hiburo shel Rabi Sha`ul Siriro. [History of Fez: Misfortunes and Events of Moroccan Jewry as Recorded by Ibn Danan's Family and Descendents.]* Tel Aviv: Diaspora Research Institute, 1993.

Benéch, José. *Essai d'Explication d'un Mellah.* Paris: Maisonneuve Larose, 1940.

Bensusan, S.L. "In Red Marrakesh." *The Fortnightly Review* 82 (1904): 422–433.

Bertrand, Louis. *Le mirage oriental.* Paris: Perrin et Cie, 1910.

Bianca, Stefano. *Urban Form in the Arab World: Past and Present.* London: Thames & Hudson, 2000.

Bilu, Yoram. *Without Bounds: The Life and Death of Rabbi Ya'aqov Wazana.* Detroit: Wayne State University Press, 2000.

Bonfil, Robert. *Jewish Life in Renaissance Italy.* Berkeley and Los Angeles: University of California Press, 1994.

Botte, Louis. "Marrakech une année après la conquête." *L'Afrique française* 12 (1913): 429–433.

Bourqia, Rahma. "Don et théatralité: Réflexion sur le rituel du don (*Hadiyya*) offert au Sultan au XIXe siècle." *Hespéris-Tamuda* 31 (1993): 61–75.

Boyer, M. Christine. *The City of Collective Memory: Its Historical Imagery and Architectural Entertainments.* Cambridge, MA: MIT Press, 1994.

Braude, Benjamin, and Bernard Lewis, eds. *Christians and Jews in the Ottoman Empire: The Functioning of a Plural Society*. 2 vols. New York: Holmes and Meier, 1982.

Braudel, Fernand. *The Mediterranean and the Mediterranean World in the Age of Philip II.*, Translated by Siân Reynolds. 2 vols. London: Collins,1973.

Brauer, Ralph W. "Boundaries and Frontiers in Medieval Muslim Geography." *Transactions of the American Philosophical Society*. vol. 85, part 6. Philadelphia: The American Philosophical Society, 1995: 1–73.

Brignon, J. et al. *Histoire du Maroc*. Paris: Hatier, 1967.

Brown, Kenneth. "An Urban View of Moroccan History: Salé 1000–1800." *Hespéris-Tamuda* 12 (1971): 5–106.

Brunot, Louis, and Elie Malka. *Textes judéo-arabes de Fès: Textes, transcription, traduction annotée*. Rabat: Ecole du Livre, 1939.

Calabi, Donatella. "Les quartiers juifs en Italie entre 15e et 17e siècle; quelques hypothèses de travail." *Annales ESC* 4 (1997): 777–797.

—. "La cité des juifs en Italie entre XVe et XVIe siècle." In *Les étrangers dans la ville: minorités et espace urbain du bas Moyen Age à l'époque moderne*. Edited by Jacques Bottin and Donatella Calabi, 25–40. Paris: Editions de la Maison des sciences de l'homme, 1999.

Capozzi, Salvatore Carlo. *Guida di Trani*. Trani: Ditta tipografica editrice vecchi, 1915.

Carmi, T., ed. *The Penguin Book of Hebrew Verse*. New York: Penguin Books, 1981.

Cassuto, David. "La Meschita di Palermo." In *Architettura judaica in Italia: ebraismo, sito, memoria dei luoghi*. Edited by Rosalia La Franca. 29–39. Palermo: Flaccovio, 1994.

Cassuto, Noemi. "The Italian Synagogue through the Ages." In *Synagogues Without Jews and the Communities That Built and Used Them*. Edited by Rivka and Ben-Zion Dorfman, 300–307. Philadelphia: Jewish Publication Society, 2000.

Cassuto, Umberto. "Iscrizioni ebraiche a Trani." *Rivista degli studi orientali* 13, 2 (1932): 172–178.

Çelik, Zeynep. *The Remaking of Istanbul : Portrait of an Ottoman City in the Nineteenth Century*. Berkeley: University of California Press, 1993.

Cigar, Norman. "Société et vie politique à Fès sous les premiers 'Alaouites (c 1660/1830)." *Hespéris-Tamuda* 18 (1978–79): 93–172.

—, ed. *Muhammad al-Qâdiri's Nashr al-mathâni: The Chronicles*. Oxford: Oxford University Press, 1981.

Clogg, Richard. *A Concise History of Greece*. New York: Cambridge University Press, 1992.

Cohen, Mark. *Under Crescent and Cross: The Jews in the Middle Ages*. Princeton, NJ: Princeton University Press, 1994.

Colafemmina, Cesare. "Gli ebrei nel Mezzagiorno d'Italia." In *Architettura Judaica in Italia: ebraismo, sito, memoria dei luoghi*. Edited by Rosalia La Franca, 247–255. Palermo: Flaccovio, 1994.

—. "Gli Ebrei in Puglia al tempo di Federico II di Svevia." In *Aspetti della storia degli Ebrei in Trani e in Biscelie e vicende tranesi dal secolo IX*. Edited by Cesare Colafemmina and Luigi Palmiotti, 11–24. Trani: Centro regionale di servizi educativi e culturali, 1999.

Cornell, Vincent J. *Realm of the Saint : Power and Authority in Moroccan Sufism*. Austin, TX: University of Texas Press, 1998.

De Amicis, Edmondo. *Constantinople*. Translated by Caroline Tilton. New York: G.P. Putnam, 1878.

—. *Constantinopoli*. Milan: Touring Club Italiano, 1997.

De Paule, J.-Ch. et al. *Actualité de l'habitat ancien au Caire : le Rab' Qizlar*. Cairo: Centre d'Études et de Documentation Économiques, Juridiques, et Sociales, 1985.

De Robertis, Francesco Maria. *Federico II di Svevia nel mito e nella realta: notazioni critiche e ricostruttive sulla figura e l'opera, spesso tutt'altro che esaltanti, del maggior dinasta dell'Occidente*. Documenti e monografie, Societa di storia patria per la Puglia, 49. Bari: Societa di storia patria per la Puglia, 1998.

De Simone, Adalgisa. "Palermo nei geografi e viaggiatori arabi del Medioevo." *Studi Magrebini* 2 (1968): 129–189.

Deleon, Jak. *Ancient Districts on the Golden Horn: Balat, Haskoy, Fener, Ayvansaray* Istanbul: Gözlem Gazetecilik Basın ve Yayın, 1991.

Deshen, Shlomo. *The Mellah Society: Jewish Community Life in Sherifian Morocco.* Chicago: University of Chicago Press, 1989.

Deverdun, Gaston. *Marrakech des Origines à 1912.* 2 vols. Rabat: Éditions Techniques Nord-africaines, 1959.

Di Giovanni, Vincenzo. *La Topografia antica di Palermo.* 2 vols. Palermo: Tipografia e Lagatoria del Boccone del Povero, 1889.

Di Matteo, Salvo. "La Giudecca di Palermo dal X al XV secolo." In *Fonti per la storia dell'espulsione degli ebrei dalla Sicilia.* Edited by R. Giuffrida, A. Sparti and S. Di Matteo, 62–84. Palermo: Accademia nazionale di Palermo, 1992.

Documenti per la storia degli Ebrei in Puglia nell' archivio di stato di Napoli. Bari: Regione Puglia assessorato alla cultura Istituto Ecumenico S. Nicola, 1990.

Dünden Bugüne İstanbul Ansiklopedisi [Encyclopedia of Istanbul from Yesterday to Today]. Istanbul: Kültür Bakanlığı ve Tarih Vakfı, 1993.

Doutté, Edmond. *Missions au Maroc. En tribu.* Paris: P. Geuthner, 1914.

Eickelman, Dale F. *Knowledge and Power in Morocco: The Education of a Twentieth-Century Notable.* Princeton, N.J.: Princeton University Press, 1985.

Elalouf, David. "Une Architecture juive? Regards sur une identité perdue." In *Les Juifs du Maroc.* Edited by A. Goldenberg, 303–307. Paris: Editions du Scribe, 1992.

Ennaji, Mohammed. *Serving the Master: Slavery and Society in Nineteenth-Century Morocco.* Translated by Seth Graebner. New York: St. Martin's Press, 1999.

Erckmann, Jules. *Le Maroc moderne.* Paris: Challamal Ainé, 1885.

Falcandus, Hugo. *The History of the Tyrants of Sicily by 'Hugo Falcandus' (1154–69).* Translated and edited by Graham A. Loud and Thomas Wiedemann. Manchester: Manchester University Press, 1998.

Fernandes, Leonor. "Habitat et prescriptions légales." In *L'Habitat traditionnel dans les pays musulmans autour de la Mediterranee : rencontre d'Aix-en-Provence (6–8 juin 1984),* 2: 419–426. Cairo: Institut francais d'archéologie orientale, 1984.

Foucauld, Charles de. *Reconnaissance au Maroc: Journal de route.* Paris: Société d'editions, 1939.

Franco, Moïse. *Essai sur l'histoire des Israélites de l'Empire Ottoman depuis les origines jusqu'à nos jours.* Paris: Centre d'Etudes Don Isaac Abravanel, 1981.

Fromerz, Allen. "Marrakech: City as Doctrine." Paper presented at the Middle East Studies Association Annual Meeting. Washington, D.C., 2005.

Gaignebet, Jean. "Marrakech: Grand carrefour des routes marocaines." *Revue de Géographie Marocaine* 7 (1928): 272–304.

Galanté, Abraham "Les Synagogues d'Istanbul." *Ha-Menora* (July-August 1937): 100–112.

—. *Histoire des Juifs de Turquie.* Istanbul: Editions Isis, 1985.

García-Arenal, Mercedes. "The Revolution of Fas in 869/1465 and the Death of Sultan 'Abd al-Haqq al-Marini." *BSOAS* 41, part 1 (1978): 43–66.

—. "Les Bildiyyîn de Fès, un groupe de néo-musulmans d'origine juive." *Studia Islamica* 66 (1987): 113–143.

—. "Jewish Converts to Islam in the Muslim West." In *Dhimmis and Others: Jews and Christians and the World of Classical Islam.* Edited by Uri Rubin and David Wasserstein, 227–248. Winona Lake, Indiana: Eisenbraus, 1997.

— and Gerard Albert Wiegers. *A Man of Three Worlds : Samuel Pallache, a Moroccan Jew in Catholic and Protestant Europe.* Baltimore: Johns Hopkins University Press, 2003.

Gellner, Ernest. *Saints of the Atlas.* Chicago: University of Chicago Press, 1969.

Gerber, Jane. *Jewish Society in Fez, 1450–1700. Studies in Communal and Economic Life.* Leiden: Brill,1980.

Gil, Moshe. *Jews in the Islamic Countries in the Middle Ages.* Translated by David Strassler. Leiden: Brill, 2004.

Goitein, S.D. *A Mediterranean Society: The Jewish Communities of the Arab World as Portrayed in the Documents of the Cairo Geniza.* 5 vols. Berkeley: University of California Press, 1967–1988.

— "Sicily and Southern Italy in the Cairo Geniza Documents." *Archivio storico per la Sicilia Orientale,* 67. Catania: Societa di Storia Patria per la Sicilia Orientale, 1971: 9–33.

Goldberg, Harvey E., ed. *Sephardi and Middle Eastern Jewries: History and Culture in the Modern Era.* Bloomington: Indiana University Press, 1996.

Gottreich, Emily. "On the Origins of the Mellah of Marrakesh." *International Journal of Middle Eastern Studies* 35 (2003): 287–305.

—. "Rethinking the Islamic City from the Perspective of Jewish Space." *Jewish Social Studies* 11, 1 (2004): 118–46.

—. *The Mellah of Marrakesh : Jewish and Muslim Space in Morocco's Red City.* Bloomington: Indiana University Press, 2007.

Gradeva, Rossitsa. "Ottoman Policy towards Christian Church Buildings." *Etudes Balkaniques* 30,4 (1994): 14–36.

Güleryüz, Naim. *İstanbul Sinagogları [The Synagogues of Istanbul].* Istanbul: Naim Güleryüz, 1992.

—. *The History of the Turkish Jews.* Istanbul: Gözlem Gazetecilik Basın ve Yayın, 2000.

Hadziiossif, Jacqueline. "Les conversions des juifs à l'islam et au christianisme en Méditerranée XIe-XVe siècles." In *Mutations d'identités en Méditerranée : Moyen Age et époque contemporaine.* Edited by Christiane Veauvy, Eliane Dupuy, and Henri Bresc, 159–173. [Saint-Denis]: Bouchène, 2000.

Hanna, Nelly. "Social Implications of Housing Types in 17th and 18th century Cairo." In *Sciences sociales et phénomènes urbains dans le monde arabe : actes du colloque de l'Association de liaison entre les Centres de recherches et documentations sur le monde arabe (ALMA), Casablanca, 30 novembre–2 décembre 1994.* Edited by Mohamed Naciri and André Raymond, 85–92. Casablanca: Fondation du Roi Abdul-Aziz Al-Saoud, 1997.

Harvey, David. *Paris, Capital of Modernity.* London: Routledge, 2006.

Hirschberg, H. Z. *A History of the Jews in North Africa.* 2 vols. Leiden: Brill, 1974–81.

Hodgkin, Thomas. *Narrative of a Journey to Morocco, in 1863 and 1864.* London: T.C. Newby, 1866.

Hourani, Albert Habib, Philip S. Khoury, and Mary C. Wilson. *The Modern Middle East: A Reader.* London: I.B. Tauris, 1993.

Hovannisian, Richard G, and David N. Myers, eds. *Enlightenment and Diaspora: The Armenian and Jewish Cases.* Atlanta, GA: Scholars Press, 1999.

Humphreys, R. Stephen. *Islamic History : A Framework for Inquiry.* Minneapolis: Bibliotheca Islamica, 1988.

Hunwick, J.O. "The Rights of Dhimmîs to Maintain a Place of Worship: A 15th Century Fatwâ from Tlemcen." *al-Qantara* 12, 1 (1991): 133–155.

Iancu, Danièle. *Les Juifs en Provence (1475–1501); de l'insertion à l'expulsion.* Marseille: Institut historique de Provence, Archives communales, 1981.

Ibn ʾAbi Zarʾ al-Fâsî, ʾAli b. ʾAbd Allah. *Anîs al-mutrib bî-rawd al-qîrtas fî akhbâr mulûk al-Maghrib wa-tarîkh madînat Fâs.* Rabat: Dâr al-Mansûr, 1972.

Ibn Hawqal, Abû al-Qâsim. *Surat al-ard.* Beirut: Dâr Maktabat al-Hayât, 1979.

Ibn Jubayr, Muhammad b. Ahmad. *Rihla.* Beirut: Dâr Sâdir, 1964.

Idel, Moshe "The ecstatic Kabbalah of Abraham Abulafia in Sicilia and its Transmission during the Renaissance." In *Italia Judaica: Gli Ebrei in Sicilia sino all'espulsione del 1492: atti del V convegno internazionale, Palermo, 15–19 giungo, 1992,* 330–340. Rome: Fratelli Palombi Editori, 1995.

al-Idrîsî, Abû ʾAbdallah. *Description de l'Afrique et de l'Espagne.* Edited by R.P.A. Dozy and M.J. Goeje. 2 vols. Leiden: E.J. Brill, 1866.

—. *Nuzhat al-mushtâq fî ikhtirâq al-afâq.* Cairo: Maktabat al-thaqâfa al-dîniya, 1990.

İnciciyan, P.G. *XVIII. Asırda İstanbul [Istanbul in the Eighteenth Century].* Translated by Hrand Andreasyan. Istanbul: Istanbul Fethi Derneği Yayınları, 1956.

Kahera, Akel, and Omar Benmira. "Damages in Islamic Law: Maghribî Muftîs and the Built Environment (9th–15th Centuries C.E.)." *Islamic Law and Society* 5, 2 (1998): 131–164.

Karmi, Ilan. *The Jewish Community of Istanbul in the Nineteenth Century: Social, Legal and Administrative Transformations.* Istanbul: Isis Press, 1996.

Katz, Jacob. *Exclusiveness and Tolerance*. New York: Oxford University Press, 1961.

Kenbib, Mohammed. "Changing Aspects of State and Society in Nineteenth Century Morocco." In *The Moroccan State in Historical Perspective, 1850–1985*. Edited by Abdelali Doumou, 11–27. Dakar: Codesria, 1990.

—. *Juifs et Musulmans au Maroc, 1859–1948*. Rabat: Université Mohammed V, 1994.

Koçu, Reşad Ekrem ed. *İstanbul Ansiklopedisi [Encyclopedia of Istanbul]*. Istanbul: İstanbul Ansiklopedisi ve Neşriyat Kollektif Şirketi, 1958–1971.

Kohn, David. *Rabi Avraham Ibn Ezra: Kovets hokhmat ha-Raba', shirav u-melitsotav, hidotav u-mikhtamav` im toladeto*.Warsaw: Hotsa'at Ahi'asaf, 1894.

Koehler, Henry. "La Kasba saadienne de Marrakech, d'après un plan manuscrit de 1585." *Hespéris* 27 (1940): 1–19.

Kömürciyan, Eremya Çelebi. *İstanbul Tarihi: XVII. Asırda İstanbul [History of Istanbul: Istanbul in the Seventeenth Century]*. Translated by Hrand Andreasyan. Istanbul: Eren Yayıncılık, 1988.

Kostof, Spiro. *The City Shaped: Urban Patterns and Meanings Through History*. Boston: Little, Brown, 1991.

Krinsky, Carol H. *Synagogues of Europe: Architecture, History, Meaning*. New York, N.Y.: Architectural History Foundation, 1985.

La Duca, Rosario. "Vicende topographiche del centro storico di Palermo." In *Bibliografia dell'Urbanistica e dell'Architettura Palermitana*. Quaderno no. 2–3, tavola 2, 7–29. Palermo: Facolta di Architettura, 1964.

La Franca, Rosalia, ed. *Architettura judaica in Italia: ebraismo, sito, memoria dei luoghi*. Palermo: Flaccovio, 1994.

Lagardère, Vincent. *Les Almoravides jusqu'au règne de Yûsuf b. Tasfîn, (1039–1106)*. Paris: L'Harmattan, 1989.

Lambert, Paul. "Notice sur la ville de Maroc." *Bulletin de la Société Géographie de Paris* 16 (July–Dec. 1868): 430–447.

Lapidus, Ira. *Muslim Cities in the Later Middle Ages*. Cambridge: Cambridge University Press, 1984.

Larner, John. *Italy in the Age of Dante and Petrarch, 1216–1380*. London and New York: Longman, 1980.

Le Tourneau, Roger. "Notes sur les lettres latines de Nicolas Clénard relatant son séjour dans le royaume de Fès (1540–41)." *Hespéris* 19 (1934): 45–62.

—. *Fès avant le protectorat: étude économique et sociale d'une ville de l'occident musulman*. Casablanca: SMLE, 1949; Rabat: Ed. La Porte, 1987.

— and M. Vicaire. "L'Industrie du fil d'or au mellah de Fès." *Bulletin economique et social du Maroc* 3,13 (1936): 185–190.

—. "La Fabrication du fil d'or à Fès." *Hespéris* 2,1–2 (1937): 67–88.

Leal, Karen A. "The Ottoman State and the Greek Orthodox of Istanbul: Sovereignty and Identity at the Turn of the Eighteenth Century." Ph.D. diss. Harvard University, 2003.

Lévi-Provençal, Evariste *Las ciudades y las instituciones urbanas del Occidente musulman en la Edad Media*. Tetuán, Morocco: Editora Marroqui, 1950.

Levy, André. "To Morocco and Back: Tourism and Pilgrimage among Moroccan-born Israelis." In *Grasping Land : Space and Place in Contemporary Israeli Discourse and Experience*. Edited by Eyal Ben-Ari and Yoram Bilu, 25–46. Albany, NY: SUNY Press, 1997.

Levy, Avigdor. *The Sephardim in the Ottoman Empire*. Princeton, NJ: The Darwin Press, 1992.

— ed. *The Jews of the Ottoman Empire*. Princeton, NJ: Darwin Press, 1994.

Levy, Simon. "Hara et Mellah: Les mots, l'histoire et l'institution." In *Histoire et Linguistique*. Edited by Abdelahad Sebti, 41–50. Rabat: Université Mohammed V, 1992.

—. "Arabófonos e hispanófonos (beldiyin y 'azmiyin) en la judería de Fez, dos siglos después de la expulsión." In *El siglo XVII Hispanomarroqui*. Edited Mohammed Salhi, 333–51. Rabat: Facultad de Letras de Rabat, 1997.

—. "Fès et ses synagogues." [n.p,, n.d.]

—. *La synagogue Danan restaurée*. Casablanca: Fondation du Patrimoine Culturel Judéo-marocain, [n.d.]

Lewis, Bernard. *The Emergence of Modern Turkey*. New York: Oxford University Press, 1968.

—. *Islam from the Prophet Muhammad to the Capture of Constantinople*. 2 vols. New York: Harper and Row, 1974.

Loti, Pierre. *Au Maroc*. Paris: Boîte à documents, 1988.

Malcangi, Guido. *Trani: pagine di storia, ricordi di vita e altre divagazioni pugliesi*. [Fasano]: Schena, 1983.

Mansel, Peter. *Constantinople: City of the World's Desire, 1453–1924*. New York: St. Martin's Press, 1998.

Mantran, Robert. *17. Yüzyılın İkinci Yarısında İstanbul: Kurumsal, İktisadi, Toplumsal Tarih Denemesi [Istanbul in the Second Half of the 17th Century: An Essay on Institutional, Economic, and Social History.]* Translated by Mehmet Ali Kılıçbay and Enver Özcan, vol. 1. Ankara: Türk Tarih Kurumu, 1990.

Marçais, Georges. "La conception des villes de l'Islam." *Revue d'Alger* 2, 10 (1945): 517–533.

Marçais, William. "L'islamisme et la vie urbaine." *Comptes Rendus de l'Academie des Inscriptions et Belles Lettres* (Jan–March 1928): 86–100.

Matham, Adrien. "Le Palais d'el Bedi et l'oeuvre de Matham." *Les sources inédites de l'histoire du Maroc [S.I.H.M.] première série, Pays Bas*. Edited by Henry de Castries, 4: 570–596. Paris: Ernest Leroux, 1906–1923.

Mazzamuto, Antonella. "L'insediamento ebraico in Sicilia dal periodo arabo all'espulsione del 1492." In *Architettura judaica in Italia: ebraismo, sito, memoria dei luoghi*. Edited by Rosaria La Franca, 83–95. Palermo: Flaccovio, 1994.

Messier, Ronald. "Rereading Medieval Sources through Multidisciplinary Glasses." In *The Maghrib in Question: Essays in History and Historiography*. Edited by Michel Le Gall and Kenneth Perkins, 174–200. Austin, TX: University of Texas Press, 1997.

Meunié, Jacques, Henri Terrasse, and Gaston Deverdun. *Nouvelles recherches archéologiques à Marrakech*. Publications de l'Institut des hautes-études marocaines, [I.H.E.M.] 62. Paris: Arts et métiers graphiques, 1957.

Michaux-Bellaire, E., ed. *Les Habous de Tanger: Registre officiel d'actes et de documents, part 2, Analyses et extraits*. Paris: Ernest Leroux, 1914.

Miège, Jean-Louis. *Le Maroc et L'Europe (1830–1894)*. 4 vols. Rabat: Editions La Porte, 1989.

—. *Morocco*. Translated by O. C. Warden. Paris: Arthaud, 1952.

Miller, Susan Gilson. "Watering the Garden of Tangier: Colonial Contestations in a Moroccan City." In *The Walled Arab City in Architecture, Literature and History: The Living Medina*. Edited by S. Slyomovics, 26–50. London: Frank Cass, 2001.

_____. "Apportioning Sacred Space in a Moroccan City: The Case of Tangier, 1860–1912." *City & Society*. 13, 1(2001): 57–83.

_____. "Finding Order in the City; The Hubûs of the Great Mosque of Tangier as an Agent of Urban Change." *Muqarnas* 22 (2005): 262–280.

Mocquet, Jean. "Voyage de Jean Mocquet au Maroc." *Les sources inédites de l'histoire du Maroc [S.I.H.M.] première série, France*. Edited by Henry de Castries, et al., 383–417. Paris: E. Leroux, 1909.

Munkácsi, Ernst. *Der Jude von Neapel*. Zurich: Verlag Die Lica, 1939.

Nahon, Moïse I. "Les Israélites du Maroc." *Revue des études ethnographiques et sociologiques* 2 (1909): 258–279.

Nirenberg, David. *Communities of Violence: Persecution of Minorities in the Middle Ages*. Princeton, NJ: Princeton University Press, 1996.

Noin, Daniel. *La population rurale du Maroc*. Publications de l'Université de Rouen, 8. Paris: Presses universitaires de France, 1970.

Nora, Pierre, and Lawrence D. Kritzman. *Realms of Memory : Rethinking the French Past*. 3 vols. New York: Columbia University Press, 1996.

Onesti, Francesa. *La Campana di Trani*. Trani: CRSEC Trani, 1999.

Ovadia of Bertenura. *Pathway to Jerusalem: The Travel Letters of Rabbi Ovadia of Bertenura*. Translated by Yaakov Shulman. New York: CIS Publishers, 1992.

Oyhon, Edith, and Bente Etingü. *Churches in Istanbul*. İstanbul: Yapı Kredi Yayınları, 1999.

Paparrigopoulos, Constantinos. *Historia tou Hellenikou Ethnous [History of the Hellenic Nation]*. Athens: Ekdotikē Hermes E.P.E, 1970.

Pascon, Paul. *Le Haouz de Marrakech*. Rabat: [s.n.], 1977.

— and John R. Hall. *Capitalism and Agriculture in the Haouz of Marrakesh*. London: KPI, 1986.

Qâdirî, Muhammad b. al-Tayyib. *Nashr al-mathâni lî-ahl al-qarn al-hâdî ashar wa-al-thâni*. Edited by Ahmad Tawfîq and Muhammad Hajji. 4 vols. Rabat: Maktabat al-Tâlib, 1977–86.

Quatriglio, Giuseppe. *A Thousand Years in Sicily*. Translated by Justin Vitiello. New York: Legas, 1991.

Ravid, Benjamin. "A Tale of three Cities and their Raison d'Etat: Ancona, Venice and Livorno and the Competition for Jewish Merchants in the Sixteenth Century." *Mediterranean Historical Review* 6, 2 (1991): 139–162.

Raymond, A. "Les caractéristiques d'une ville arabe `moyenne' au XVIIIe siécle. Le cas de Constantine." *Revue de l'Occident Musulman et de la Méditerranée* 44 (1987): 134–147.

—. "Islamic City, Arab City: Orientalist Myths and Recent Views." *British Journal of Middle Eastern Studies* 21,1 (1994): 3–18.

—. "La structure spatiale de la ville." In *Sciences sociales et phénomènes urbains dans le monde arabe : actes du colloque de l'Association de Liaison entre les Centres de recherches et documentations sur le monde arabe (ALMA), Casablanca, 30 novembre–2 décembre 1994*. Edited by Mohamed Naciri and André Raymond, 75–84. Casablanca: Fondation du Roi Abdul-Aziz Al-Saoud, 1997.

Refik [Altınay], Ahmed. *Onuncu Asr-ı Hicrî'de İstanbul Hayatı (1495–1591) [Life in Istanbul (1495–1591)]*. Istanbul: Enderun Kitabevi, 1988.

—. *Onikinci Asr-ı Hicrî'de İstanbul Hayatı (1689–1785) [Life in Istanbul (1689–1785)]*. Istanbul: Enderun Kitabevi, 1988.

René-Leclerc, Charles. *Le Maroc septentrional: souvenirs et impressions (été 1904)*. Algiers: Imp. Algérienne, 1905.

—. *La Commerce et l'industrie à Fès: Rapport au Comité du Maroc*. Paris: Comité du Maroc, 1905.

Revault, Jacques, Lucien Golvin, and Ali Amahan. *Palais et demeures de Fès*. Paris: C.N.R.S., 1985.

Rodrigue, Aron. *French Jews, Turkish Jews: The Alliance Israélite Universelle and the Politics of Jewish Schooling in Turkey, 1860–1925*. Bloomington: Indiana University Press, 1990.

—. *Ottoman and Turkish Jewry: Community and Leadership*. Bloomington: Indiana University Press, 1992.

—. *Jews and Muslims: Images of Sephardi and Eastern Jewries in Modern Times*. Seattle: University of Washington Press, 2003.

Ronchi, Benedetto. *Indagine sullo sviluppo urbanistico di Trani dall'XI al XVIII secolo*. [Fasano]: Schena, 1984.

Rosen, Lawrence. *Bargaining for Reality: The Construction of Social Relations in a Muslim Community*. Chicago: University of Chicago Press, 1984.

Roth, Cecil. *The History of the Jews of Italy*. Philadelphia: Jewish Publication Society, 1946.

Rozen, Minna. "Public Space and Private Space Among the Jews of Istanbul in the Sixteenth and Seventeenth Centuries." *Turcica* 30 (1998): 331–346.

—. *A History of the Jewish Community in Istanbul: The Formative Years, 1453–1566*. Leiden: Brill, 2002.

Ruderman, David B. "At the Intersection of Cultures: The Historical Legacy of Italian Jewry." In *Gardens and Ghettos: The Art of Jewish Life in Italy*. Edited by Vivian Mann, 1–23. Berkeley: University of California Press, 1989.

Runciman, Steven. *The Great Church in Captivity: A Study of the Patriarchate of Constantinople from the Eve of the Turkish Conquest to the Greek War of Independence*. Cambridge: Cambridge University Press, 1968.

Saisset, Pascale. *Heures juives au Maroc*. Paris: Rieder, 1930.

Salmon, Georges "Le culte de Muley Idrîs et la Mosquée des Chorfa à Fès." *Archives marocaines [AM]* 3 (1905): 423–429.

———. "Notes sur les superstitions populaires dans la région de Tanger." *AM* 2 (1904): 262–272.

———. "Les mariages musulmans à Tanger." *AM* 2 (1904): 273–289.

———. "Marabouts de Tanger." *AM* 2 (1905): 115–126.

———. "Confréries et zaouiyas de Tanger." *AM* 2 (1905): 100–114.

———. "L'administration marocaine à Tanger." *AM* 1 (1904): 1–55.

———. "Le commerce indigène et le marché de Tanger." *AM* 1 (1904): 38–55.

Sayed, Hazem I. "The *rab'* in Cairo : a window on Mamluk architecture and urbanism." Ph.D. diss. Massachusetts Institute of Technology, 1987.

Schroeter, Daniel J. *Merchants of Essaouira: Urban Society and Imperialism in Southwestern Morocco, 1844–1886*. Cambridge: Cambridge University Press, 1988.

—. "The Jewish Quarter and the Moroccan City." In *New Horizons in Sephardic Studies*. Edited by Yedida Stillman and George Zucker, 67–81. Binghamton, NY: SUNY Press, 1993.

—. *The Sultan's Jew : Morocco and the Sephardi World*. Stanford: Stanford University Press, 2002.

Schwerdtfeger, Friedrich W. *Traditional Housing in African Cities : A Comparative Study of Houses in Zaria, Ibadan, and Marrakech*. Chichester [Eng.]; New York: J. Wiley, 1982.

Sebag, Paul, avec Robert Attal. *La hara de Tunis; l'évolution d'un ghetto nord-africain*. Paris: Presses universitaires de France, 1959.

Segre, Renata. "Sephardic Settlements in Sixteenth Century Italy: A Historical and Geographical Survey." *Mediterranean Historical Review* 6, 2 (1991): 112–137.

Sémach, Y.D. "Un rabbin voyageur marocain: Mardochée Aby Serrour." *Hespéris* 8, 3–4 (1928): 385–399.

—. "Une Chronique juive de Fès: Le "Yahas Fès" de Ribbi Abner Hassarfaty." *Hespéris* 19 (1934): 79–94.

Şer'iye Sicilleri: mahiyeti, toplu kataloğu ve seçme hükümler [The Şer'iye Records: Their Nature, Compact Catalogue and Selection of Decrees. Edited by Ahmet Akgündüz and Türk Dünyasi Arastırmaları Vakfı İlim Hey'eti. vol I. Istanbul: Türk Dünyası Araştırmaları Vakfı, 1988.

Şer'iyye Sicilleri'ne göre İstanbul tarihi: İstanbul mahkemesi 121 numaralf Şer'iyye Sicili tarih: 1231–1232/1816–1817 (Halil İnalcık Araştırma Projesi) [The History of Istanbul According to the Law Registers: Istanbul Law Court Register No. 121, 1816–1817 (The Halil İnalcık Research Project). Edited by Şevki Nezihi Aykut and Nejdet Ertuğ. Istanbul: Sabancı University Press/Packard Humanities Institute, 2006.

Şer'iye Sicilleri: Seçme Hükümler [The Şer'iye Records: Selection of Decrees], vol. 2. Edited by İlim Hey'eti, Istanbul: Türk Dünyası Araştırmaları Vakfı, 1989.

Sezgin, Haluk. "Les maisons en pierre de Fener." *Observatoire urbain de l'Istanbul: Lettre de l'information* 5 (1993): 6–9.

Shahbar, Abd al-Aziz, ed. *al-Kitâb al-tawârîkh aw tarîkh Fâs*. Tetuan: Association Tetuan Asmir, 2002.

Simonsohn, Shlomo. "The Hebrew Revival Among Early Medieval European Jews." In *Salo Wittmayer Baron Jubilee Volume*, 2: 843–848. Jerusalem: American Academy for Jewish Research, 1975.

—. *The Jews in Sicily*. Leiden: Brill, 1997.

Şişman, Cengiz. "A Jewish Messiah in the Ottoman Court: Sabbetai Sevi and the Emergence of a Judeo-Islamic Community, 1666–1720." Ph. D. diss. Harvard University, 2004.

Slousch, Nahum "Elegie de Moise Rimos: martyr juif a Palerme au XVI siècle." In *Centenario della Nascita di Michele Amari*. Edited by G. Salvo Cozzo, 2: 186–204. Palermo: Stablimento Tipografico Virzi, 1910.

Stathis, Pinelopi, ed. *19. Yüzyıl İstanbul'unda Gayrimüslimler [Non-Muslims in Nineteenth Century Istanbul]*. Istanbul: Türkiye Ekonomik ve Toplumsal Tarih Vakfı, 1999.

Stern, S.M. "A Twelfth Century Circle of Hebrew Poets in Sicily." *Journal of Jewish Studies* 5 (1954): 60–79.

Stillman, Norman A. *The Jews of Arab Lands: A History and Source Book*. Philadelphia: Jewish Publication Society, 1979.

—. "Saddiq and Marabout in Morocco." In *The Sephardic and Oriental Jewish Heritage*. Edited by Issachar Ben-Ami, 489–500. Jerusalem: Magnes Press, 1982.

Stoquart, Rémi. *Réhabilitation des quartiers de Balat et de Fener (péninsule historique d'Istanbul): diagnostic et propositions d'aménagement février 1998*. [Turkey?]: UNESCO, 1998.

Taylor, Julie. *Muslims in Medieval Italy: The Colony at Lucera*. Lanham: Lexington Books, 2003.

Tharaud, Jérôme, and Jean Tharaud. *Marrakech; ou, les seigneurs de l'Atlas*. Paris: Plon Nourrit, 1920.

Thomson, Joseph. *Travels in the Atlas and Southern Morocco : A Narrative of Exploration*. London: George Philip, 1889.

Torres, Diego de. *Relación del origen y suceso de los xarifes y del estado de los reinos de Marruecos, Fez y Tarudante*. Edited by Mercedes García-Arenal. Madrid: Siglo Veintiuno, 1980.

Triki, Hamid, and Bernard Rosenberger. "Famines et épidémies au Maroc aux XVIe et XVIIe siècles." *Hespéris-Tamuda* 14, 15 (1974): 14: 109–175; 15: 5–103.

Tuğlacı, Pars. *İstanbul Ermeni Kiliseleri [The Armenian Churches of Istanbul]*. Istanbul: Pars Yayın, 1991.

Tudela, Benjamin of. *The Itinerary of Benjamin of Tudela*. Edited by Marcus Nathan Adler. London: Henry Frowde, 1907: Malibu, CA: Joseph Simon, 1983.

Twersky, Isadore. "The Contribution of Italian Sages to Rabbinic Literature." In *Italia judaica : atti del I Convegno internazionale : Bari 18–22, maggio 1981,* 383–400. Roma: Ministero per i beni culturali e ambientali, 1983.

Udovitch, Abraham L. and Lucette Valensi. *The Last Arab Jews: The Communities of Jerba, Tunisia*. Chur, Switzerland: Harwood, 1984.

Vajda, Georges. "Un Recueil de textes historiques judéo-marocains." *Hespéris* 35–36 (1948–1949): 35 (1948): 311–358 and 36 (1949):139–188.

Valensi, Lucette. "Inter-Communal Relations and Changes in Religious Affiliation in the Middle East (Seventeenth to Nineteenth Centuries)." *Comparative Studies in Society and History* 39,1 (1997): 251–269.

Varol, Marie-Christine. *Balat, faubourg juif d'Istanbul*. Istanbul: Editions Isis, 1989.

Vivanti, Corrado. "The History of the Jews in Italy and the History of Italy." *Journal of Modern History* 67, 2 (1995): 309–357.

Weiker, Walter F. *Ottomans, Turks and the Jewish Polity: A History of the Jews of Turkey*. Lanham: University Press of America, 1992.

Westermarck, Edward. *Ritual and Belief in Morocco*. New Hyde Park, NY: University Books, 1968.

Wheatley, Paul. *The Places Where Men Pray Together : Cities in Islamic Lands, Seventh Through the Tenth Centuries*. Chicago: University of Chicago Press, 2000.

Woodhouse, C.M. *Modern Greece: A Short History*. Boston: Faber & Faber, Ltd., 1991.

Yerasimos, Stéphane. "La communauté juive à Istanbul à la fin du XVIe siècle." *Turcica* 27 (1995): 101–130.

Yıldız, Sara Nur. "Review" of *The History of the Jewish Community in Istanbul: The Formative Years, 1453–1566* by Minna Rozen. Boston: Brill, 2002." *H-Mideast-Medieval,* March, 2003.

Zack, Joel. *The Synagogues of Morocco: An Architectural and Preservation Survey*. New York: World Monuments Fund, 1995.

Zeldes, Nadia, and Miriam Frenkel. "The Sicilian Trade: Jewish Merchants in the Mediterranean in the Twelfth and Thirteenth Centuries." In *Gli Ebrei in Sicilia dal tardoantico al Medioevo*. Edited by N. Bucaria, 243–256. Palermo: Flaccovio, 1998.

Zerbib, T. "Slave Caravans in Morocco." *Anti-Slavery Reporter* 7, 3 (1887): 36–59.

GLOSSARY

`adl (Ar.) an adjunct to the qâdî who witnesses and notarizes contracts

aron kodesh or **heikhal** (Heb.) the closet-like receptacle in the synagogue in which the Torah scrolls are kept

`attârîn (Ar.) the spice market

bâb, bâb al-mallâh (Ar.) gate; the gate of the *mallâh*

bâbûj (Ar.) Moroccan slippers made of cloth or leather

bar-mitzvah (Heb.) the confirmation ceremony of a Jewish boy at the age of thirteen, regarded as the age of religious responsibility

baraka (Ar.) divine beneficence, one of the qualities of a saint

bayt (Ar.) a room; the primary unit of a house

bugnato (It.) a masonry style in which stones are hewn to protrude outward from the wall to create a monumental effect

burj (Ar.) a fortified tower, usually part of the city wall, used as a point of defense

castrum (Lat.) a Roman camp with its distinctive cross-axis street pattern

dâr (Ar.) a house

darb (Ar.) a narrow street

darîba (Ar.) a cul-de-sac

dhimmî (Ar.) a "protected" person; a Jew or a Christian under Islamic rule

divan (Tur.) the Ottoman council of state presided over by the Sultan, or in his absence, by the grand vizier

eruv (Heb.) lit. "mixing"; an actual physical boundary that defines the space within which goods may be transported on the Sabbath and religious holidays

expulsado (Sp.) an exiled person, especially Jews and Muslims banished from Catholic Spain in the 15th–17th centuries

faqîh (Ar.) a person learned in *fiqh*, or Islamic jurisprudence; a teacher

fatwâ, pl. **fatâwâ** (Ar.) a religious opinion based on Islamic law

firman (Tur.) an edict issued by the Ottoman Sultan

funduq, pl. **fanâdiq** (Ar.) storehouses, dormitories, or workshops built around a central courtyard

genizah (Heb.) a store-room for disused books and papers attached to a synagogue

giudecca, pl. **giudecche** (It.) the Jewish quarter of the Italian city

habûs, pl. **ahbâs** (Ar., esp. North Africa) a Muslim public endowment ; a *waqf*

hahambaşı (Tur.) the Chief Rabbi of the Jewish community

hajj (Ar.) pilgrimage to Mecca

halâl (Ar.) lit., permitted; an animal slaughtered in the manner prescribed by Muslim law

hammâm (Ar. and Tur.) a public bathhouse

hâra (Ar.) quarter of the city, as in hârat al-yahûd, the "Jewish quarter"

hawma (Ar.) neighborhood or quarter

jibs (Ar., *gibs* in the Moroccan dialect) plaster of Paris sculpted to form an ornamental surface element

jihâd (Ar.) waging a struggle in defense of Islamic principles

jinn (Ar.) creature from the spirit world who exercises power over human beings

jizya (Ar.) **cizye** (Tur.) the poll tax imposed on non-Muslims

judería (Sp.) the Jewish quarter of a Spanish town

madîna (Ar.) lit. "the city," especially the pre-modern Middle Eastern city

madrasa (Ar.) an institution of higher learning where the Islamic sciences are taught

mahalle (Tur.) neighborhood; the basic unit of social organization in the Ottoman city

mahiya (Ar.) a fig brandy distilled by Jews in Morocco

makhzan (Ar.) lit., storehouse; a name for the Moroccan ruling authority

mallâh (Ar.) the Jewish quarter of a Moroccan city

marrano (Sp.) in medieval Iberia, a Jew converted to Christianity to avoid persecution

mashrabîya (Ar.) a window grille or screen of turned wood

mashwâr (Ar.) the parade ground adjacent to a Moroccan royal palace

masjid (Ar.) a mosque

matzah, pl. **matzot** (Heb.) unleavened bread eaten during Passover

megorashim (Heb.) the Jews exiled from Spain in 1492

menorah (Heb.) a seven-branched candelabrum which, according to the Bible, was a prominent feature of the Temple in Jerusalem; hence, a symbol of the Jewish faith

mesquita (Sp.), **meschita** (It.) from the Ar. **masjid**; a mosque

mezuzah, **mezuzot** (Heb.) a piece of parchment inscribed with Hebrew texts (Deuteronomy 6:4-9 and 11:13-21) enclosed in a case and attached to the doorpost of a Jewish house

mikveh (Heb.) a bath for ritual immersion and purification

millet (Tur.) a religious community under the authority of the Ottoman government

minhag (Heb.) customary practices that have become binding and assume the force of law

minyan (Heb.) lit. "number"; the quorum of ten male adults, aged 13 years or over, necessary for public synagogue service and other religious ceremonies

minzah (Ar.) a pavilion; a summer house

mithqâl (Ar.) an amount of money equal to 10 *dirham*s (Morocco, c. 1900)

mudéjar (Sp.) An architectural style developed in Muslim Spain

muhtasib (Ar.) the inspector of weights and measures in the marketplace

mujâhid, pl. **mujâhidîn** (Ar.) a warrior for the faith

mukhaznî (Ar.) a government soldier in Morocco

mulkîya (Ar.) an official title to a piece of property

nahiye (Tur.) neighborhood

nawâla, pl. **nawâwil** (Ar.) a hut made of thatch and reeds

oreil, a polygonal recess with a window projecting from the upper storey of a building

pasha (Ar.) the governor of a large Moroccan city

palazzo, pl. **palazzi** (It.) a mansion

protégé (Fr.) a non-European who has acquired legal status from a European nation

qâdî (Ar.) **kadi** (Tur.) a judge in an Islamic court

qahal (Heb.) a congregation; a group of Jews who worship together

qâ`id (Ar.) a tribal chief

qasba (Ar.) citadel; the quarter of the Moroccan town that housed the royal guard and served as the sultan's residence

qasr, **qusûr** (Ar.) a palace or a fortified settlement

qaysariya (Ar.) the main market of a large city

rab' (Ar.) a multifamily dwelling

responsa (Heb. *tshuvoth*) an epistolary exchange in which one party consults another on a legal matter

riyâdh (Ar.) a garden; a house with a central courtyard

sabât (Ar.) extension of a house overhanging the street and supported by the facing wall

saddiq, saddiqim (Judeo-Arabic) lit., "friend"; a holy man

saqîfa (Ar.) the corridor giving entry to a house, often bent at an angle

semt (Tur.) a large district of the city

serarah (Heb.) the right to a religious office through patrilineal descent

shammash (Heb.) the sexton or beadle of the synagogue

sharîf, pl. **shurafâ'** (Ar.) a descendent of the Prophet Muhammad through his daughter Fatîma

shaykh al-yahûd (Ar.) the Jewish community's representative vis-à-vis the Muslim authority

shehita (Heb.) the Jewish method of slaughtering meat

simchat torah (Heb.) a celebration marking the end of one annual cycle of public Torah readings and the beginning of another

slâ (Judeo-Arabic, Morocco) a small neighborhood synagogue

sqalli (Ar., Morocco) embroidery executed with silver or gold thread

sukkot (Heb.) the Jewish Feast of Tabernacles

sunna (Ar.) the right "path," following the example of the Prophet Muhammad

sûq, pl. **aswâq** (Ar.) the market; **sûq al-däkhil**—the "inner" market in Tangier

tâbiya (Ar.) a building material made from earth

tâjir pl. **tujjâr** (Ar.) a wealthy merchant; **tâjir al-sultân**, in Morocco, a rich merchant, Jewish or Muslim, who acted as an agent for the sultan

tanzimat (Tur.) a series of reform edicts issued by the Ottoman government between 1839 and 1876 aimed at rationalizing the army and the administration and granting equal rights to all citizens

tarik-i am (Tur.) the main street of a quarter

tarîqa (Ar.) a religious brotherhood

talîth (Heb.) a prayer shawl

tevah (Heb.) the podium in the synagogue from which the prayer leader conducts the service

thaghr (Ar.) a port city, especially one on the frontier of Islam

toshavim (Heb.) the autochthonic Jewish inhabitants of Morocco

`ulamâ'**, sing. **`âlim (Ar.) the educated class, made up of scholars learned in Islamic law and practice

vakfiye (Tur.) endowment deed

yahas (Heb.) prestige acquired through family connections

yehudihane (Tur.) a multi-storied tenement specifically intended for Jewish families

yali (Tur.) a waterside summer house along the Bosphorus

yeshivah, pl. **yeshivot** (Heb.) Orthodox Jewish seminary; a Talmudic academy.

zanqa(t) (Ar.) a street in the madîna

zâwiya (Ar.) lit. "corner"; in Morocco, a lodge belonging to a religious order, often erected on the site of the founding saint's tomb

zulaij (Ar.; *zalîj* in the Moroccan dialect) ornamental tile work worked into brilliant and intricate patterns, used as a surface element in traditional building types

ziyâra (Ar.) pilgrimage to a saint's shrine or tomb

CONTRIBUTORS

MAURO BERTAGNIN is an architect and urban planner who teaches in the Faculty of Architecture at the University of Udine, Italy. He holds a Master's degree in architecture from the Instituto Universitario di Architettura of Venice, where he studied under Giancarlo De Carlo. His areas of expertise are earthen architecture, sustainable design, and historic conservation. He serves as a consultant to UNESCO and has contributed to rehabilitation projects in Tunisia, Malta, Hungary, Morocco, Syria, Mali and Eritrea.

EMILY GOTTREICH is Adjunct Associate Professor in the Department of History and International and Area Studies Teaching Program at U.C. Berkeley, where she also serves as Vice Chair of the Center for Middle Eastern Studies. Her research interests include Moroccan Jewish history, Muslim-Jewish relations, and North African cities. She is author of *The Mellah of Marrakesh: Jewish and Muslim Space in Morocco's Red City* (University of Indiana Press, 2006) and co-editor with Daniel J. Schroeter of the forthcoming *Rethinking Jewish Culture and Society in North Africa*.

WILLIAM GRANARA is Gordon Gray Professor of the Practice of Arabic at Harvard University where he teaches Arabic language and literature. He specializes in the history and cultures of Muslim Sicily and Spain and writes about cross-cultural encounters between Islam and Christendom throughout the Middle Ages, as well as on medieval Arabic poetics and historiography. A recent publication is "Islamic Education & the Transmission of Knowledge in Medieval Sicily," in *Law and Education in Medieval Islam: Studies in Honor of George Makdisi*. London: E.J.W. Gibb Memorial Trust, 2004.

ILHAM KHURI-MAKDISI is Assistant Professor of Middle East and World History at Northeastern University in Boston. Her current research focuses on the movement of people and ideas in the late nineteenth century Eastern Mediterranean. Her publications include *The Eastern Mediterranean and the Making of Global Radicalism, 1860–1914* (Berkeley: University of California Press, 2010), "Theater and Radical Politics in Beirut, Cairo and Alexandria 1860-1914," CCAS Occasional Papers (Center for Contemporary Arab Studies, Georgetown University, Fall 2006.)

KAREN A. LEAL is the Managing Editor of *Muqarnas: An Annual on the Visual Culture of the Islamic World*. She received her A.B. in the Classics and her A.M. and Ph.D. in History and Middle Eastern Studies from Harvard University. After completing her dissertation, *The Ottoman State and the Greek Orthodox of Istanbul: Sovereignty and Identity at the Turn of the Eighteenth Century*, she worked as an editor and translator for the Ottoman Court Records Project sponsored by Harvard University and the Packard Humanities Institute. She also taught at St. John's University in New York, where she was named a Vincentian Research Fellow. Her current research uses philological analyses of archival and literary sources to examine the ties that bound Muslims and non-Muslims to one another and the Ottoman state.

SUSAN GILSON MILLER is Associate Professor of History at the University of California, Davis, where she teaches courses on North Africa and Mediterranean Jewish history. She was formerly Director of the Moroccan Studies Program at Harvard University. Her current research centers on North African urbanism in the colonial and post-colonial periods, with an emphasis on patterns of multiethnicity. A recent publication is "The Mellah of Fez: Reflections on the Spatial Turn in Moroccan Jewish History," in *Jewish Topographies; Visions of Space, Traditions of Place*, A. Nocke, J. Brauch, A. Lipphardt. eds. (Ashgate, 2008).

ATTILIO PETRUCCIOLI is Chief Editor of *Environmental Design* and author of numerous publications on urban architecture, Islamic architecture, and the methodology of design. He is Dean of the Faculty of Architecture, Polytechnic University of Bari, Italy, and was formerly the Director of the Aga Khan Program in Islamic Architecture at MIT. His recent publications include *After Amnesia: Learning from the Islamic Mediterranean Urban Fabric* (ICAR, 2007), *Fathpur Sikri: la capitale dell'impero Moghul, la meraviglia di Akbar* (Electa, 2007), and *The City in the Islamic World,* with Salma K. Jayyusi, Renata Holod, and André Raymond (Brill, 2008).

ILLUSTRATION CREDITS

1. PHOTOGRAPHS

A. PHOTOGRAPHS TAKEN FOR THIS BOOK

Mauro Bertagnin   Cover photo; 69, 70, 74 top, 142, 152, 153, 154 below left, 155 below right, 158 below, 161 below, 162 above, 163, 165, 186 below, 187 above, 187 below, 189, 190 above, 190 below, 191 above right, 191 middle left, 196.

Susan Gilson Miller   46, 51 top, 61, 66 below, 67, 74 right, 92, 93, 96, 101, 126, 128 below, 129 below, 131 right, 132, 186 top, 195, 198, 205.

William Granara 44 top, 51 below

Enrico Pietrogrande 114

B. ARCHIVAL COLLECTIONS

Gerard Levy, Paris 88, 91, 95, 97, 100, 104, 105

Jamil Simon/Spectrum Media 122, 126

2. MAPS AND PLANS

A. PUBLISHED MAPS:

Rosalia La Franca, *Architettura judaica in Italia: ebraismo, sito, memoria dei luoghi.* Palermo: Flaccovio editore, 1994. 38.

Vincenzo Di Giovanni, *La Topografia Antica di Palermo.* Palermo: Tipografia e Lagatoria del Boccone del Povero, 1889. 42

B. ARCHIVAL AND PERSONAL COLLECTIONS

Francesca Fatta 39, 41

Aziza Chaouni 10, 82, 112

Susan Gilson Miller 185

Tangier American Legation Institute for Moroccan Studies (TALIM) 143

C. MAPS, PLANS AND SURVEYS DRAWN ESPECIALLY FOR THIS BOOK

Mauro Bertagnin 89

Enrico Pietrogrande 58, 60, 65, 116, 120, 124, 125 top, 128 top, 129 top, 131 top, middle, and below left, 146, 176, 179.

Vincenzo Arena 44 bottom, 50.

 Stefania Lanzidei and Roberto DiTolla 64, 66, 68, 141, 154 top, middle, and below right, 155 top and below left, 156, 157, 158 top, 159, 188, 191 below, 199.

Zachary Hinchliffe 86

INDEX

The Aga Khan Program for Islamic Architecture at Harvard and MIT

Based at Harvard University and the Massachusetts Institute of Technology, the Aga Khan Program for Islamic Architecture (AKPIA) is dedicated to the study of Islamic art and architecture, urbanism, landscape design, and conservation, and the application of that knowledge to contemporary design projects.

The goals of the program are to improve the teaching of Islamic art and architecture, promote excellence in advanced research, enhance the understanding of Islamic architecture, urbanism, and visual culture in light of contemporary theoretical, historical, critical, and developmental issues, and increase the visibility of Islamic cultural heritage in the modern Muslim world. Established in 1979, AKPIA is supported by an endowment from His Highness the Aga Khan. AKPIA's faculty, students, and alumni have played a substantial role in advancing the practice, analysis, and understanding of Islamic architecture as a discipline and cultural force.

The Aga Khan Program at the Harvard University Graduate School of Design

Established in 2003, the main aim of the Aga Khan Program at the GSD is to study the impact of development on the shaping of landscapes, cities, and regional territories in the Muslim world and to generate the means by which design at this scale could be improved.

The program focuses on the emerging phenomena that characterize these settings and on issues related to the design of public spaces and landscapes, environmental concerns, and land use and territorial settlement patterns. The process entails a study of their current conditions, their recent history (from World War II to the present), and, most important, the exploration of appropriate design approaches. The program sponsors new courses, option studios, faculty research, workshops, conferences, student activities, and publications. It is supported by a generous grant from the Aga Khan Trust for Culture.

TITLES IN THE AGA KHAN PROGRAM BOOK SERIES

Two Squares: Martyrs Square, Beirut, and Sirkeci Square, Istanbul, edited by Hashim Sarkis, with Mark Dwyer and Pars Kibarer

A Turkish Triangle: Ankara, Istanbul, and Izmir at the Gates of Europe, edited by Hashim Sarkis, with Neyran Turan

Han Tumertekin: Recent Work, edited by Hashim Sarkis

The Superlative City: Dubai and the Urban Condition in the Early Twenty-First Century, edited by Ahmed Kanna

Landscapes of Development: The Impact of Modernization Discourses on the Physical Environment of the Eastern Mediterranean, edited by Panayiota Pyla